Praise for *Practical Object-Oriented Design in Ruby*

"This is great stuff! Your descriptions are so vibrant and vivid that I'm rediscovering the truth buried in OO principles that are otherwise so internalized that I forget to explore them. Your thoughts on design and knowing the future are especially eloquent."

—Ian McFarland, President, New Context, Inc.

"As a self-taught programmer, this was an extremely helpful dive into some OOP concepts that I could definitely stand to become better acquainted with! And, I'm not alone: there's a sign posted at work that reads, "WWSMD?—What Would Sandi Metz Do"?

—Jonathan Mukai, Pivotal in NYC

"Meticulously pragmatic and exquisitely articulate, Practical Object Oriented Design in Ruby *makes otherwise elusive knowledge available to an audience which desperately needs it. The prescriptions are appropriate both as rules for novices and as guidelines for experienced professionals."*

—Katrina Owen, developer, Bengler

"I do believe this will be the most important Ruby book of 2012. Not only is the book 100% on-point, Sandi has an easy writing style with lots of great analogies that drive every point home."

—Avdi Grimm, Author of *Exceptional Ruby and Objects on Rails*

"While Ruby is an object-oriented language, little time is spent in the documentation on what OO truly means or how it should direct the way we build programs. Here Metz brings it to the fore, covering most of the key principles of OO development and design in an engaging, easy-to-understand manner. This is a must for any respectable Ruby bookshelf."

—Peter Cooper, editor, *Ruby Weekly*

"So good, I couldn't put it down! This is a must-read for anyone wanting to do object-oriented programming in any language, not to mention it has completely changed the way I approach testing."

—Charles Max Wood, video and audio show host, TeachMeToCode.com

"Distilling scary OO design practices with clear-cut examples and explanations makes this a book for novices and experts alike. It is well worth the study by anyone interested in OO design being done right and 'light.' I thoroughly enjoyed this book."

—Manuel Pais, editor, InfoQ.com

"If you call yourself a Ruby programmer, you should read this book. It's jam-packed with great nuggets of practical advice and coding techniques that you can start applying immediately in your projects."

—Ylan Segal, San Diego Ruby User Group

"This is the best OO book I've ever read. It's short, sweet, but potent. It slowly moves from simple techniques to more advanced, each example improving on the last. The ideas it presents are useful not just in Ruby but in static languages like C# too. Highly recommended!"

—Kevin Berridge, software engineering manager, Pointe Blank Solutions, and organizer, Burning River Developers Meetup

PRACTICAL OBJECT-ORIENTED DESIGN IN RUBY

PRACTICAL OBJECT-ORIENTED DESIGN IN RUBY

An Agile Primer

Sandi Metz

✦✦Addison-Wesley

Upper Saddle River, NJ • Boston • Indianapolis • San Francisco
New York • Toronto • Montreal • London • Munich • Paris • Madrid
Capetown • Sydney • Tokyo • Singapore • Mexico City

> U.S. Corporate and Government Sales
> (800) 382-3419
> corpsales@pearsontechgroup.com

For sales outside the United States, please contact:

> International Sales
> international@pearson.com

Visit us on the Web: informit.com/aw

Library of Congress Cataloging-in-Publication Data

Metz, Sandi.
  Practical object-oriented design in Ruby : an agile primer / Sandi Metz.
    p. cm.
  Includes bibliographical references and index.
  ISBN 0-321-72133-0 (alk. paper) 05-30-13
  1. Object-oriented programming (Computer science) 2. Ruby (Computer program language) I. Title.
  QA76.64.M485 2013
  005.1'17—dc23   2012026008

ISBN-13: 978-0-321-72133-4
ISBN-10:   0-321-72133-0
Text printed in the United States at RR Donnelley in Crawfordsville, Indiana.
Second printing, April 2013

Editor-in-Chief
Mark Taub

Acquisitions Editor
Debra Williams Cauley

Development Editor
Michael Thurston

Managing Editor
John Fuller

Project Editor
Elizabeth Ryan

Packager
Laserwords

Copy Editor
Phyllis Crittenden

Indexer
Constance A. Angelo

Proofreader
Gina Delaney

Publishing Coordinator
Kim Boedigheimer

Cover Designer
Chuti Prasertsith

Compositor
Laserwords

For Amy, who read everything first

Contents

Foreword

One of the core truisms of software development is that as your code grows and requirements for the system that you are building change, additional logic will be added that is not yet present in the current system. In almost all cases, maintainability over the life of the code is more important than optimizing its present state.

The promise of using object-oriented (OO) design is that your code will be easier to maintain and evolve than otherwise. If you are new to programming, how do you unlock these secrets to maintainability using OO? The fact is that many of us have never had holistic training in writing clean object-oriented code, instead picking up our techniques through osmosis from colleagues and a myriad of older books and online sources. Or if we were given a primer in OO during school, it was done in languages such as Java or C++. (The lucky ones were taught using Smalltalk!)

Sandi Metz's *Practical Object-Oriented Design in Ruby* covers all of the basics of OO using the Ruby language, meaning that it's ready to usher countless Ruby and Rails newcomers to the next steps in their professional development as mature programmers.

Ruby itself, like Smalltalk, is a completely object-oriented (OO) language. Everything in it, even primitive data constructs such as strings and numbers, is represented by objects with behavior. When you write your own applications in Ruby, you do so by coding your own objects, each encapsulating some state and defining its own behavior. If you don't already have OO experience, it can feel daunting to know how to start the process. This book guides you every step of the way, from the most basic questions of what to put in a class, through basic concepts such as the Single Responsibility Principle, all the way through to making tradeoffs between inheritance and composition, and figuring out how to test objects in isolation.

The best part, though, is Sandi's voice. She's got a ton of experience and is one of the nicest members of the community you'll ever meet, and I think she did a great job getting that feeling across in her writing. I've known Sandi for several years now, and I wondered if her manuscript would live up to the pleasure of actually getting to know Sandi in real life. I'm glad to say that it does, in spades, which is why I'm glad to welcome her as our newest author to the Professional Ruby Series.

—Obie Fernandez, Series Editor
Addison Wesley Professional Ruby Series

Introduction

We want to do our best work, and we want the work we do to have meaning. And, all else being equal, we prefer to enjoy ourselves along the way.

Those of us whose work is to write software are incredibly lucky. Building software is a guiltless pleasure because we get to use our creative energy to get things done. We have arranged our lives to have it both ways; we can enjoy the pure act of writing code in sure knowledge that the code we write has use. We produce things that matter. We are modern craftspeople, building structures that make up present-day reality, and no less than bricklayers or bridge builders, we take justifiable pride in our accomplishments.

This all programmers share, from the most enthusiastic newbie to the apparently jaded elder, whether working at the lightest weight Internet startup or the most staid, long-entrenched enterprise. We want to do our best work. We want our work to have meaning. We want to have fun along the way.

And so it's especially troubling when software goes awry. Bad software impedes our purpose and interferes with our happiness. Where once we felt productive, now we feel thwarted. Where once fast, now slow. Where once peaceful, now frustrated.

This frustration occurs when it costs too much to get things done. Our internal calculators are always running, comparing total amount accomplished to overall effort expended. When the cost of doing work exceeds its value, our efforts feel wasted. If programming gives joy it is because it allows us to be useful; when it becomes painful it is a sign that we believe we could, and should, be doing more. Our pleasure follows in the footsteps of work.

This book is about designing object-oriented software. It is not an academic tome, it is a programmer's story about how to write code. It teaches how to arrange software so as to be productive today and to remain so next month and next year. It shows how to write applications that can succeed in the present and still adapt to the future. It allows you to raise your productivity and reduce your costs for the entire lifetime of your applications.

This book believes in your desire to do good work and gives you the tools you need to best be of use. It is completely practical and as such is, at its core, a book about how to write code that brings you joy.

Who Might Find This Book Useful?

This book assumes that you have at least tried to write object-oriented software. It is not necessary that you feel you succeeded, just that you made the attempt in any object-oriented (OO) language. Chapter 1 contains a brief overview of object-oriented programming (OOP) but its goal is to define common terms, not to teach programming.

If you want to learn OO design (OOD) but have not yet done any object-oriented programming, at least take a tutorial before reading this book. OO design solves problems; suffering from those problems is very nearly a prerequisite for comprehending these solutions. Experienced programmers may be able to skip this step but most readers will be happier if they write some OO code before starting this book.

This book uses Ruby to teach OOD but you do not need to know Ruby to understand the concepts herein. There are many code examples but all are quite straightforward. If you have programmed in any OO language you will find Ruby easy to understand.

If you come from a statically typed OO language like Java or C++ you have the background necessary to benefit from reading this book. The fact that Ruby is dynamically typed simplifies the syntax of the examples and distills the design ideas to their essence, but every concept in this book can be directly translated to a statically typed OO language.

How to Read This Book

Chapter 1, Object-Oriented Design, contains a general overview of the whys, whens and wherefores of OO design, followed by a brief overview of object-oriented programming. This chapter stands alone. You can read it first, last, or, frankly, skip it entirely, although if you are currently stuck with an application that suffers from lack of design you may find it a comforting tale.

If you have experience writing object-oriented applications and want to jump right in, you can safely start with Chapter 2. If you do so and then stumble upon an unfamiliar term, come back and browse the Introduction to Object-Oriented Programming section of Chapter 1, which introduces and defines common OO terms used throughout the book.

Chapters 2 through 9 progressively explain object-oriented design. Chapter 2, Designing Classes with a Single Responsibility, covers how to decide what belongs in a single class. Chapter 3, Managing Dependencies, illustrates how objects get entangled with one another and shows how to keep them apart. These two chapters are focused on objects rather than messages.

In Chapter 4, Creating Flexible Interfaces, the emphasis begins to shift away from object-centric towards message-centric design. Chapter 4 is about defining interfaces and is concerned with how objects talk to one another. Chapter 5, Reducing Costs with Duck Typing, is about duck typing and introduces the idea that objects of different classes may play common roles. Chapter 6, Acquiring Behavior Through Inheritance, teaches the techniques of classical inheritance, which are then used in Chapter 7, Sharing Role Behavior with Modules, to create duck typed roles. Chapter 8, Combining Objects with Composition, explains the technique of building objects via composition and provides guidelines for choosing among composition, inheritance, and duck-typed role sharing. Chapter 9, Designing Cost-Effective Tests, concentrates on the design of tests, which it illustrates using code from earlier chapters of the book.

Each of these chapters builds on the concepts of the last. They are full of code and best read in order.

How to Use This Book

This book will mean different things to readers of different backgrounds. Those already familiar with OOD will find things to think about, possibly encounter some new points of view, and probably disagree with a few of the suggestions. Because there is no final authority on OOD, challenges to the principles (and to this author) will improve the understanding of all. In the end you must be the arbiter of your own designs; it is up to you to question, to experiment, and to choose.

While this book should be of interest to many levels of reader, it is written with the particular goal of being accessible to novices. If you are one of those novices, this part of the introduction is especially for you. Know this: object-oriented design is not black magic. It is simply things you don't yet know. The fact that you've read this far indicates you care about design; this desire to learn is the only prerequisite for benefiting from this book.

Chapters 2 through 9 explain OOD principles and provide very explicit programming rules; these rules will mean different things to novices than they mean to experts. If you are a novice, start out by following these rules in blind faith if necessary. This early obedience will stave off disaster until you can gain enough experience to make your own decisions. By the time the rules start to chafe, you'll have enough experience to make up rules of your own and your career as a designer will have begun.

Acknowledgments

It is a wonder this book exists; the fact that it does is due to the efforts and encouragement of many people.

Throughout the long process of writing, Lori Evans and TJ Stankus provided early feedback on every chapter. They live in Durham, NC, and thus could not escape me, but this fact does nothing to lessen my appreciation for their help.

Midway through the book, after it became impossible to deny that its writing would take approximately twice as long as originally estimated, Mike Dalessio and Gregory Brown read drafts and gave invaluable feedback and support. Their encouragement and enthusiasm kept the project alive during dark days.

As it neared completion, Steve Klabnik, Desi McAdam, and Seth Wax reviewed the book and thus acted as gracious stand-ins for you, the gentle reader. Their impressions and suggestions caused changes that will benefit all who follow.

Late drafts were given careful, thorough readings by Katrina Owen, Avdi Grimm, and Rebecca Wirfs-Brock, and the book is much improved by their kind and thoughtful feedback. Before they pitched in, Katrina, Avdi, and Rebecca were strangers to me; I am grateful for their involvement and humbled by their generosity. If you find this book useful, thank them when you next see them.

I am also grateful for the Gotham Ruby Group and for everyone who expressed their appreciation for the design talks I gave at GoRuCo 2009 and 2011. The folks at GoRuCo took a chance on an unknown and gave me a forum in which to express these ideas; this book started there. Ian McFarland and Brian Ford watched those talks and their immediate and ongoing enthusiasm for this project was both infectious and convincing.

The process of writing was greatly aided by Michael Thurston of Pearson Education, who was like an ocean liner of calmness and organization chugging through the chaotic sea of my opposing rogue writing waves. You can, I expect, see the problem he faced. He insisted, with endless patience and grace, that the writing be arranged in a readable structure. I believe his efforts have paid off and hope you will agree.

My thanks also to Debra Williams Cauley, my editor at Addison-Wesley, who overheard an ill-timed hallway rant in 2006 at the first Ruby on Rails conference in Chicago and launched the campaign that eventually resulted in this book. Despite my best efforts, she would not take no for an answer. She cleverly moved from one argument to the next until she finally found the one that convinced; this accurately reflects her persistence and dedication.

I owe a debt to the entire object-oriented design community. I did not make up the ideas in this book, I am merely a translator, and I stand on the shoulders of giants. It goes without saying that while all credit for these ideas belongs to others—failures of translation are mine alone.

And finally, this book owes its existence to my partner Amy Germuth. Before this project started I could not imagine *writing* a book; her view of the world as a place where people did such things made doing so seem possible. The book in your hands is a tribute to her boundless patience and endless support.

Thank you, each and every one.

About the Author

Sandi Metz has 30 years of experience working on projects that survived to grow and change. She writes code every day as a software architect at Duke University, where her team solves real problems for customers who have large object-oriented applications that have been evolving for 15 or more years. She's committed to getting useful software out the door in extremely practical ways. *Practical Object-Oriented Design in Ruby* is the distillation of many years of whiteboard drawings and the logical culmination of a lifetime of conversations about OO design. Sandi has spoken at Ruby Nation and several times at Gotham Ruby User's Conference and lives in Durham, NC.

CHAPTER 1
Object-Oriented Design

The world is procedural. Time flows forward and events, one by one, pass by. Your morning procedure may be to get up, brush your teeth, make coffee, dress, and then get to work. These activities can be modeled using procedural software; because you know the order of events you can write code to do each thing and then quite deliberately string the things together, one after another.

The world is also object-oriented. The objects with which you interact might include a spouse and a cat, or an old car and a pile of bike parts in the garage, or your ticking heart and the exercise plan you use to keep it healthy. Each of these objects comes equipped with its own behavior and, while some of the interactions between them might be predictable, it is entirely possible for your spouse to unexpectedly step on the cat, causing a reaction that rapidly raises everyone's heart rate and gives you new appreciation for your exercise regimen.

In a world of objects, new arrangements of behavior emerge naturally. You don't have to explicitly write code for the `spouse_steps_on_cat` procedure, all you need is a spouse object that takes steps and a cat object that does not like being stepped on. Put these two objects into a room together and unanticipated combinations of behavior will appear.

This book is about designing object-oriented software, and it views the world as a series of spontaneous interactions between objects. Object-oriented design (OOD) requires that you shift from thinking of the world as a collection of predefined procedures to modeling the world as a series of messages that pass between objects. Failures of OOD might look like failures of coding technique but they are actually failures of

1

perspective. The first requirement for learning how to do object-oriented design is to immerse yourself in objects; once you acquire an object-oriented perspective the rest follows naturally.

This book guides you through the immersion process. This chapter starts with a general discussion of OOD. It argues the case for design and then proceeds to describe when to do it and how to judge it. The chapter ends with a brief overview of object-oriented programming that defines the terms used throughout the book.

In Praise of Design

Software gets built for a reason. The target application—whether a trivial game or a program to guide radiation therapy—is the entire point. If painful programming were the most cost-effective way to produce working software, programmers would be morally obligated to suffer stoically or to find other jobs.

Fortunately, you do not have to choose between pleasure and productivity. The programming techniques that make code a joy to write overlap with those that most efficiently produce software. The techniques of object-oriented design solve both the moral and the technical dilemmas of programming; following them produces cost-effective software using code that is also a pleasure to work on.

The Problem Design Solves

Imagine writing a new application. Imagine that this application comes equipped with a complete and correct set of requirements. And if you will, imagine one more thing: once written, this application need never change.

For this case, design does not matter. Like a circus performer spinning plates in a world without friction or gravity, you could program the application into motion and then stand back proudly and watch it run forever. No matter how wobbly, the plates of code would rotate on and on, teetering round and round but never quite falling.

As long as nothing changed.

Unfortunately, something *will* change. It always does. The customers didn't know what they wanted, they didn't say what they meant. You didn't understand their needs, you've learned how to do something better. Even applications that are perfect in every way are not stable. The application was a huge success, now everyone wants more. Change is unavoidable. It is ubiquitous, omnipresent, and inevitable.

Changing requirements are the programming equivalent of friction and gravity. They introduce forces that apply sudden and unexpected pressures that work against the best-laid plans. It is the need for change that makes design matter.

Applications that are easy to change are a pleasure to write and a joy to extend. They're flexible and adaptable. Applications that resist change are just the opposite; every change is expensive and each makes the next cost more. Few difficult-to-change applications are pleasant to work on. The worst of them gradually become personal horror films where you star as a hapless programmer, running madly from one spinning plate to the next, trying to stave off the sound of crashing crockery.

Why Change Is Hard

Object-oriented applications are made up of parts that interact to produce the behavior of the whole. The parts are *objects;* interactions are embodied in the *messages* that pass between them. Getting the right message to the correct target object requires that the sender of the message know things about the receiver. This knowledge creates dependencies between the two and these dependencies stand in the way of change.

Object-oriented design is about *managing dependencies*. It is a set of coding techniques that arrange dependencies such that objects can tolerate change. In the absence of design, unmanaged dependencies wreak havoc because objects know too much about one another. Changing one object forces change upon its collaborators, which in turn, forces change upon its collaborators, *ad infinitum*. A seemingly insignificant enhancement can cause damage that radiates outward in overlapping concentric circles, ultimately leaving no code untouched.

When objects know too much they have many expectations about the world in which they reside. They're picky, they need things to be "just so." These expectations constrain them. The objects resist being reused in different contexts; they are painful to test and susceptible to being duplicated.

In a small application, poor design is survivable. Even if everything is connected to everything else, if you can hold it all in your head at once you can still improve the application. The problem with poorly designed *small* applications is that if they are successful they grow up to be poorly designed *big* applications. They gradually become tar pits in which you fear to tread lest you sink without a trace. Changes that should be simple may cascade around the application, breaking code everywhere and requiring extensive rewriting. Tests are caught in the crossfire and begin to feel like a hindrance rather than a help.

A Practical Definition of Design

Every application is a collection of code; the code's arrangement is the *design*. Two isolated programmers, even when they share common ideas about design, can be relied upon to solve the same problem by arranging code in different ways. Design is not an assembly line where similarly trained workers construct identical widgets; it's a studio where like-minded artists sculpt custom applications. Design is thus an art, the art of arranging code.

Part of the difficulty of design is that every problem has two components. You must not only write code for the feature you plan to deliver today, you must also create code that is amenable to being changed later. For any period of time that extends past initial delivery of the beta, the cost of change will eventually eclipse the original cost of the application. Because design principles overlap and every problem involves a shifting timeframe, design challenges can have a bewildering number of possible solutions. Your job is one of synthesis; you must combine an overall understanding of your application's requirements with knowledge of the costs and benefits of design alternatives and then devise an arrangement of code that is cost effective in the present and will continue to be so in the future.

Taking the future into consideration might seem to introduce a need for psychic abilities normally considered outside the realm of programming. Not so. The future that design considers is not one in which you anticipate unknown requirements and preemptively choose one from among them to implement in the present. Programmers are not psychics. Designs that anticipate specific future requirements almost always end badly. Practical design does not anticipate what will happen to your application, it merely accepts that something will and that, in the present, you cannot know what. It doesn't guess the future; it preserves your options for accommodating the future. It doesn't choose; it leaves you room to move.

The purpose of design is to allow you to do design *later* and its primary goal is to reduce the cost of change.

The Tools of Design

Design is not the act of following a fixed set of rules, it's a journey along a branching path wherein earlier choices close off some options and open access to others. During design you wander through a maze of requirements where every juncture represents a decision point that has consequences for the future.

Just as a sculptor has chisels and files, an object-oriented designer has tools—principles and patterns.

Design Principles

The SOLID acronym, coined by Michael Feathers and popularized by Robert Martin, represents five of the most well known principles of object-oriented design: **S**ingle Responsibility, **O**pen-Closed, **L**iskov Substitution, **I**nterface Segregation, and **D**ependency Inversion. Other principles include Andy Hunt and Dave Thomas's DRY (Don't Repeat Yourself) and the Law of Demeter (LoD) from the Demeter project at Northeastern University.

The principles themselves will be dealt with throughout this book; the question for now is "Where on earth did they come from?" Is there empirical proof that these principles have value or are they merely someone's opinion that you may freely discount? In essence, who says?

All of these principles got their start as choices someone made while writing code. Early OO programmers noticed that some code arrangements made their lives easier while others made them harder. These experiences led them to develop opinions about how to write good code.

Academics eventually got involved and, needing to write dissertations, decided to quantify "goodness." This desire is laudable. If we could count things, that is, compute *metrics* about our code and correlate these metrics to high- or low-quality applications (for which we also need an objective measure), we could do more of the things that lower costs and fewer of things that raise them. Being able to measure quality would change OO design from infinitely disputed opinion into measurable science.

In the 1990s Chidamber and Kemerer[1] and Basili[2] did exactly this. They took object-oriented applications and tried to quantify the code. They named and measured things like the overall size of classes, the entanglements that classes have with one another, the depth and breadth of inheritance hierarchies, and the number of methods that get invoked as a result of any message sent. They picked code arrangements they thought might matter, devised formulas to count them, and then correlated the resulting metrics to the quality of the enclosing applications. Their research shows a definite correlation between use of these techniques and high-quality code.

---

1. Chidamber, S. R., & Kemerer, C. F. (1994). A metrics suite for object-oriented design. *IEEE Trans. Softw. Eng. 20*(6): 476–493.

2. Basili Technical Report (1995). Univ. of Maryland, Dep. of Computer Science, College Park, MD, 20742 USA. April 1995. *A Validation of Object-Oriented Design Metrics as Quality Indicators.*

While these studies seem to prove the validity of the design principles, they come, for any seasoned programmer, with a caveat. These early studies examined very small applications written by graduate students; this alone is enough to justify viewing the conclusions with caution. The code in these applications may not be representative of real-world OO applications.

However, it turns out caution is unnecessary. In 2001, Laing and Coleman examined several NASA Goddard Space Flight Center applications (rocket science) with the express intention of finding "a way to produce cheaper and higher quality software."[3] They examined three applications of varying quality, one of which had 1,617 classes and more than 500,000 lines of code. Their research supports the earlier studies and further confirms that design principles matter.

Even if you never read these studies you can be assured of their conclusions. The principles of good design represent measurable truths and following them will improve your code.

Design Patterns

In addition to principles, object-oriented design involves *patterns*. The so-called Gang of Four (Gof), Erich Gamma, Richard Helm, Ralph Johnson, and Jon Vlissides, wrote the seminal work on patterns in 1995. Their *Design Patterns* book describes patterns as "simple and elegant solutions to specific problems in object-oriented software design" that you can use to "make your own designs more flexible, modular, reusable and understandable."[4]

The notion of design patterns is incredibly powerful. To name common problems and to solve the problems in common ways brings the fuzzy into focus. *Design Patterns* gave an entire generation of programmers the means to communicate and collaborate.

Patterns have a place in every designer's toolbox. Each well-known pattern is a near perfect open-source solution for the problem it solves. However, the popularity of patterns led to a kind of pattern abuse by novice programmers, who, in an excess of well-meaning zeal, applied perfectly good patterns to the wrong problems. Pattern misapplication results in complicated and confusing code but this result is not the

---

3. Laing, Victor & Coleman, Charles. (2001). Principal Components of Orthogonal Object-Oriented Metrics (323-08-14).

4. Gamma, E., Helm, R., Johnson, R., & Vlissides, J. (1995). *Design Patterns, Elements of Reusable Object-Oriented Software.* New York, NY: Addison-Wesley Publishing Company, Inc.

fault of the pattern itself. A tool cannot be faulted for its use, the user must master the tool.

This book is not about patterns; however, it will prepare you to understand them and give you the knowledge to choose and use them appropriately.

The Act of Design

With the discovery and propagation of common design principles and patterns, all OOD problems would appear to have been solved. Now that the underlying rules are known, how hard can designing object-oriented software be?

Pretty hard, it turns out. If you think of software as custom furniture, then principles and patterns are like woodworking tools. Knowing how software should look when it's done does not cause it to build itself; applications come into existence because some programmer applied the tools. The end result, be it a beautiful cabinet or a rickety chair, reflects its programmer's experience with the tools of design.

How Design Fails

The first way design fails is due to lack of it. Programmers initially know little about design. This is not a deterrent, however, as it is possible to produce working applications without knowing the first thing about design.

This is true of any OO language but some languages are more susceptible than others and an approachable language like Ruby is especially vulnerable. Ruby is very friendly; the language permits nearly anyone to create scripts to automate repetitive tasks, and an opinionated framework like Ruby on Rails puts web applications within every programmer's reach. The syntax of the Ruby language is so gentle that anyone blessed with the ability to string thoughts into logical order can produce working applications. Programmers who know nothing about object-oriented design can be very successful in Ruby.

However, successful but *undesigned* applications carry the seeds of their own destruction; they are easy to write but gradually become impossible to change. A programmer's past experience does not predict the future. The early promise of painless development gradually fails and optimism turns to despair as programmers begin to greet every change request with "Yes, I can add that feature, *but it will break everything.*"

Slightly more experienced programmers encounter different design failures. These programmers are aware of OO design techniques but do not yet understand how to apply them. With the best of intentions, these programmers fall into the trap of overdesign. A little bit of knowledge is dangerous; as their knowledge increases and hope returns, they *design* relentlessly. In an excess of enthusiasm they apply principles inappropriately and see patterns where none exist. They construct complicated, beautiful castles of code and then are distressed to find themselves hemmed in by stone walls. You can recognize these programmers because they begin to greet change requests with "No, I can't add that feature; *it wasn't designed to do that.*"

Finally, object-oriented software fails when the act of design is separated from the act of programming. Design is a process of progressive discovery that relies on a feedback loop. This feedback loop should be timely and incremental; the iterative techniques of the Agile software movement (http://agilemanifesto.org/) are thus perfectly suited to the creation of well-designed OO applications. The iterative nature of Agile development allows design to adjust regularly and to evolve naturally. When design is dictated from afar none of the necessary adjustments can occur and early failures of understanding get cemented into the code. Programmers who are forced to write applications that were designed by isolated *experts* begin to say, "Well, I can certainly write this, *but it's not what you really want and you will eventually be sorry.*"

When to Design

Agile believes that your customers can't define the software they want before seeing it, so it's best to show them sooner rather than later. If this premise is true, then it logically follows that you should build software in tiny increments, gradually iterating your way into an application that meets the customer's true need. Agile believes that the most cost-effective way to produce what customers really want is to collaborate with them, building software one small bit at a time such that each delivered bit has the opportunity to alter ideas about the next. The Agile experience is that this collaboration produces software that differs from what was initially imagined; the resulting software could not have been anticipated by any other means.

If Agile is correct, two other things are also true. First, there is absolutely no point in doing a Big Up Front Design (BUFD) (because it cannot possibly be correct), and second, no one can predict when the application will be done (because you don't know in advance what it will eventually do).

It should come as no surprise that some people are uncomfortable with Agile. "We don't know what we're doing" and "We don't know when we'll be done" can be a difficult sell. The desire for BUFD persists because, for some, it provides a feeling of control that would otherwise be lacking. Comforting though this feeling may be, it is a temporary illusion that will not survive the act of writing the application.

BUFD inevitably leads to an adversarial relationship between customers and programmers. Because any big design created in advance of working software cannot be correct, to write the application as specified guarantees that it will not meet the customer's needs. Customers discover this when they attempt to use it. They then request changes. Programmers resist these changes because they have a schedule to meet, one that they are very likely already behind. The project gradually becomes doomed as participants switch from working to make it succeed to striving to avoid being blamed for its failure.

The rules of this engagement are clear to all. When a project misses its delivery deadline, even if this happened because of changes to the specification, the programmers are at fault. If, however, it is delivered on time but doesn't fulfill the actual need, the specification must have been wrong, so the customer gets the blame. The design documents of BUFD start out as roadmaps for application development but gradually become the focus of dissent. They do not produce quality software, instead they supply fiercely parsed words that will be invoked in the final, scrambling defense against being the person who ends up holding the hot potato of blame.

If insanity is doing the same thing over and over again and expecting different results, the Agile Manifesto was where we collectively began to regain our senses. Agile works because it acknowledges that certainty is unattainable *in advance* of the application's existence; Agile's acceptance of this truth allows it to provide strategies to overcome the handicap of developing software while knowing neither the target nor the timeline.

However, just because Agile says "don't do a big up front design" doesn't mean it tells you to do no design at all. The word *design* when used in BUFD has a different meaning than when used in OOD. BUFD is about completely specifying and totally documenting the anticipated future inner workings of all of the features of the proposed application. If there's a software architect involved this may extend to deciding, in advance, how to arrange all of the code. OOD is concerned with a much narrower domain. It is about arranging what code you have so that it will be easy to change.

Agile processes *guarantee change* and your ability to make these changes depends on your application's design. If you cannot write well-designed code you'll have to rewrite your application during every iteration.

Agile thus does not prohibit design, it requires it. Not only does it require design, it requires really good design. It needs your best work. Its success relies on simple, flexible, and malleable code.

Judging Design

In the days of yore, programmers were sometimes judged by the number of lines of code (referred to as *source lines of code* or SLOC) they produced. It's obvious how this metric came to be; any boss who thinks of programming as an assembly line where similarly trained workers labor to construct identical widgets can easily develop a belief that individual productivity can be judged by simply weighing output. For managers in desperate need of a reliable way to compare programmers and evaluate software, SLOC, for all its obvious problems, was far better than nothing; it was at least a reproducible measure of *something*.

This metric was clearly not developed by programmers. While SLOC may provide a yardstick by which to measure individual effort and application complexity, it says nothing about overall quality. It penalizes the efficient programmer while rewarding the verbose and is ripe to be gamed by the expert to the detriment of the underlying application. If you know that the novice programmer sitting next to you will be thought more productive because he or she writes a lot of code to produce a feature that you could produce with far fewer lines, what is your response? This metric alters the reward structure in ways that harm quality.

In the modern world, SLOC is a historical curiosity that has largely been replaced by newer metrics. There are numerous Ruby gems (a google search on *ruby metrics* will turn up the most recent) that assess how well your code follows OOD principles. Metrics software works by scanning source code and counting things that predict quality. Running a metrics suite against your own code can be illuminating, humbling, and sometimes alarming. Seemingly well-designed applications can rack up impressive numbers of OOD violations.

Bad OOD metrics are indisputably a sign of bad design; code that scores poorly *will* be hard to change. Unfortunately, good scores don't prove the opposite, that is, they don't guarantee that the next change you make will be easy or cheap. The problem is that it is possible to create beautiful designs that over-anticipate the future. While these designs may generate very good OOD metrics, if they anticipate the *wrong* future they will be expensive to fix when the real future finally arrives. OOD metrics cannot identify designs that do the wrong thing in the right way.

The cautionary tale about SLOC gone wrong therefore extends to OOD metrics. Take them with a grain of salt. Metrics are useful because they are unbiased and produce numbers from which you can infer something about software; however, they are not direct indicators of quality, but are proxies for a deeper measurement. The ultimate software metric would be *cost per feature over the time interval that matters*, but this is not easy to calculate. Cost, feature, and time are individually difficult to define, track, and measure.

Even if you could isolate an individual feature and track all of its associated costs, the *time interval that matters* affects how code should be judged. Sometimes the value of having the feature right now is so great that it outweighs any future increase in costs. If lack of a feature will force you out of business today it doesn't matter how much it will cost to deal with the code tomorrow; you must do the best you can in the time you have. Making this kind of design compromise is like borrowing time from the future and is known as taking on *technical debt*. This is a loan that will eventually need to be repaid, quite likely with interest.

Even when you are not intentionally taking on technical debt, design takes time and therefore costs money. Because your goal is to write software with the lowest cost per feature, your decision about how much design to do depends on two things: your skills and your timeframe. If design takes half your time this month and does not start returning dividends for a year, it may not be worth it. When the act of design prevents software from being delivered on time, you have lost. Delivering half of a well-designed application might be the same as delivering no application at all. However, if design takes half of your time this morning, pays that time back this afternoon, and then continues to provide benefits for the lifetime of the application, you get a kind of daily compounding interest on your time; this design effort pays off forever.

The break-even point for design depends on the programmer. Inexperienced programmers who do a lot of anticipatory design may never reach a point where their earlier design efforts pay off. Skilled designers who write carefully crafted code this morning may save money this afternoon. Your experience likely lies somewhere between these extremes, and the remainder of this book teaches skills you can use to shift the break-even point in your favor.

A Brief Introduction to Object-Oriented Programming

Object-oriented applications are made up of objects and the messages that pass between them. Messages will turn out to be the more important of the two, but in this brief introduction (and in the first few chapters of the book) the concepts will get equal weight.

Procedural Languages

Object-oriented programming is *object-oriented* relative to non object-oriented, or *procedural*, programming. It's instructive to think of these two styles in terms of their differences. Imagine a generic procedural programming language, one in which you create simple scripts. In this language you can define variables, that is, make up names and associate those names with bits of data. Once assigned, the associated data can be accessed by referring to the variables.

Like all procedural languages, this one knows about a small, fixed set of different kinds of data, things like strings, numbers, arrays, files, and so on. These different kinds of data are known as *data types*. Each data type describes a very specific kind of thing. The *string* data type is different from the *file* data type. The syntax of the language contains built-in operations to do reasonable things to the various data types. For example, it can concatenate strings and read files.

Because *you* create variables, you know what kind of thing each holds. Your expectations about which operations you can use are based on your knowledge of a variable's data type. You know that you can append to strings, do math with numbers, index into arrays, read files, and so on.

Every possible data type and operation already exists; these things are built into the syntax of the language. The language might let you create functions (group some of the predefined operations together under a new name) or define complex data structures (assemble some of the predefined data types into a named arrangement), but you can't make up wholly new operations or brand new data types. What you see is all you get.

In this language, as in all procedural languages, there is a chasm between data and behavior. Data is one thing, behavior is something completely different. Data gets packaged up into variables and then passed around to behavior, which could, frankly, do anything to it. Data is like a child that behavior sends off to school every morning; there is no way of knowing what actually happens while it is out of sight. The influences on data can be unpredictable and largely untraceable.

Object-Oriented Languages

Now imagine a different kind of programming language, a class-based object-oriented one like Ruby. Instead of dividing data and behavior into two separate, never-the-twain-shall-meet spheres, Ruby combines them together into a single thing, an *object*. Objects have behavior and may contain data, data to which they alone control access. Objects invoke one another's behavior by sending each other *messages*.

Ruby has a string *object* instead of a string *data type*. The operations that work with strings are built into the string objects themselves instead of into the syntax of the language. String objects differ in that each contains its own personal *string* of data, but are similar in that each behaves like the others. Each string *encapsulates*, or hides, its data from the world. Every object decides for itself how much, or how little, of its data to expose.

Because string objects supply their own operations, Ruby doesn't have to know anything in particular about the string data type; it need only provide a general way for objects to send messages. For example, if strings understand the concat message, Ruby doesn't have to contain syntax to concatenate strings, it just has to provide a way for one object to send concat to another.

Even the simplest application will probably need more than one string or number or file or array. As a matter of fact, while it's true that you may occasionally need a unique, individual snowflake of an object, it's far more common to desire to manufacture a bunch of objects that have identical behavior but encapsulate different data.

Class-based OO languages like Ruby allow you to define a *class* that provides a blueprint for the construction of similar objects. A class defines *methods* (definitions of behavior) and *attributes* (definitions of variables). Methods get invoked in response to messages. The same method name can be defined by many different objects; it's up to Ruby to find and invoke the right method of the correct object for any sent message.

Once the String class exists it can be used to repeatedly *instantiate*, or create, new *instances* of a string object. Every newly instantiated String *implements* the same methods and uses the same attribute names but each contains its own personal data. They share the same methods so they all behave like Strings; they contain different data so they represent different ones.

The String class defines a type that is more than mere *data*. Knowing an object's type lets you have expectations about how it will behave. In a procedural language variables have a single data type; knowledge of this data type lets you have expectations about which operations are valid. In Ruby an object may have many types, one of which will always come from its class. Knowledge of an object's type(s) therefore lets you have expectations about the messages to which it responds.

Ruby comes with a number of predefined classes. The most immediately recognizable are those that overlap the data types used by procedural languages. For example, the String class defines strings, the Fixnum class, integers. There's a pre-existing class for every data type that you would expect a programming language to supply. However, object-oriented languages are themselves built using objects and here's where things begin to get interesting.

The `String` class, that is, the blueprint for new string objects, *is itself an object*; it's an instance of the `Class` class. Just as every string object is a data-specific instance of the `String` class, every class object (`String`, `Fixnum`, *ad infinitum*) is a data-specific instance of the `Class` class. The `String` class manufactures new strings, the `Class` class manufactures new classes.

OO languages are thus open-ended. They don't limit you to a small set of built-in types and pre-predefined operations; you can invent brand new types of your own. Each OO application gradually becomes a unique programming language that is specifically tailored to your domain.

Whether this language ultimately brings you pleasure or gives you pain is a matter of design and the concern of this book.

Summary

If an application lives long enough, that is, if it succeeds, its biggest problem will become that of dealing with change. Arranging code to efficiently accommodate change is a matter of design. The most visible elements of design are principles and patterns, but unfortunately even applying principles correctly and using patterns appropriately does not guarantee the creation of an easy-to-change application.

OO metrics expose how well an application follows OO design principles. Bad metrics strongly imply future difficulties; however, good metrics are less helpful. A design that does the wrong thing might produce great metrics but may still be costly to change.

The trick to getting the most bang for your design buck is to acquire an understanding of the theories of design and to apply these theories appropriately, at the right time, and in the right amounts. Design relies on your ability to translate theory into practice.

What is the difference between theory and practice?

In theory, there is none. If theory *were* practice you could learn the rules of OOD, apply them consistently, and create perfect code from this day forward; your work here would be done.

However, no matter how deeply theory believes this to be true, practice knows better. Unlike theory, practice gets its hands dirty. It is practice that lays bricks, builds bridges, and writes code. Practice lives in the real world of change, confusion, and uncertainty. It faces competing choices and, grimacing, chooses the lesser evil; it dodges, it hedges, it robs Peter to pay Paul. It makes a living by doing the best it can with what it has.

Theory is useful and necessary and has been the focus of this chapter. But enough already; it's time for practice.

CHAPTER 2

Designing Classes with a Single Responsibility

The foundation of an object-oriented system is the *message,* but the most visible organizational structure is the *class.* Messages are at the core of design, but because classes are so obvious this chapter starts small and concentrates on how to decide what belongs in a class. The design emphasis will gradually shift from classes to messages over the next several chapters.

What are your classes? How many should you have? What behavior will they implement? How much do they know about other classes? How much of themselves should they expose?

These questions can be overwhelming. Every decision seems both permanent and fraught with peril. Fear not. At this stage your first obligation is to take a deep breath and *insist that it be simple.* Your goal is to model your application, using classes, such that it does what it is supposed to do *right now* and is also easy to change *later.*

These are two very different criteria. Anyone can arrange code to make it work right now. Today's application can be beat into submission by sheer force of will. It's a standing target at a known range. It is at your mercy.

Creating an easy-to-change application, however, is a different matter. Your application needs to work right now just once; it must be easy to change forever. This quality of easy changeability reveals the craft of programming. Achieving it takes knowledge, skill, and a bit of artistic creativity.

Fortunately, you don't have to figure everything out from scratch. Much thought and research has gone into identifying the qualities that make an application easy to change. The techniques are simple; you only need to know what they are and how to use them.

Deciding What Belongs in a Class

You have an application in mind. You know what it should do. You may even have thought about how to implement the most interesting bits of behavior. The problem is not one of technical knowledge but of organization; you know how to write the code but not where to put it.

Grouping Methods into Classes

In a class-based OO language like Ruby, methods are defined in classes. The classes you create will affect how you think about your application forever. They define a virtual world, one that constrains the imagination of everyone downstream. You are constructing a box that may be difficult to think outside of.

Despite the importance of correctly grouping methods into classes, at this early stage of your project you cannot possibly get it right. You will never know less than you know right now. If your application succeeds many of the decisions you make today will need to be changed later. When that day comes, your ability to successfully make those changes will be determined by your application's design.

Design is more the art of preserving changeability than it is the act of achieving perfection.

Organizing Code to Allow for Easy Changes

Asserting that code should be easy to change is akin to stating that children should be polite; the statement is impossible to disagree with yet it in no way helps a parent raise an agreeable child. The idea of *easy* is too broad; you need concrete definitions of *easiness* and specific criteria by which to judge code.

If you define *easy to change* as

- Changes have no unexpected side effects

- Small changes in requirements require correspondingly small changes in code

- Existing code is easy to reuse

- The easiest way to make a change is to add code that in itself is easy to change

Then the code you write should have the following qualities. Code should be

- **Transparent** The consequences of change should be obvious in the code that is changing and in distant code that relies upon it

- **Reasonable** The cost of any change should be proportional to the benefits the change achieves

- **Usable** Existing code should be usable in new and unexpected contexts

- **Exemplary** The code itself should encourage those who change it to perpetuate these qualities

Code that is *T*ransparent, *R*easonable, *U*sable, and *Ex*emplary (TRUE) not only meets today's needs but can also be changed to meet the needs of the future. The first step in creating code that is TRUE is to ensure that each class has a single, well-defined responsibility.

Creating Classes That Have a Single Responsibility

A class should do the smallest possible useful thing; that is, it should have a single responsibility.

Illustrating how to create a class that has a single responsibility and explaining why it matters requires an example, which in turn requires a small divergence into the domain of bicycles.

An Example Application: Bicycles and Gears

Bicycles are wonderfully efficient machines, in part because they use gears to provide humans with mechanical advantage. When riding a bike you can choose between a small gear (which is easy to pedal but not very fast) or a big gear (which is harder to pedal but sends you zooming along). Gears are great because you can use small ones to creep up steep hills and big ones to fly back down.

Gears work by changing how far the bicycle travels each time your feet complete one circle with the pedals. More specifically, your gear controls how many times the wheels rotate for each time the pedals rotate. In a small gear your feet spin around several times to make the wheels rotate just once; in a big gear each complete pedal rotation may cause the wheels to rotate multiple times. See Figure 2.1.

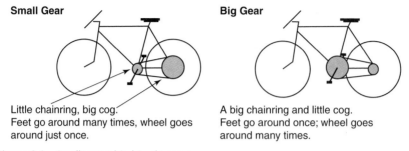

Figure 2.1   Small versus big bicycle gears.

The terms *small* and *big* are not very precise. To compare different gears, bicyclists use the ratio of the numbers of their teeth. These ratios can be calculated with this simple Ruby script:

```
1  chainring = 52                        # number of teeth
2  cog       = 11
3  ratio     = chainring / cog.to_f
4  puts ratio                            # -> 4.72727272727273
5
6  chainring = 30
7  cog       = 27
8  ratio     = chainring / cog.to_f
9  puts ratio                            # -> 1.11111111111111
```

The gear created by combining a 52-tooth chainring with an 11-tooth cog (a 52 × 11) has a ratio of about 4.73. Each time your feet push the pedals around *one* time your wheels will travel around almost *five* times. The 30 × 27 is a much easier gear; each pedal revolution causes the wheels to rotate a little more than once.

Believe it or not, there are people who care deeply about bicycle gearing. You can help them out by writing a Ruby application to calculate gear ratios.

The application will be made of Ruby classes, each representing some part of the domain. If you read through the description above looking for nouns that represent objects in the domain you'll see words like *bicycle* and *gear*. These nouns represent the simplest candidates to be classes. Intuition says that *bicycle* should be a class, but nothing in the above description lists any behavior for bicycle, so, as yet, it does not qualify. *Gear*, however, has chainrings, cogs, and ratios, that is, it has both data and behavior. It deserves to be a class. Taking the behavior from the script above, you create this simple Gear class:

```
1  class Gear
2    attr_reader :chainring, :cog
3    def initialize(chainring, cog)
4      @chainring = chainring
5      @cog       = cog
6    end
7
8    def ratio
9      chainring / cog.to_f
10   end
11 end
12
13 puts Gear.new(52, 11).ratio      # -> 4.72727272727273
14 puts Gear.new(30, 27).ratio      # -> 1.11111111111111
```

This Gear class is simplicity itself. You create a new Gear instance by providing the numbers of teeth for the chainring and cog. Each instance implements three methods: chainring, cog, and ratio.

Gear is a subclass of Object and thus inherits many other methods. A Gear consists of everything it directly implements plus everything it inherits, so the complete set of behavior, that is, the total set of messages to which it can respond, is fairly large. Inheritance matters to your application's design, but this simple case where *Gear* inherits from object is so basic that, at least for now, you can act as if these inherited methods do not exist. More sophisticated forms of inheritance will be covered in Chapter 6, Acquiring Behavior Through Inheritance.

You show your Gear calculator to a cyclist friend and she finds it useful but immediately asks for an enhancement. She has two bicycles; the bicycles have exactly the same gearing but they have different wheel sizes. She would like you to also calculate the effect of the difference in wheels.

A bike with huge wheels travels much farther during each wheel rotation than one with tiny wheels, as shown in Figure 2.2.

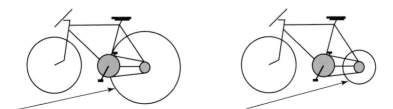

Big wheel — one rotation goes a long way.   Small wheel — one rotation goes hardly anywhere.

Figure 2.2   Effect of wheel size on distance traveled.

Cyclists (at least those in the United States) use something called *gear inches* to compare bicycles that differ in both gearing and wheel size. The formula follows:

gear inches = wheel diameter * gear ratio

where

wheel diameter = rim diameter + twice tire diameter.

You change the Gear class to add this new behavior:

```ruby
class Gear
  attr_reader :chainring, :cog, :rim, :tire
  def initialize(chainring, cog, rim, tire)
    @chainring = chainring
    @cog       = cog
    @rim       = rim
    @tire      = tire
  end

  def ratio
    chainring / cog.to_f
  end

  def gear_inches
      # tire goes around rim twice for diameter
    ratio * (rim + (tire * 2))
  end
end

puts Gear.new(52, 11, 26, 1.5).gear_inches
# -> 137.090909090909

puts Gear.new(52, 11, 24, 1.25).gear_inches
# -> 125.272727272727
```

The new gear_inches method assumes that rim and tire sizes are given in inches, which may or may not be correct. With that caveat, the Gear class meets the specifications (such as they are) and the code, with the exception of the following bug, works.

```ruby
puts Gear.new(52, 11).ratio  # didn't this used to work?
# ArgumentError: wrong number of arguments (2 for 4)
#        from (irb):20:in 'initialize'
```

```
4  #          from (irb):20:in 'new'
5  #          from (irb):20
6
```

The bug above was introduced when the `gear_inches` method was added. `Gear.initialize` was changed to require two additional arguments, `rim` and `tire`. Altering the number of arguments that a method requires breaks all existing callers of the method. This would normally be a terrible problem that would have to be dealt with instantly, but because the application is so small that `Gear.initialize` currently has no other callers, the bug can be ignored for now.

Now that a rudimentary `Gear` class exists, it's time to ask the question: Is this the best way to organize the code?

The answer, as always, is: it depends. If you expect the application to remain static forever, `Gear` in its current form may be good enough. However, you can already foresee the possibility of an entire application of calculators for bicyclists. `Gear` is the first of many classes of an application that will *evolve*. To efficiently evolve, code must be easy to change.

Why Single Responsibility Matters

Applications that are easy to change consist of classes that are easy to reuse. Reusable classes are pluggable units of well-defined behavior that have few entanglements. An application that is easy to change is like a box of building blocks; you can select just the pieces you need and assemble them in unanticipated ways.

A class that has more than one responsibility is difficult to reuse. The various responsibilities are likely thoroughly entangled *within* the class. If you want to reuse some (but not all) of its behavior, it is impossible to get at only the parts you need. You are faced with two options and neither is particularly appealing.

If the responsibilities are so coupled that you cannot use just the behavior you need, you could duplicate the code of interest. This is a terrible idea. Duplicated code leads to additional maintenance and increases bugs. If the class is structured such that you *can* access only the behavior you need, you could reuse the entire class. This just substitutes one problem for another.

Because the class you're reusing is confused about what it does and contains several tangled up responsibilities, it has many reasons to change. It may change for a reason that is unrelated to your use of it, and each time it changes there's a possibility of breaking every class that depends on it. You increase your application's chance of breaking unexpectedly if you depend on classes that do too much.

Determining If a Class Has a Single Responsibility

How can you determine if the `Gear` class contains behavior that belongs somewhere else? One way is to pretend that it's sentient and to interrogate it. If you rephrase every one of its methods as a question, asking the question ought to make sense. For example, *"Please Mr. Gear, what is your ratio?"* seems perfectly reasonable, while *"Please Mr. Gear, what are your gear_inches?"* is on shaky ground, and *"Please Mr. Gear, what is your tire (size)?"* is just downright ridiculous.

Don't resist the idea that *"what is your tire?"* is a question that can legitimately be asked. From inside the `Gear` class, `tire` may feel like a different kind of thing than `ratio` or `gear_inches`, but that means nothing. From the point of view of every other object, anything that `Gear` can respond to is just another message. If `Gear` responds to it, someone will send it, and that sender may be in for a rude surprise when `Gear` changes.

Another way to hone in on what a class is actually doing is to attempt to describe it in one sentence. Remember that a class should do the smallest possible useful thing. That thing ought to be simple to describe. If the simplest description you can devise uses the word "and," the class likely has more than one responsibility. If it uses the word "or," then the class has more than one responsibility and they aren't even very related.

OO designers use the word *cohesion* to describe this concept. When everything in a class is related to its central purpose, the class is said to be *highly cohesive* or to have a single responsibility. The Single Responsibility Principle (SRP) has its roots in Rebecca Wirfs-Brock and Brian Wilkerson's idea of Responsibility-Driven Design (RDD). They say "A class has responsibilities that fulfill its purpose." SRP doesn't require that a class do only one very narrow thing or that it change for only a single nitpicky reason, instead SRP requires that a class be cohesive—that everything the class does be highly related to its purpose.

How would you describe the responsibility of the `Gear` class? How about *"Calculate the ratio between two toothed sprockets"*? If this is true, the class, as it currently exists, does too much. Perhaps *"Calculate the effect that a gear has on a bicycle"*? Put this way, `gear_inches` is back on solid ground, but `tire` size is still quite shaky.

The class doesn't feel right. `Gear` has more than one responsibility but it's not obvious what should be done.

Determining When to Make Design Decisions

It's common to find yourself in a situation where you know something isn't quite right with a class. Is this class really a *Gear*? It has rims and tires, for goodness sake! Perhaps *Gear* should be *Bicycle*? Or maybe there's a *Wheel* in here somewhere?

If you only knew what feature requests would arrive in the future you could make perfect design decisions today. Unfortunately, you do not. Anything might happen. You can waste a lot of time being torn between equally plausible alternatives before rolling the dice and choosing the wrong one.

Do not feel compelled to make design decisions prematurely. Resist, even if you fear your code would dismay the design gurus. When faced with an imperfect and muddled class like Gear, ask yourself: *"What is the future cost of doing nothing today?"*

This is a (very) small application. It has one developer. You are intimately familiar with the Gear class. The future is uncertain and you will never know less than you know right now. The most cost-effective course of action may be to wait for more information.

The code in the Gear class is both *transparent* and *reasonable,* but this does not reflect excellent design, merely that the class has no dependencies so changes to it have no consequences. If it were to acquire dependencies it would suddenly be in violation of both of those goals and should be reorganized *at that time.* Conveniently, the new dependencies will supply the exact information you need to make good design decisions.

When the future cost of doing nothing is the same as the current cost, postpone the decision. Make the decision only when you must with the information you have at that time.

Even though there's a good argument for leaving Gear as is for the time being, you could also make a defensible argument that it should be changed. The structure of every class is a message to future maintainers of the application. It reveals your design intentions. For better or for worse, the patterns you establish today will be replicated forever.

Gear *lies* about your intentions. It is neither *usable* nor *exemplary.* It has multiple responsibilities and so should not be reused. It is not a pattern that should be replicated.

There is a chance that someone else will reuse Gear, or create new code that follows its pattern while you are waiting for better information. Other developers believe that your intentions are reflected in the code; when the code lies you must be alert to programmers believing and then propagating that lie.

This "improve it now" versus "improve it later" tension always exists. Applications are never perfectly designed. Every choice has a price. A good designer understands this tension and minimizes costs by making informed tradeoffs between the needs of the present and the possibilities of the future.

Writing Code That Embraces Change

You can arrange the code so that Gear will be easy to change even if you don't know what changes will come. Because change is inevitable, coding in a changeable style has big future payoffs. As an additional bonus, coding in these styles will improve your code, today, at no extra cost.

Here are a few well-known techniques that you can use to create code that embraces change.

Depend on Behavior, Not Data

Behavior is captured in methods and invoked by sending messages. When you create classes that have a single responsibility, every tiny bit of behavior lives in one and only one place. The phrase "Don't Repeat Yourself" (DRY) is a shortcut for this idea. DRY code tolerates change because any change in behavior can be made by changing code in just one place.

In addition to behavior, objects often contain data. Data is held in an instance variable and can be anything from a simple string or a complex hash. Data can be accessed in one of two ways; you can refer directly to the instance variable or you can wrap the instance variable in an accessor method.

Hide Instance Variables

Always wrap instance variables in accessor methods instead of directly referring to variables, like the ratio method does below:

```
 1  class Gear
 2    def initialize(chainring, cog)
 3      @chainring = chainring
 4      @cog       = cog
 5    end
 6
 7    def ratio
 8      @chainring / @cog.to_f      # <-- road to ruin
 9    end
10  end
```

Hide the variables, even from the class that defines them, by wrapping them in methods. Ruby provides attr_reader as an easy way to create the encapsulating methods:

```
 1  class Gear
 2    attr_reader :chainring, :cog   # <-------
 3    def initialize(chainring, cog)
 4      @chainring = chainring
 5      @cog       = cog
 6    end
 7
 8    def ratio
 9      chainring / cog.to_f           # <-------
10    end
11  end
```

Using `attr_reader` caused Ruby to create simple wrapper methods for the variables. Here's a virtual representation of the one it created for cog:

```
 1    # default implementation via attr_reader
 2    def cog
 3      @cog
 4    end
```

This cog method is now the only place in the code that understands what cog means. *Cog* becomes the result of a message send. Implementing this method changes cog from data (which is referenced all over) to behavior (which is defined once).

If the `@cog` instance variable is referred to ten times and it suddenly needs to be adjusted, the code will need many changes. However, if `@cog` is wrapped in a method, you can change what cog means by implementing your own version of the method. Your new method might be as simple as the first implementation below, or more complicated, like the second:

```
 1    # a simple reimplementation of cog
 2    def cog
 3      @cog * unanticipated_adjustment_factor
 4    end
```

```
 1    # a more complex one
 2    def cog
 3      @cog * (foo? ? bar_adjustment : baz_adjustment)
 4    end
```

The first example could arguably have been done by making one change to the value of the instance variable. However, you can never be sure that you won't eventually need something like the second example. The second adjustment is a simple behavior change when done in a method, but a code destroying mess when applied to a bunch of instance variable references.

Dealing with data as if it's an object that understands messages introduces two new issues. The first issue involves visibility. Wrapping the @cog instance variable in a *public* cog method exposes this variable to the other objects in your application; any other object can now send cog to a Gear. It would have been just as easy to create a *private* wrapping method, one that turns the data into behavior without exposing that behavior to the entire application. Choosing between these two alternatives is covered in Chapter 4, Creating Flexible Interfaces.

The second issue is more abstract. Because it's possible to wrap every instance variable in a method and to therefore treat any variable as if it's just another object, the distinction between *data* and a regular *object* begins to disappear. While it's sometimes expedient to think of parts of your application as behavior-less data, most things are better thought of as plain old objects.

Regardless of how far your thoughts move in this direction, you should hide data from yourself. Doing so protects the code from being affected by unexpected changes. Data very often has behavior that you don't yet know about. Send messages to access variables, even if you think of them as data.

Hide Data Structures

If being attached to an instance variable is bad, depending on a complicated data structure is worse. Consider the following ObscuringReferences class:

```ruby
1  class ObscuringReferences
2    attr_reader :data
3    def initialize(data)
4      @data = data
5    end
6
7    def diameters
8      # 0 is rim, 1 is tire
9      data.collect {|cell|
10        cell[0] + (cell[1] * 2)}
11    end
12    # ... many other methods that index into the array
13  end
```

This class expects to be initialized with a two-dimensional array of rims and tires:

```
1 # rim and tire sizes (now in millimeters!) in a 2d array
2 @data = [[622, 20], [622, 23], [559, 30], [559, 40]]
```

`ObscuringReferences` stores its initialization argument in the variable `@data` and obediently uses Ruby's `attr_reader` to wrap the `@data` instance variable in a method. The `diameters` method sends the `data` message to access the contents of the variable. This class certainly does everything necessary to hide the instance variable from itself.

However, since `@data` contains a complicated data structure, just hiding the instance variable is not enough. The `data` method merely returns the array. To do anything useful, each sender of `data` must have complete knowledge of what piece of data is at which index in the array.

The `diameters` method knows not only how to calculate diameters, but also where to find rims and tires in the array. It explicitly knows that if it iterates over `data` that rims are at [0] and tires are at [1].

It *depends* upon the array's structure. If that structure changes, then this code must change. When you have data in an array it's not long before you have references to the array's structure all over. The references are *leaky*. They escape encapsulation and insinuate themselves throughout the code. They are not DRY. The knowledge that rims are at [0] should not be duplicated; it should be known in just one place.

This simple example is bad enough; imagine the consequences if `data` returned an array of hashes that were referenced in many places. A change to its structure would cascade throughout your code; each change represents an opportunity to create a bug so stealthy that your attempts to find it will make you cry.

Direct references into complicated structures are confusing, because they obscure what the data really is, and they are a maintenance nightmare, because every reference will need to be changed when the structure of the array changes.

In Ruby it's easy to separate structure from meaning. Just as you can use a method to wrap an instance variable, you can use the Ruby `Struct` class to wrap a structure. In the following example, `RevealingReferences` has the same interface as the previous class. It takes a two-dimensional array as an initialization argument and it implements the `diameters` method. Despite these external similarities, its internal implementation is very different.

```ruby
class RevealingReferences
  attr_reader :wheels
  def initialize(data)
    @wheels = wheelify(data)
  end

  def diameters
    wheels.collect {|wheel|
      wheel.rim + (wheel.tire * 2)}
  end
  # ... now everyone can send rim/tire to wheel

  Wheel = Struct.new(:rim, :tire)
  def wheelify(data)
    data.collect {|cell|
      Wheel.new(cell[0], cell[1])}
  end
end
```

The `diameters` method above now has no knowledge of the internal structure of the array. All `diameters` knows is that the message `wheels` returns an enumerable and that each enumerated thing responds to `rim` and `tire`. What were once references to `cell[1]` have been transformed into message sends to `wheel.tire`.

All knowledge of the structure of the incoming array has been isolated inside the `wheelify` method, which converts the array of `Arrays` into an array of `Structs`. The official Ruby documentation (http://ruby-doc.org/core/classes/Struct.html) defines Struct as "a convenient way to bundle a number of attributes together, using accessor methods, without having to write an explicit class." This is exactly what `wheelify` does; it creates little lightweight objects that respond to `rim` and `tire`.

The `wheelify` method contains the only bit of code that understands the structure of the incoming array. If the input changes, the code will change in just this one place. It takes four new lines of code to create the `Wheel` Struct and to define the `wheelify` method, but these few lines of code are a minor inconvenience compared to the permanent cost of repeatedly indexing into a complex array.

This style of code allows you to protect against changes in externally owned data structures and to make your code more readable and intention revealing. It trades indexing into a structure for sending messages to an object. The `wheelify` method above isolates the messy structural information and DRYs out the code. It makes this class far more tolerant of change.

Although it might be easier to just have an array of Wheels to begin with, it is not always possible. If you can control the input, pass in a useful object, but if you are compelled to take a messy structure, hide the mess even from yourself.

Enforce Single Responsibility Everywhere

Creating classes with a single responsibility has important implications for design, but the idea of single responsibility can be usefully employed in many other parts of your code.

Extract Extra Responsibilities from Methods

Methods, like classes, should have a single responsibility. All of the same reasons apply; having just one responsibility makes them easy to change and easy to reuse. All the same design techniques work; ask them questions about what they do and try to describe their responsibilities in a single sentence.

Look at the diameters method of class RevealingReferences:

```
1   def diameters
2     wheels.collect {|wheel|
3       wheel.rim + (wheel.tire * 2)}
4   end
```

This method clearly has two responsibilities: it iterates over the wheels and it calculates the diameter of each wheel.

Simplify the code by separating it into two methods, each with one responsibility. This next refactoring moves the calculation of a single wheel's diameter into its own method. The refactoring introduces an additional message send but at this point in your design you should act as if sending a message is free. Performance can be improved later, if need be. Right now the most important design goal is to write code that is easily changeable.

```
1   # first - iterate over the array
2   def diameters
3     wheels.collect {|wheel| diameter(wheel)}
4   end
5
6   # second - calculate diameter of ONE wheel
7   def diameter(wheel)
8     wheel.rim + (wheel.tire * 2))
9   end
```

Will you ever need to get the diameter of just one wheel? Look at the code again; you already do. This refactoring is not a case of overdesign, it merely reorganizes code that is currently in use. The fact that the singular *diameter* method can now be called from other places is a free and happy side effect.

Separating iteration from the action that's being performed on each element is a common case of multiple responsibility that is easy to recognize. In other cases the problem is not so obvious.

Recall the gear_inches method of the Gear class:

```
1   def gear_inches
2       # tire goes around rim twice for diameter
3     ratio * (rim + (tire * 2))
4   end
```

Is gear_inches a responsibility of the Gear class? It is reasonable that it would be. But if it is, why does this method feel so wrong? It is muddled and uncertain and seems likely to cause trouble later. The root cause of the problem is that the method *itself* has more than one responsibility.

Hidden inside gear_inches is the calculation for wheel diameter. Extracting that calculation into this new diameter method will make it easier to examine the class's responsibilities.

```
1   def gear_inches
2     ratio * diameter
3   end
4
5   def diameter
6     rim + (tire * 2)
7   end
```

The gear_inches method now sends a message to get wheel diameter. Notice that the refactoring does not alter how diameter is calculated; it merely isolates the behavior in a separate method.

Do these refactorings even when you do not know the ultimate design. They are needed, not because the design is clear, but because it isn't. You do not have to know where you're going to use good design practices to get there. Good practices reveal design.

This simple refactoring makes the problem obvious. Gear is definitely responsible for calculating gear_inches but Gear should not be calculating wheel diameter.

The impact of a single refactoring like this is small, but the cumulative effect of this coding style is huge. Methods that have a single responsibility confer the following benefits:

- **Expose previously hidden qualities** Refactoring a class so that all of its methods have a single responsibility has a clarifying effect on the class. Even if you do not intend to reorganize the methods into other classes today, having each of them serve a single purpose makes the set of things the class does more obvious.

- **Avoid the need for comments** How many times have you seen a comment that is out of date? Because comments are not executable, they are merely a form of decaying documentation. If a bit of code inside a method needs a comment, extract that bit into a separate method. The new method name serves the same purpose as did the old comment.

- **Encourage reuse** Small methods encourage coding behavior that is healthy for your application. Other programmers will reuse the methods instead of duplicating the code. They will follow the pattern you have established and create small, reusable methods in turn. This coding style propagates itself.

- **Are easy to move to another class** When you get more design information and decide to make changes, small methods are easy to move. You can rearrange behavior without doing a lot of method extraction and refactoring. Small methods lower the barriers to improving your design.

Isolate Extra Responsibilities in Classes

Once every method has a single responsibility, the scope of your class will be more apparent. The Gear class has some wheel-like behavior. Does this application need a Wheel class?

If circumstances allow you to create a separate Wheel class, perhaps you should. For now, imagine that you choose not to create a new, permanent, publicly available class at this moment. Perhaps some design restriction has been imposed upon you, or perhaps you are so uncertain about where you're going that you don't want to create a new class that others might start depending on, lest you change your mind.

It may seem impossible for Gear to have a single responsibility unless you remove its wheel-like behavior; the extra behavior is either in Gear or it's not. However, casting the design choice in either/or terms is shortsighted. There are other choices. Your goal is to preserve single responsibility in Gear while making the fewest design commitments possible. Because you are writing changeable code, you are best served by postponing decisions until you are absolutely forced to make them. Any decision you make in advance of an explicit requirement is just a guess. Don't decide; preserve your ability to make a decision *later*.

Ruby allows you to remove the responsibility for calculating tire diameter from Gear without committing to a new class. The following example extends the previous Wheel Struct with a block that adds a method to calculate diameter.

```ruby
 1  class Gear
 2    attr_reader :chainring, :cog, :wheel
 3    def initialize(chainring, cog, rim, tire)
 4      @chainring = chainring
 5      @cog       = cog
 6      @wheel     = Wheel.new(rim, tire)
 7    end
 8
 9    def ratio
10      chainring / cog.to_f
11    end
12
13    def gear_inches
14      ratio * wheel.diameter
15    end
16
17    Wheel = Struct.new(:rim, :tire) do
18      def diameter
19        rim + (tire * 2)
20      end
21    end
22  end
```

Now you have a Wheel that can calculate its own diameter. Embedding this Wheel in Gear is obviously not the long-term design goal; it's more an experiment in code organization. It cleans up Gear but defers the decision about Wheel.

Embedding Wheel inside of Gear suggests that you expect that a Wheel will only exist in the context of a Gear. If you lift your head from this book for a moment and look out at the real world, common sense suggests otherwise. In this case, enough information exists right now to support the creation of an independent Wheel class. However, every domain isn't this clear-cut.

If you have a muddled class with too many responsibilities, separate those responsibilities into different classes. Concentrate on the primary class. Decide on its responsibilities and enforce your decision fiercely. If you identify extra responsibilities that you cannot yet remove, isolate them. Do not allow extraneous responsibilities to leak into your class.

Finally, the Real Wheel

While you're pondering the design of the Gear class, the future arrives. You show your calculator to your cyclist friend again and she tells you that it's very nice but that while you're writing calculators she would also like to have one for "bicycle wheel circumference." She has a computer on her bike that calculates speed; this computer has to be configured with the bicycle's wheel circumference to do its job.

This is the information you've been waiting for; it's a new feature request that supplies the exact information you need to make the next design decision.

You know that the circumference of a wheel is PI times its diameter. Your embedded Wheel already calculates diameter; it's a simple matter to add a new method to calculate circumference. These changes are minor; the real change here is that now your application has an explicit need for a Wheel class that it can use independently of Gear. It's time to set Wheel free to be a separate class of it's own.

Because you have already carefully isolated the Wheel behavior inside of the Gear class, this change is painless. Simply convert the Wheel Struct to an independent Wheel class and add the new circumference method:

```
1  class Gear
2    attr_reader :chainring, :cog, :wheel
3    def initialize(chainring, cog, wheel=nil)
4      @chainring = chainring
5      @cog       = cog
6      @wheel     = wheel
7    end
8
9    def ratio
10     chainring / cog.to_f
11   end
12
13   def gear_inches
14     ratio * wheel.diameter
15   end
16 end
17
```

```
18  class Wheel
19    attr_reader :rim, :tire
20
21    def initialize(rim, tire)
22      @rim        = rim
23      @tire       = tire
24    end
25
26    def diameter
27      rim + (tire * 2)
28    end
29
30    def circumference
31      diameter * Math::PI
32    end
33  end
34
35  @wheel = Wheel.new(26, 1.5)
36  puts @wheel.circumference
37  # -> 91.106186954104
38
39  puts Gear.new(52, 11, @wheel).gear_inches
40  # -> 137.090909090909
41
42  puts Gear.new(52, 11).ratio
43  # -> 4.72727272727273
```

Both classes have a single responsibility. The code is not perfect, but in some ways it achieves a higher standard: it is *good enough*.

Summary

The path to changeable and maintainable object-oriented software begins with classes that have a single responsibility. Classes that do one thing *isolate* that thing from the rest of your application. This isolation allows change without consequence and reuse without duplication.

CHAPTER 3
Managing Dependencies

Object-oriented programming languages contend that they are efficient and effective because of the way they model reality. Objects reflect qualities of a real-world problem and the interactions between those objects provide solutions. These interactions are inescapable. A single object cannot know everything, so inevitably it will have to talk to another object.

If you could peer into a busy application and watch the messages as they pass, the traffic might seem overwhelming. There's a lot going on. However, if you stand back and take a global view, a pattern becomes obvious. Each message is initiated by an object to invoke some bit of behavior. All of the behavior is dispersed among the objects. Therefore, for any desired behavior, an object either knows it personally, inherits it, or knows another object who knows it.

The previous chapter concerned itself with the first of these, that is, behaviors that a class should personally implement. The second, inheriting behavior, will be covered in Chapter 6, Acquiring Behavior Through Inheritance. This chapter is about the third, getting access to behavior when that behavior is implemented in *other* objects.

Because well designed objects have a single responsibility, their very nature requires that they collaborate to accomplish complex tasks. This collaboration is powerful and perilous. To collaborate, an object must know something know about others. *Knowing* creates a dependency. If not managed carefully, these dependencies will strangle your application.

Understanding Dependencies

An object depends on another object if, when one object changes, the other might be forced to change in turn.

Here's a modified version of the `Gear` class, where `Gear` is initialized with four familiar arguments. The `gear_inches` method uses two of them, `rim` and `tire`, to create a new instance of `Wheel`. `Wheel` has not changed since you last you saw it in Chapter 2, Designing Classes with a Single Responsibility.

```ruby
 1 class Gear
 2   attr_reader :chainring, :cog, :rim, :tire
 3   def initialize(chainring, cog, rim, tire)
 4     @chainring = chainring
 5     @cog       = cog
 6     @rim       = rim
 7     @tire      = tire
 8   end
 9
10   def gear_inches
11     ratio * Wheel.new(rim, tire).diameter
12   end
13
14   def ratio
15     chainring / cog.to_f
16   end
17 # ...
18 end
19
20 class Wheel
21   attr_reader :rim, :tire
22   def initialize(rim, tire)
23     @rim       = rim
24     @tire      = tire
25   end
26
27   def diameter
28     rim + (tire * 2)
29   end
30 # ...
31 end
32
33 Gear.new(52, 11, 26, 1.5).gear_inches
```

Examine the code above and make a list of the situations in which `Gear` would be forced to change because of a change to `Wheel`. This code seems innocent but it's sneakily complex. `Gear` has at least four dependencies on `Wheel`, enumerated as follows. Most of the dependencies are unnecessary; they are a side effect of the coding style. `Gear` does not need them to do its job. Their very existence weakens `Gear` and makes it harder to change.

Recognizing Dependencies

An object has a dependency when it knows

- The name of another class. `Gear` expects a class named `Wheel` to exist.

- The name of a message that it intends to send to someone other than `self`. `Gear` expects a `Wheel` instance to respond to `diameter`.

- The arguments that a message requires. `Gear` knows that `Wheel.new` requires a `rim` and a `tire`.

- The order of those arguments. `Gear` knows the first argument to `Wheel.new` should be `rim`, the second, `tire`.

Each of these dependencies creates a chance that `Gear` will be forced to change because of a change to `Wheel`. Some degree of dependency between these two classes is inevitable, after all, they *must* collaborate, but most of the dependencies listed above are unnecessary. These unnecessary dependencies make the code less *reasonable.* Because they increase the chance that `Gear` will be forced to change, these dependencies turn minor code tweaks into major undertakings where small changes cascade through the application, forcing many changes.

Your design challenge is to manage dependencies so that each class has the fewest possible; a class should know just enough to do its job and not one thing more.

Coupling Between Objects (CBO)

These dependencies *couple* `Gear` to `Wheel`. Alternatively, you could say that each coupling *creates* a dependency. The more `Gear` knows about `Wheel`, the more tightly coupled they are. The more tightly coupled two objects are, the more they behave like a single entity.

If you make a change to `Wheel` you may find it necessary to make a change to `Gear`. If you want to reuse `Gear`, `Wheel` comes along for the ride. When you test `Gear`, you'll be testing `Wheel` too.

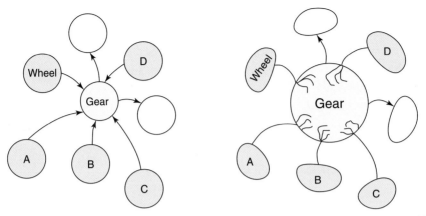

Gear depends on wheel, A, B, C and D   Gear and its dependencies act like one thing

Figure 3.1   Dependencies entangle objects with one another.

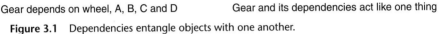

Figure 3.1 illustrates the problem. In this case, Gear depends on Wheel and four other objects, coupling Gear to five different things. When the underlying code was first written everything worked fine. The problem lies dormant until you attempt to use Gear in another context or to change one of the classes upon which Gear depends. When that day comes the cold hard truth is revealed; despite appearances, Gear is not an independent entity. Each of its dependencies is a place where another object is stuck to it. The dependencies cause these objects to act like a single thing. They move in lockstep; they change together.

When two (or three or more) objects are so tightly coupled that they behave as a unit, it's impossible to reuse just one. Changes to one object force changes to all. Left unchecked, unmanaged dependencies cause an entire application to become an entangled mess. A day will come when it's easier to rewrite everything than to change anything.

Other Dependencies

The remainder of this chapter examines the four kinds of dependencies listed above and suggests techniques for avoiding the problems they create. However, before going forward it's worth mentioning a few other common dependency related issues that will be covered in other chapters.

One especially destructive kind of dependency occurs where an object knows another who knows another who knows something; that is, where many messages are chained together to reach behavior that lives in a distant object. This is the "knowing the name of a message you plan to send to someone other than *self*" dependency, only magnified. Message chaining creates a dependency between the original object and every object and message along the way to its ultimate target. These additional couplings greatly increase the chance that the first object will be forced to change because a change to *any* of the intermediate objects might affect it.

This case, a Law of Demeter violation, gets its own special treatment in Chapter 4, Creating Flexible Interfaces.

Another entire class of dependencies is that of tests on code. In the world outside of this book, tests come first. They drive design. However, they refer to code and thus depend on code. The natural tendency of "new-to-testing" programmers is to write tests that are too tightly coupled to code. This tight coupling leads to incredible frustration; the tests break every time the code is refactored, even when the fundamental behavior of the code does not change. Tests begin to seem costly relative to their value. Test-to-code over-coupling has the same consequence as code-to-code over-coupling. These couplings are dependencies that cause changes to the code to cascade into the tests, forcing them to change in turn.

The design of tests is examined in Chapter 9, Designing Cost-Effective Tests.

Despite these cautionary words, your application is not doomed to drown in unnecessary dependencies. As long as you recognize them, avoidance is quite simple. The first step to this brighter future is to understand dependencies in more detail; therefore, it's time to look at some code.

Writing Loosely Coupled Code

Every dependency is like a little dot of glue that causes your class to stick to the things it touches. A few dots are necessary, but apply too much glue and your application will harden into a solid block. Reducing dependencies means recognizing and removing the ones you don't need.

The following examples illustrate coding techniques that reduce dependencies by decoupling code.

Inject Dependencies

Referring to another class by its name creates a major sticky spot. In the version of Gear we've been discussing (repeated below), the gear_inches method contains an explicit reference to class Wheel:

```
1  class Gear
2    attr_reader :chainring, :cog, :rim, :tire
3    def initialize(chainring, cog, rim, tire)
4      @chainring = chainring
```

```
 5     @cog      = cog
 6     @rim      = rim
 7     @tire     = tire
 8   end
 9
10   def gear_inches
11     ratio * Wheel.new(rim, tire).diameter
12   end
13 # ...
14 end
15
16 Gear.new(52, 11, 26, 1.5).gear_inches
```

The immediate, obvious consequence of this reference is that if the name of the Wheel class changes, Gear's gear_inches method must also change.

On the face of it this dependency seems innocuous. After all, if a Gear needs to talk to a Wheel, something, somewhere, must create a new instance of the Wheel class. If Gear itself knows the name of the Wheel class, the code in Gear must be altered if Wheel's name changes.

In truth, dealing with the name change is a relatively minor issue. You likely have a tool that allows you to do a global find/replace within a project. If Wheel's name changes to Wheely, finding and fixing all of the references isn't that hard. However, the fact that line 11 above must change if the name of the Wheel class changes is the least of the problems with this code. A deeper problem exists that is far less visible but significantly more destructive.

When Gear hard-codes a reference to Wheel deep inside its gear_inches method, it is explicitly declaring that it is only willing to calculate gear inches for instances of Wheel. Gear refuses to collaborate with any other kind of object, even if that object has a diameter and uses gears.

If your application expands to include objects such as disks or cylinders and you need to know the gear inches of gears which use them, *you cannot*. Despite the fact that disks and cylinders naturally have a diameter you can never calculate their gear inches because Gear is stuck to Wheel.

The code above exposes an unjustified attachment to static types. It is not the class of the object that's important, it's the *message* you plan to send to it. Gear needs access to an object that can respond to diameter; a duck type, if you will (see Chapter 5, Reducing Costs with Duck Typing). Gear does not care and should not know about the class of that object. It is not necessary for Gear to know about the existence of the Wheel class in order to calculate gear_inches. It doesn't need to know that Wheel expects to be initialized with a rim and then a tire; it just needs an object that knows diameter.

Hanging these unnecessary dependencies on Gear simultaneously reduces Gear's reusability and increases its susceptibility to being forced to change unnecessarily. Gear becomes less useful when it knows too much about *other* objects; if it knew less it could do more.

Instead of being glued to Wheel, this next version of Gear expects to be initialized with an object that can respond to diameter:

```ruby
 1  class Gear
 2    attr_reader :chainring, :cog, :wheel
 3    def initialize(chainring, cog, wheel)
 4      @chainring = chainring
 5      @cog       = cog
 6      @wheel     = wheel
 7    end
 8
 9    def gear_inches
10      ratio * wheel.diameter
11    end
12  # ...
13  end
14
15  # Gear expects a 'Duck' that knows 'diameter'
16  Gear.new(52, 11, Wheel.new(26, 1.5)).gear_inches
```

Gear now uses the @wheel variable to hold, and the wheel method to access, this object, but don't be fooled, Gear doesn't know or care that the object might be an instance of class Wheel. Gear only knows that it holds an object that responds to diameter.

This change is so small it is almost invisible, but coding in this style has huge benefits. Moving the creation of the new Wheel instance outside of Gear decouples the two classes. Gear can now collaborate with any object that implements diameter. As an extra bonus, this benefit was free. Not one additional line of code was written; the decoupling was achieved by rearranging existing code.

This technique is known as *dependency injection*. Despite its fearsome reputation, dependency injection truly is this simple. Gear previously had explicit dependencies on the Wheel class and on the type and order of its initialization arguments, but through injection these dependencies have been reduced to a single dependency on the diameter method. Gear is now smarter because it knows less.

Using dependency injection to shape code relies on your ability to recognize that the responsibility for knowing the name of a class and the responsibility for knowing the name of a message to send to that class may belong in different objects. Just because `Gear` needs to send `diameter` somewhere does not mean that `Gear` should know about `Wheel`.

This leaves the question of where the responsibility for knowing about the actual `Wheel` class lies; the example above conveniently sidesteps this issue, but it is examined in more detail later in this chapter. For now, it's enough to understand that this knowledge does *not* belong in `Gear`.

Isolate Dependencies

It's best to break all unnecessary dependences but, unfortunately, while this is always *technically* possible it may not be *actually* possible. When working on an existing application you may find yourself under severe constraints about how much you can actually change. If prevented from achieving perfection, your goals should switch to improving the overall situation by leaving the code better than you found it.

Therefore, if you cannot remove unnecessary dependencies, you should isolate them within your class. In Chapter 2, Designing Classes with a Single Responsibility, you isolated extraneous responsibilities so that they would be easy to recognize and remove when the right impetus came; here you should isolate unnecessary dependences so that they are easy to spot and reduce when circumstances permit.

Think of every dependency as an alien bacterium that's trying to infect your class. Give your class a vigorous immune system; quarantine each dependency. Dependencies are foreign invaders that represent vulnerabilities, and they should be concise, explicit, and isolated.

Isolate Instance Creation

If you are so constrained that you cannot change the code to inject a `Wheel` into a `Gear`, you should isolate the creation of a new `Wheel` inside the `Gear` class. The intent is to explicitly expose the dependency while reducing its reach into your class.

The next two examples illustrate this idea.

In the first, creation of the new instance of `Wheel` has been moved from `Gear`'s `gear_inches` method to `Gear`'s initialization method. This cleans up the `gear_inches` method and publicly exposes the dependency in the `initialize` method. Notice that this technique unconditionally creates a new `Wheel` each time a new `Gear` is created.

```
 1  class Gear
 2    attr_reader :chainring, :cog, :rim, :tire
 3    def initialize(chainring, cog, rim, tire)
 4      @chainring = chainring
 5      @cog      = cog
 6      @wheel    = Wheel.new(rim, tire)
 7    end
 8
 9    def gear_inches
10      ratio * wheel.diameter
11    end
12  # ...
```

The next alternative isolates creation of a new Wheel in its own explicitly defined wheel method. This new method lazily creates a new instance of Wheel, using Ruby's ||= operator. In this case, creation of a new instance of Wheel is deferred until gear_inches invokes the new wheel method.

```
 1  class Gear
 2    attr_reader :chainring, :cog, :rim, :tire
 3    def initialize(chainring, cog, rim, tire)
 4      @chainring = chainring
 5      @cog      = cog
 6      @rim      = rim
 7      @tire     = tire
 8    end
 9
10    def gear_inches
11      ratio * wheel.diameter
12    end
13
14    def wheel
15      @wheel ||= Wheel.new(rim, tire)
16    end
17  # ...
```

In both of these examples Gear still knows far too much; it still takes rim and tire as initialization arguments and it still creates its own new instance of Wheel. Gear is still stuck to Wheel; it can calculate the gear inches of no other kind of object.

However, an improvement *has* been made. These coding styles reduce the number of dependencies in gear_inches while publicly exposing Gear's dependency on

Wheel. They reveal dependencies instead of concealing them, lowering the barriers to reuse and making the code easier to refactor when circumstances allow. This change makes the code more agile; it can more easily adapt to the unknown future.

The way you manage dependencies on external class names has profound effects on your application. If you are mindful of dependencies and develop a habit of routinely injecting them, your classes will naturally be loosely coupled. If you ignore this issue and let the class references fall where they may, your application will be more like a big woven mat than a set of independent objects. An application whose classes are sprinkled with entangled and obscure class name references is unwieldy and inflexible, while one whose class name dependencies are concise, explicit, and isolated can easily adapt to new requirements.

Isolate Vulnerable External Messages

Now that you've isolated references to external class names it's time to turn your attention to external *messages*, that is, messages that are "sent to someone other than self." For example, the gear_inches method below sends ratio and wheel to self, but sends diameter to wheel:

```
1 def gear_inches
2   ratio * wheel.diameter
3 end
```

This is a simple method and it contains Gear's only reference to wheel.diameter. In this case the code is fine, but the situation could be more complex. Imagine that calculating gear_inches required far more math and that the method looked something like this:

```
1 def gear_inches
2   #... a few lines of scary math
3   foo = some_intermediate_result * wheel.diameter
4   #... more lines of scary math
5 end
```

Now wheel.diameter is embedded deeply inside a complex method. This complex method depends on Gear responding to wheel and on wheel responding to diameter. Embedding this external dependency inside the gear_inches method is unnecessary and increases its vulnerability.

Any time you change *anything* you stand the chance of breaking it; gear_inches is now a complex method and that makes it both more likely to need changing and more susceptible to being damaged when it does. You can reduce your chance of being forced to make a change to gear_inches by removing the external dependency and encapsulating it in a method of its own, as in this next example:

```
1  def gear_inches
2    #... a few lines of scary math
3    foo = some_intermediate_result * diameter
4    #... more lines of scary math
5  end
6
7  def diameter
8    wheel.diameter
9  end
```

The new diameter method is exactly the method that you would have written if you had many references to wheel.diameter sprinkled throughout Gear and you wanted to DRY them out. The difference here is one of timing; it would normally be defensible to defer creation of the diameter method until you had a need to DRY out code; however, in this case the method is created preemptively to remove the dependency from gear_inches.

In the original code, gear_inches knew that wheel had a diameter. This knowledge is a dangerous dependency that couples gear_inches to an external object and one of *its* methods. After this change, gear_inches is more abstract. Gear now isolates wheel.diameter in a separate method and gear_inches can depend on a message sent to self.

If Wheel changes the name or signature of *its* implementation of diameter, the side effects to Gear will be confined to this one simple wrapping method.

This technique becomes necessary when a class contains embedded references to a *message* that is likely to change. Isolating the reference provides some insurance against being affected by that change. Although not every external method is a candidate for this preemptive isolation, it's worth examining your code, looking for and wrapping the most vulnerable dependencies.

An alternative way to eliminate these side effects is to avoid the problem from the very beginning by reversing the direction of the dependency. This idea will be addressed soon but first there's one more coding technique to cover.

Remove Argument-Order Dependencies

When you send a message that requires arguments, you, as the sender, cannot avoid having knowledge of those arguments. This dependency is unavoidable. However, passing arguments often involves a second, more subtle, dependency. Many method signatures not only require arguments, but they also require that those arguments be passed in a specific, fixed order.

In the following example, Gear's initialize method takes three arguments: chainring, cog, and wheel. It provides no defaults; each of these arguments is required. In lines 11–14, when a new instance of Gear is created, the three arguments must be passed and they must be passed *in the correct order*.

```
1  class Gear
2    attr_reader :chainring, :cog, :wheel
3    def initialize(chainring, cog, wheel)
4      @chainring = chainring
5      @cog       = cog
6      @wheel     = wheel
7    end
8    ...
9  end
10
11 Gear.new(
12   52,
13   11,
14   Wheel.new(26, 1.5)).gear_inches
```

Senders of new depend on the order of the arguments as they are specified in Gear's initialize method. If that order changes, all the senders will be forced to change.

Unfortunately, it's quite common to tinker with initialization arguments. Especially early on, when the design is not quite nailed down, you may go through several cycles of adding and removing arguments and defaults. If you use fixed-order arguments each of these cycles may force changes to many dependents. Even worse, you may find yourself avoiding making changes to the arguments, even when your design calls for them because you can't bear to change all the dependents yet again.

Use Hashes for Initialization Arguments

There's a simple way to avoid depending on fixed-order arguments. If you have control over the Gear initialize method, change the code to take a hash of options instead of a fixed list of parameters.

The next example shows a simple version of this technique. The `initialize` method now takes just one argument, `args`, a hash that contains all of the inputs. The method has been changed to extract its arguments from this hash. The hash itself is created in lines 11–14.

```
1  class Gear
2    attr_reader :chainring, :cog, :wheel
3    def initialize(args)
4      @chainring = args[:chainring]
5      @cog       = args[:cog]
6      @wheel     = args[:wheel]
7    end
8    ...
9  end
10
11 Gear.new(
12   :chainring => 52,
13   :cog       => 11,
14   :wheel     => Wheel.new(26, 1.5)).gear_inches
```

The above technique has several advantages. The first and most obvious is that it removes every dependency on argument order. `Gear` is now free to add or remove initialization arguments and defaults, secure in the knowledge that no change will have side effects in other code.

This technique adds verbosity. In many situations verbosity is a detriment, but in this case it has value. The verbosity exists at the intersection between the needs of the present and the uncertainty of the future. Using fixed-order arguments requires less code today but you pay for this decrease in volume of code with an increase in the risk that changes will cascade into dependents later.

When the code in line 11 changed to use a hash, it lost its dependency on argument order but it gained a dependency on the names of the keys in the argument hash. This change is healthy. The new dependency is more stable than the old, and thus this code faces less risk of being forced to change. Additionally, and perhaps unexpectedly, the hash provides one new, secondary benefit: The *key* names in the hash furnish explicit documentation about the arguments. This is a byproduct of using a hash but the fact that it is unintentional makes it no less useful. Future maintainers of this code will be grateful for the information.

The benefits you achieve by using this technique vary, as always, based on your personal situation. If you are working on a method whose parameter list is lengthy and wildly unstable, in a framework that is intended to be used by others, it will likely lower overall costs if you specify arguments in a hash. However, if you are writing a method for your own use that divides two numbers, it's far simpler and perhaps ultimately cheaper to merely pass the arguments and accept the dependency on order. Between these two extremes lies a common case, that of the method that requires a few very stable arguments and optionally permits a number of less stable ones. In this case, the most cost-effective strategy may be to use both techniques; that is, to take a few fixed-order arguments, followed by an options hash.

Explicitly Define Defaults

There are many techniques for adding defaults. Simple non-boolean defaults can be specified using Ruby's || method, as in this next example:

```
1  # specifying defaults using ||
2  def initialize(args)
3    @chainring = args[:chainring] || 40
4    @cog       = args[:cog]       || 18
5    @wheel     = args[:wheel]
6  end
```

This is a common technique but one you should use with caution; there are situations in which it might not do what you want. The || method acts as an or condition; it first evaluates the left-hand expression and then, if the expression returns false or nil, proceeds to evaluate and return the result of the right-hand expression. The use of || above therefore, relies on the fact that the [] method of Hash returns nil for missing keys.

In the case where args contains a :boolean_thing key that defaults to true, use of || in this way makes it impossible for the caller to ever explicitly set the final variable to false or nil. For example, the following expression sets @bool to true when :boolean_thing is missing *and* also when it is present but set to false or nil:

```
@bool = args[:boolean_thing] || true
```

This quality of || means that if you take boolean values as arguments, or take arguments where you need to distinguish between false and nil, it's better to use the fetch method to set defaults. The fetch method *expects* the key you're fetching to be in the hash and supplies several options for explicitly handling missing keys. Its advantage over || is that it does not automatically return nil when it fails to find your key.

In the example below, line 3 uses `fetch` to set `@chainring` to the default, 40, only if the `:chainring` key is not in the `args` hash. Setting the defaults in this way means that callers can actually cause `@chainring` to get set to `false` or `nil`, something that is not possible when using the `||` technique.

```
1    # specifying defaults using fetch
2    def initialize(args)
3      @chainring = args.fetch(:chainring, 40)
4      @cog       = args.fetch(:cog, 18)
5      @wheel     = args[:wheel]
6    end
```

You can also completely remove the defaults from `initialize` and isolate them inside of a separate wrapping method. The `defaults` method below defines a second hash that is merged into the options hash during initialization. In this case, `merge` has the same effect as `fetch`; the defaults will get merged only if their keys are not in the hash.

```
1    # specifying defaults by merging a defaults hash
2    def initialize(args)
3      args = defaults.merge(args)
4      @chainring = args[:chainring]
5 #     ...
6    end
7
8    def defaults
9      {:chainring => 40, :cog => 18}
10   end
```

This isolation technique is perfectly reasonable for the case above but it's especially useful when the defaults are more complicated. If your defaults are more than simple numbers or strings, implement a `defaults` method.

Isolate Multiparameter Initialization

So far all of the examples of removing argument order dependencies have been for situations where *you* control the signature of the method that needs to change. You will not always have this luxury; sometimes you will be forced to depend on a method that requires fixed-order arguments where you do not own and thus cannot change the method itself.

Imagine that `Gear` is part of a framework and that its initialization method requires fixed-order arguments. Imagine also that your code has many places where you must create a new instance of `Gear`. `Gear`'s `initialize` method is *external* to your application; it is part of an external interface over which you have no control.

As dire as this situation appears, you are not doomed to accept the dependencies. Just as you would DRY out repetitive code inside of a class, DRY out the creation of new `Gear` instances by creating a single method to wrap the external interface. The classes in your application should depend on code that you own; use a wrapping method to isolate external dependencies.

In this example, the `SomeFramework::Gear` class is not owned by your application; it is part of an external framework. Its initialization method requires fixed-order arguments. The `GearWrapper` module was created to avoid having multiple dependencies on the order of those arguments. `GearWrapper` isolates all knowledge of the external interface in one place and, equally importantly, it provides an improved interface for your application.

As you can see in line 24, `GearWrapper` allows your application to create a new instance of `Gear` using an options hash.

```ruby
1  # When Gear is part of an external interface
2  module SomeFramework
3    class Gear
4      attr_reader :chainring, :cog, :wheel
5      def initialize(chainring, cog, wheel)
6        @chainring = chainring
7        @cog       = cog
8        @wheel     = wheel
9      end
10     # ...
11   end
12 end
13
14 # wrap the interface to protect yourself from changes
15 module GearWrapper
16   def self.gear(args)
17     SomeFramework::Gear.new(args[:chainring],
18                             args[:cog],
19                             args[:wheel])
20   end
21 end
22
```

```
23  # Now you can create a new Gear using an arguments hash.
24  GearWrapper.gear(
25    :chainring => 52,
26    :cog       => 11,
27    :wheel     => Wheel.new(26, 1.5)).gear_inches
```

There are two things to note about `GearWrapper`. First, it is a Ruby module instead of a class (line 15). `GearWrapper` is responsible for creating new instances of `SomeFramework::Gear`. Using a module here lets you define a separate and distinct object to which you can send the `gear` message (line 24) while simultaneously conveying the idea that you don't expect to have instances of `GearWrapper`. You may already have experience with including modules into classes; in the example above `GearWrapper` is not meant to be included in another class, it's meant to directly respond to the `gear` message.

The other interesting thing about `GearWrapper` is that its sole purpose is to create instances of some other class. Object-oriented designers have a word for objects like this; they call them *factories*. In some circles the term factory has acquired a negative connotation, but the term as used here is devoid of baggage. An object whose purpose is to create other objects is a factory; the word factory implies nothing more, and use of it is the most expedient way to communicate this idea.

The above technique for substituting an options hash for a list of fixed-order arguments is perfect for cases where you are forced to depend on external interfaces that you cannot change. Do not allow these kinds of external dependencies to permeate your code; protect yourself by wrapping each in a method that is owned by your own application.

Managing Dependency Direction

Dependencies always have a direction; earlier in this chapter it was suggested that one way to manage them is to reverse that direction. This section delves more deeply into how to decide on the direction of dependencies.

Reversing Dependencies

Every example used thus far shows `Gear` depending on `Wheel` or `diameter`, but the code could easily have been written with the direction of the dependencies reversed. `Wheel` could instead depend on `Gear` or `ratio`. The following example illustrates one possible form of the reversal. Here `Wheel` has been changed to depend on `Gear` and gear_inches. Gear is still responsible for the actual calculation but it expects a diameter argument to be passed in by the caller (line 8).

```ruby
 1 class Gear
 2   attr_reader :chainring, :cog
 3   def initialize(chainring, cog)
 4     @chainring = chainring
 5     @cog       = cog
 6   end
 7
 8   def gear_inches(diameter)
 9     ratio * diameter
10   end
11
12   def ratio
13     chainring / cog.to_f
14   end
15 #  ...
16 end
17
18 class Wheel
19   attr_reader :rim, :tire, :gear
20   def initialize(rim, tire, chainring, cog)
21     @rim       = rim
22     @tire      = tire
23     @gear      = Gear.new(chainring, cog)
24   end
25
26   def diameter
27     rim + (tire * 2)
28   end
29
30   def gear_inches
31     gear.gear_inches(diameter)
32   end
33 #  ...
34 end
35
36 Wheel.new(26, 1.5, 52, 11).gear_inches
```

This reversal of dependencies does no apparent harm. Calculating gear_inches still requires collaboration between Gear and Wheel and the result of the calculation is unaffected by the reversal. One could infer that the direction of the dependency does not matter, that it makes no difference whether `Gear` depends on `Wheel` or vice versa.

Indeed, in an application that never changed, your choice would not matter. However, your application *will* change and it's in that dynamic future where this present decision has repercussions. The choices you make about the direction of dependencies have far reaching consequences that manifest themselves for the life of your application. If you get this right, your application will be pleasant to work on and easy to maintain. If you get it wrong then the dependencies will gradually take over and the application will become harder and harder to change.

Choosing Dependency Direction

Pretend for a moment that your classes are people. If you were to give them advice about how to behave you would tell them to *depend on things that change less often than you do*.

This short statement belies the sophistication of the idea, which is based on three simple truths about code:

- Some classes are more likely than others to have changes in requirements.
- Concrete classes are more likely to change than abstract classes.
- Changing a class that has many dependents will result in widespread consequences.

There are ways in which these truths intersect but each is a separate and distinct notion.

Understanding Likelihood of Change

The idea that some classes are more likely to change than others applies not only to the code that you write for your own application but also to the code that you use but did *not* write. The Ruby base classes and the other framework code that you rely on both have their own inherent likelihood of change.

You are fortunate in that Ruby base classes change a great deal less often than your own code. This makes it perfectly reasonable to depend on the * method, as `gear_inches` quietly does, or to expect that Ruby classes `String` and `Array` will continue to work as they always have. Ruby base classes always change less often than your own classes and you can continue to depend on them without another thought.

Framework classes are another story; only you can assess how mature your frameworks are. In general, any framework you use will be more stable than the code you write, but it's certainly possible to choose a framework that is undergoing such rapid development that its code changes more often than yours.

Regardless of its origin, every class used in your application can be ranked along a scale of how likely it is to undergo a change relative to all other classes. This ranking is one key piece of information to consider when choosing the direction of dependencies.

Recognizing Concretions and Abstractions

The second idea concerns itself with the concreteness and abstractness of code. The term *abstract* is used here just as Merriam-Webster defines it, as "disassociated from any specific instance," and, as so many things in Ruby, represents an idea about code as opposed to a specific technical restriction.

This concept was illustrated earlier in the chapter during the section on injecting dependencies. There, when `Gear` depended on `Wheel` and on `Wheel.new` and on `Wheel.new(rim, tire)`, it depended on extremely concrete code. After the code was altered to inject a `Wheel` into `Gear`, `Gear` suddenly begin to depend on something far more abstract, that is, the fact that it had access to an object that could respond to the `diameter` message.

Your familiarity with Ruby may lead you to take this transition for granted, but consider for a moment what would have been required to accomplish this same trick in a statically typed language. Because statically typed languages have compilers that act like unit tests for types, you would not be able to inject just any random object into `Gear`. Instead you would have to declare an *interface*, define `diameter` as part of that interface, include the interface in the `Wheel` class, and tell `Gear` that the class you are injecting is a *kind of* that interface.

Rubyists are justifiably grateful to avoid these gyrations, but languages that force you to be explicit about this transition do offer a benefit. They make it painfully, inescapably, and explicitly clear that you are defining an abstract interface. It is impossible to create an abstraction unknowingly or by accident; in statically typed languages defining an interface is *always* intentional.

In Ruby, when you inject `Wheel` into `Gear` such that `Gear` then depends on a *Duck* who responds to `diameter`, you are, however casually, defining an interface. This interface is an abstraction of the idea that a certain category of things will have a diameter. The abstraction was harvested from a concrete class; the idea is now "disassociated from any specific instance."

The wonderful thing about abstractions is that they represent common, stable qualities. They are less likely to change than are the concrete classes from which they were extracted. Depending on an abstraction is always safer than depending on a concretion because by its very nature, the abstraction is more stable. Ruby does not make you explicitly declare the abstraction in order to define the interface, but for design purposes you can behave as if your virtual interface is as real as a class. Indeed, in the rest of this discussion, the term "class" stands for both *class* and this kind of *interface*. These interfaces can have dependents and so must be taken into account during design.

Avoiding Dependent-Laden Classes

The final idea, the notion that having dependent-laden objects has many consequences, also bears deeper examination. The consequences of changing a dependent-laden class are quite obvious—not so apparent are the consequences of even *having* a dependent-laden class. A class that, if changed, will cause changes to ripple through the application, will be under enormous pressure to *never* change. Ever. Under any circumstances whatsoever. Your application may be permanently handicapped by your reluctance to pay the price required to make a change to this class.

Finding the Dependencies That Matter

Imagine each of these truths as a continuum along which all application code falls. Classes vary in their likelihood of change, their level of abstraction, and their number of dependents. Each quality matters, but the interesting design decisions occur at the place where *likelihood of change* intersects with *number of dependents*. Some of the possible combinations are healthy for your application; others are deadly.

Figure 3.2 summarizes the possibilities.

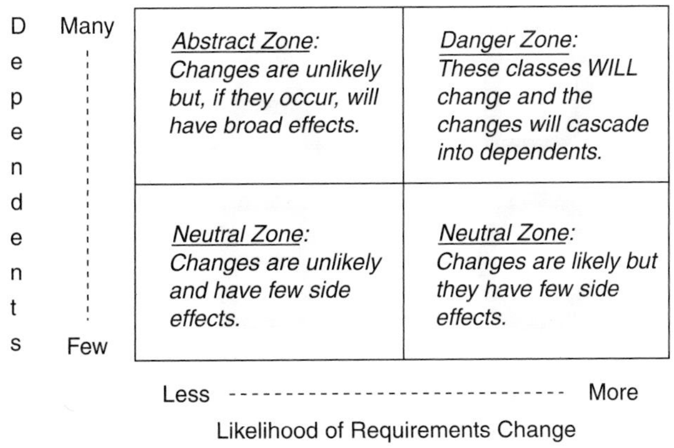

Figure 3.2   Likelihood of change versus number of dependents

The likelihood of requirements change is represented on the horizontal axis. The number of dependents is on the vertical. The grid is divided into four zones, labeled A through D. If you evaluate all of the classes in a well-designed application and place them on this grid, they will cluster in Zones A, B, and C.

Classes that have little likelihood of change but contain many dependents fall into Zone A. This Zone usually contains abstract classes or interfaces. In a thoughtfully designed application this arrangement is inevitable; dependencies cluster around abstractions because abstractions are less likely to change.

Notice that classes do not become abstract because they are in Zone A; instead they wind up here precisely because they are *already* abstract. Their abstract nature makes them more stable and allows them to safely acquire many dependents. While residence in Zone A does not guarantee that a class is abstract, it certainly suggests that it ought to be.

Skipping Zone B for a moment, Zone C is the opposite of Zone A. Zone C contains code that is quite likely to change but has few dependents. These classes tend to be more concrete, which makes them more likely to change, but this doesn't matter because few other classes depend on them.

Zone B classes are of the least concern during design because they are almost neutral in their potential future effects. They rarely change and have few dependents.

Zones A, B, and C are legitimate places for code; Zone D, however, is aptly named the Danger Zone. A class ends up in Zone D when it is guaranteed to change *and* has many dependents. Changes to Zone D classes are costly; simple requests become coding nightmares as the effects of every change cascade through each dependent. If you have a very specific *concrete* class that has many dependents and you believe it resides in Zone A, that is, you believe it is unlikely to change, think again. When a concrete class has many dependents your alarm bells should be ringing. That class might actually be an occupant of Zone D.

Zone D classes represent a danger to the future health of the application. These are the classes that make an application painful to change. When a simple change has cascading effects that force many other changes, a Zone D class is at the root of the problem. When a change breaks some far away and seemingly unrelated bit of code, the design flaw originated here.

As depressing as this is, there is actually a way to make things worse. You can guarantee that any application will gradually become unmaintainable by making its Zone D classes *more* likely to change than their dependents. This maximizes the consequences of every change.

Fortunately, understanding this fundamental issue allows you to take preemptive action to avoid the problem.

Depend on things that change less often than you do is a heuristic that stands in for all the ideas in this section. The zones are a useful way to organize your thoughts but in the fog of development it may not be obvious which classes go where. Very often you are exploring your way to a design and at any given moment the future is unclear. Following this simple rule of thumb at every opportunity will cause your application to evolve a healthy design.

Summary

Dependency management is core to creating future-proof applications. Injecting dependencies creates loosely coupled objects that can be reused in novel ways. Isolating dependencies allows objects to quickly adapt to unexpected changes. Depending on abstractions decreases the likelihood of facing these changes.

The key to managing dependencies is to control their direction. The road to maintenance nirvana is paved with classes that depend on things that change less often than they do.

CHAPTER 4

Creating Flexible Interfaces

It's tempting to think of object-oriented applications as being the sum of their classes. Classes are so very visible; design discussions often revolve around class responsibilities and dependencies. Classes are what you see in your text editor and what you check in to your source code repository.

There *is* design detail that must be captured at this level but an object-oriented application is more than just classes. It is *made up of classes* but *defined* by messages. Classes control what's in your source code repository; messages reflect the living, animated application.

Design, therefore, must be concerned with the messages that pass between objects. It deals not only with what objects know (their responsibilities) and who they know (their dependencies), but how they talk to one another. The conversation between objects takes place using their *interfaces;* this chapter explores creating flexible interfaces that allow applications to grow and to change.

Understanding Interfaces

Imagine two running applications, as illustrated in Figure 4.1. Each consists of objects and the messages that pass between them.

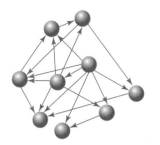 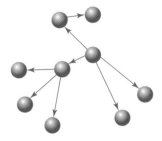

Figure 4.1　Communication patterns.

In the first application, the messages have no apparent pattern. Every object may send any message to any other object. If the messages left visible trails, these trails would eventually draw a woven mat, with each object connected to every other.

In the second application, the messages have a clearly defined pattern. Here the objects communicate in specific and well-defined ways. If these messages left trails, the trails would accumulate to create a set of islands with occasional bridges between them.

Both applications, for better or worse, are characterized by the patterns of their messages.

The objects in the first application are difficult to reuse. Each one exposes too much of itself and knows too much about its neighbors. This excess knowledge results in objects that are finely, explicitly, and disastrously tuned to do only the things that they do right now. No object stands alone; to reuse any you need all, to change one thing you must change everything.

The second application is composed of plug-able, component-like objects. Each reveals as little about itself, and knows as little about others, as possible.

The design issue in the first application is not necessarily a failure of dependency injection or single responsibility. Those techniques, while necessary, are not enough to prevent the construction of an application whose design causes you pain. The roots of this new problem lie not in what each class *does* but with what it *reveals*. In the first application each class reveals all. Every method in any class is fair game to be invoked by any other object.

Experience tells you that all the methods in a class are not the same; some are more general or more likely to change than others. The first application takes no notice of this. It allows all methods of any object, regardless of their granularity, to be invoked by others.

In the second application, the message patterns are visibly constrained. This application has some agreement, some bargain, about which messages may pass between its objects. Each object has a clearly defined set of methods that it expects others to use.

These exposed methods comprise the class's *public interface*.

The word *interface* can refer to a number of different concepts. Here the term is used to refer to the kind of interface that is *within* a class. Classes implement methods, some of those methods are intended to be used by others and these methods make up its public interface.

An alternative kind of interface is one that spans across classes and that is independent of any single class. Used in this sense, the word *interface* represents a set of messages where the messages themselves define the interface. Many different classes may, as part of their whole, implement the methods that the interface requires. It's almost as if the interface defines a *virtual* class; that is, any class that implements the required methods can act like the *interface* kind of thing.

The remainder of this chapter will address the first kind of interface, that is, methods within a class and how and what to expose to others. Chapter 5, Reducing Costs with Duck Typing, explores the second kind of interface, the one that represents a concept that is broader than a class and is defined by a set of messages.

Defining Interfaces

Imagine a restaurant kitchen. Customers order food off a menu. These orders come into the kitchen through a little window (the one with the bell beside it, "order up!") and the food eventually comes out. To a naïve imagination it may seem as if the kitchen is filled with magical plates of food that are waiting, pining to be ordered, but in reality the kitchen is full of people, food, and frenzied activity and each order triggers a new construction and assembly process.

The kitchen does many things but does not, thankfully, expose them all to its customers. It has a *public* interface that customers are expected to use; the menu. Within the kitchen many things happen, many other messages get passed, but these messages are *private* and thus invisible to customers. Even though they may have ordered it, customers are not welcome to come in and stir the soup.

This distinction between public and private exists because it is the most effective way to do business. If customers directed the cooking, they would have to be re-educated whenever the kitchen ran low on an ingredient and needed to make a substitution. Using a menu avoids this problem by letting each customer ask for *what* they want without knowing anything about *how* the kitchen makes it.

Each of your classes is like a kitchen. The class exists to fulfill a single responsibility but implements many methods. These methods vary in scale and granularity and range from broad, general methods that expose the main responsibility of the class to tiny utility methods that are only meant to be used internally. Some of these methods represent the menu for your class and should be public; others deal with internal implementation details and are private.

Public Interfaces

The methods that make up the public interface of your class comprise the face it presents to the world. They:

- Reveal its primary responsibility
- Are expected to be invoked by others
- Will not change on a whim
- Are safe for others to depend on
- Are thoroughly documented in the tests

Private Interfaces

All other methods in the class are part of its private interface. They:

- Handle implementation details
- Are not expected to be sent by other objects
- Can change for any reason whatsoever
- Are unsafe for others to depend on
- May not even be referenced in the tests

Responsibilities, Dependencies, and Interfaces

Chapter 2, Designing Classes with a Single Responsibility, was about creating classes that have a single responsibility—a single purpose. If you think of a class as having a single purpose, then the things it does (its more specific responsibilities) are what allows it to fulfill that purpose. There is a correspondence between the statements you might make about these more specific responsibilities and the classes' public methods. Indeed, public methods should read like a description of responsibilities. The public interface is a contract that articulates the responsibilities of your class.

Chapter 3, Managing Dependencies, was about dependencies and its take-home message was that a class should depend only on classes that change less often than it does. Now that you are dividing every class into a public part and a private part, this idea of depending on less changeable things also applies to the methods *within* a class.

The public parts of a class are the stable parts; the private parts are the changeable parts. When you mark methods as public or private you tell users of your class upon which methods they may safely depend. When your classes use the public methods of others, you trust those methods to be stable. When you decide to depend on the private methods of others, you understand that you are relying on something that is inherently unstable and are thus increasing the risk of being affected by a distant and unrelated change.

Finding the Public Interface

Finding and defining public interfaces is an art. It presents a design challenge because there are no cut-and-dried rules. There are many ways to create "good enough" interfaces and the costs of a "not good enough" interface may not be obvious for a while, making it difficult to learn from mistakes.

The design goal, as always, is to retain maximum future flexibility while writing only enough code to meet today's requirements. Good public interfaces reduce the cost of unanticipated change; bad public interfaces raise it.

This section introduces a new application to illustrate a number of rules-of-thumb about interfaces and a new tool aid to in their discovery.

An Example Application: Bicycle Touring Company

Meet FastFeet, Inc., a bicycle touring company. FastFeet offers both road and mountain bike trips. FastFeet runs its business using a paper system. It currently has no automation at all.

Each trip offered by FastFeet follows a specific route and may occur several times during the year. Each has limitations on the number of customers who may go and requires a specific number of guides who double as mechanics.

Each route is rated according to its aerobic difficulty. Mountain bike trips have an additional rating that reflects technical difficulty. Customers have an aerobic fitness level and a mountain bike technical skill level to determine if a trip is right for them.

Customers may rent bicycles or they may choose to bring their own. FastFeet has a few bicycles available for customer rental and it also shares in a pool of bicycle rentals with local bike shops. Rental bicycles come in various sizes and are suitable for either road or mountain bike trips.

Consider the following simple requirement, which will be referred to later as a *use case*: A customer, in order to choose a trip, would like to see a list of available trips of appropriate difficulty, on a specific date, where rental bicycles are available.

Constructing an Intention

Getting started with the first bit of code in a brand new application is intimidating. When you are adding code to an existing code base you are usually extending an existing design. Here, however, you must put pen to paper (figuratively) and make decisions that will determine the patterns of this application forever. The design that gets extended later is the one that you are establishing now.

You know that you should not dive in and start writing code. You may believe that you should start writing tests, but that belief doesn't make it easy. Many novice designers have serious difficulty imagining the first test. Writing that test requires that you have an idea about what you want to test, one that you may not yet have.

The reason that test-first gurus can easily start writing tests is that they have so much design experience. At this stage, they have already constructed a mental map of possibilities for objects and interactions in this application. They are not attached to any specific idea and plan to use tests to discover alternatives, but they know so much about design that they have already formed an intention about the application. It is this intention that allows them to specify the first test.

Whether you are conscious of them or not, you have already formed some intentions of your own. The description of FastFeet's business has likely given you ideas about potential classes in this application. You probably expect to have Customer, Trip, Route, Bike, and Mechanic classes.

These classes spring to mind because they represent *nouns* in the application that have both *data* and *behavior*. Call them *domain objects*. They are obvious because they are persistent; they stand for big, visible real-world things that will end up with a representation in your database.

Domain objects are easy to find but they are not at the design center of your application. Instead, they are a trap for the unwary. If you fixate on domain objects you will tend to coerce behavior into them. Design experts *notice* domain objects without concentrating on them; they focus not on these objects but on the messages that pass between them. These messages are guides that lead you to discover other objects, ones that are just as necessary but far less obvious.

Before you sit at the keyboard and start typing you should form an intention about the objects *and* the messages needed to satisfy this use case. You would be best served if you had a simple, inexpensive communication enhancing way to explore design that did not require you to write code.

Fortunately, some very smart people have thought about this issue at great length and have devised an effective mechanism for doing just that.

Using Sequence Diagrams

There is a perfect, low-cost way to experiment with objects and messages: *sequence diagrams*.

Sequence diagrams are defined in the Unified Modeling Language (UML) and are one of many diagrams that UML supports. Figure 4.2 shows a sampling of some diagrams.

If you have joyfully embraced UML you already know the value of sequence diagrams. If you are unfamiliar with UML and find the graphic alarming, fear not. This book is not turning into a UML guide. Lightweight, agile design does not require the creation and maintenance of piles of artifacts. However, the creators of

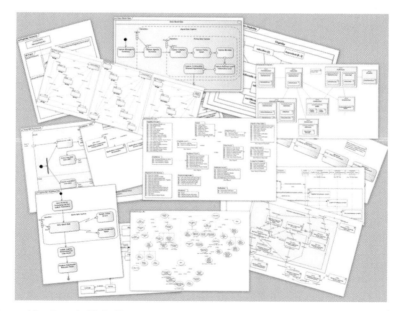

Figure 4.2   Sample UML diagrams.

UML put a great deal of thought into how to communicate object-oriented design and you can leverage off their efforts. There are UML diagrams that provide excellent, transient ways to explore and communicate design possibilities. Use them; you do not need to reinvent this wheel.

Sequence diagrams are quite handy. They provide a simple way to experiment with different object arrangements and message passing schemes. They bring clarity to your thoughts and provide a vehicle to collaborate and communicate with others. Think of them as a lightweight way to acquire an intention about an interaction. Draw them on a whiteboard, alter them as needed, and erase them when they've served their purpose.

Figure 4.3 shows a simple sequence diagram. This diagram represents an attempt to implement the use case above. It shows Moe, a `Customer` and the `Trip` class, where Moe sends the `suitable_trips` message to `Trip` and gets back a response.

Figure 4.3 illustrates the two main parts of a sequence diagram. As you can see, they show two things: *objects* and the *messages* passing between them. The following paragraphs describe the parts of this diagram but please note that the UML police will not arrest you if you vary from the official style. Do what works for you.

In the example diagram each object is represented by two identically named boxes, arranged one above the other and connected by a single vertical line. It contains two objects, the `Customer` Moe and the class `Trip`. Messages are shown as horizontal lines. When a message is sent, the line is labeled with the message name. Message lines end or begin with an arrow; this arrow points to the receiver. When an object is busy processing a received message, it is *active* and its vertical line is expanded to a vertical rectangle.

The diagram also contains a single message, `suitable_trips`, sent by Moe to the `Trip` class. Therefore, this sequence diagram can be read as follows: `Customer` Moe sends the `suitable_trips` message to the `Trip` class, which is activated to process it and then, when finished, returns a response.

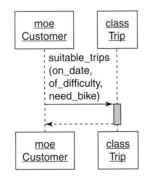

Figure 4.3   A simple sequence diagram.

This sequence diagram is very nearly an exact literal translation of the use case. The nouns in the use case became objects in the sequence diagram and the action of the use case turned into a message. The message requires three parameters: on_date, of_difficulty, and need_bike.

While this example serves quite adequately to illustrate the parts of a sequence diagram, the design that it implies should give you pause. In this sequence diagram Moe expects the Trip class to find him a suitable trip. It seems reasonable that Trip would be responsible for finding trips on a date and of a difficulty, but Moe may also need a bicycle and he clearly expects Trip to handle that too.

Drawing this sequence diagram exposes the message passing between the Customer Moe and the Trip class and prompts you to ask the question: "Should Trip be responsible for figuring out if an appropriate bicycle is available for each suitable trip?" or more generally, "Should this receiver be responsible for responding to this message?"

Therein lies the value of sequence diagrams. They explicitly specify the messages that pass between objects, and because objects should only communicate using public interfaces, sequence diagrams are a vehicle for exposing, experimenting with, and ultimately defining those interfaces.

Also, notice now that you have drawn a sequence diagram, this design conversation has been inverted. The previous design emphasis was on classes and who and what they knew. Suddenly, the conversation has changed; it is now revolving around messages. Instead of deciding on a class and then figuring out its responsibilities, you are now deciding on a message and figuring out where to send it.

This transition from class-based design to message-based design is a turning point in your design career. The message-based perspective yields more flexible applications than does the class-based perspective. Changing the fundamental design question from "I know I need this class, what should it do?" to "I need to send this message, who should respond to it?" is the first step in that direction.

You don't send messages because you have objects, you have objects because you send messages.

From a message passing point of view, it is perfectly reasonable for a Customer to send the suitable_trips message. The problem isn't that Customer should not send it, the problem is that Trip should not receive it.

Now that you have the suitable_trips message in mind but no place to send it, you must construct some alternatives. Sequence diagrams make it easy to explore the possibilities.

If the Trip class should not be figuring out if bicycles are available for a trip, perhaps there's a Bicycle class that should. Trip can be responsible for suitable_trips and

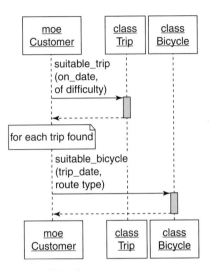

Figure 4.4   Moe talks to trip and bicycle.

Bicycle for suitable_bicycle. Moe can get the answer he needs if he talks to both of them. That sequence diagram looks like Figure 4.4.

For each of these diagrams, consider what Moe has to know.

In Figure 4.3, he knows that:

- He wants a list of trips.

- There's an object that implements the suitable_trips message.

In Figure 4.4, he knows that:

- He wants a list of trips.

- There's an object that implements the suitable_trips message.

- Part of finding a suitable trip means finding a suitable bicycle.

- There's another object that implements the suitable_bicycle message.

Sadly, Figure 4.4 is an improvement in some areas but a failure in others. This design removes extraneous responsibilities from Trip but unfortunately, it merely transfers them to Customer.

The problem in Figure 4.4 is that Moe not only knows *what* he wants, he also knows *how* other objects should collaborate to provide it. The Customer class has become the owner of the application rules that assess trip suitability.

When Moe knows how to decide if a trip is suitable, he isn't ordering behavior off of a menu, he's going into the kitchen and cooking. The Customer class is co-opting responsibilities that belong somewhere else and binding itself to an implementation that might change.

Asking for "What" Instead of Telling "How"

The distinction between a message that asks for what the sender wants and a message that tells the receiver how to behave may seem subtle but the consequences are significant. Understanding this difference is a key part of creating reusable classes with well-defined public interfaces.

To illustrate the importance of *what* versus *how*, it's time for a more detailed example. Put the customer/trip design problem aside for a bit; it will return soon. Switch your attention to a new example involving trips, bicycles, and mechanics.

In Figure 4.5, a trip is about to depart and it needs to make sure all the bicycles scheduled to be used are in good shape. The use case for this requirement is: A trip, in order to start, needs to ensure that all its bicycles are mechanically sound. Trip *could* know exactly how to make a bike ready for a trip and could ask a Mechanic to do each of those things:

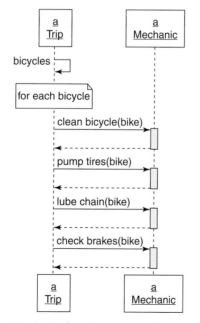

Figure 4.5 A *Trip* tells a *Mechanic* how to prepare each *Bicycle*.

In Figure 4.5:

- The public interface for `Trip` includes the method `bicycles`.

- The public interface for `Mechanic` includes methods `clean_bicycle`, `pump_tires`, `lube_chain`, and `check_brakes`.

- `Trip` expects to be holding onto an object that can respond to `clean_bicycle`, `pump_tires`, `lube_chain`, and `check_brakes`.

In this design, `Trip` knows many details about what `Mechanic` does. Because `Trip` contains this knowledge and uses it to direct `Mechanic`, `Trip` must change if `Mechanic` adds new procedures to the bike preparation process. For example, if `Mechanic` implements a method to check the bike repair kit as part of `Trip` preparation, `Trip` must change to invoke this new method.

Figure 4.6 depicts an alternative where `Trip` asks `Mechanic` to prepare each `Bicycle`, leaving the implementation details to `Mechanic`.

In Figure 4.6:

- The public interface for `Trip` includes the method `bicycles`.

- The public interface for `Mechanic` includes method `prepare_bicycle`.

- Trip expects to be holding onto an object that can respond to `prepare_bicycle`.

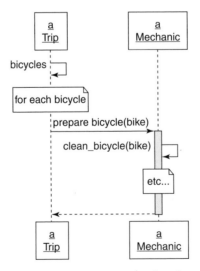

Figure 4.6   A *Trip* asks a *Mechanic* to prepare each *Bicycle*.

Trip has now relinquished a great deal of responsibility to Mechanic. Trip knows that it wants each of its bicycles to be prepared, and it trusts the Mechanic to accomplish this task. Because the responsibility for knowing *how* has been ceded to Mechanic, Trip will always get the correct behavior regardless of future improvements to Mechanic.

When the conversation between Trip and Mechanic switched from a *how* to a *what*, one side effect was that the size of the public interface in Mechanic was drastically reduced. In Figure 4.5 Mechanic exposes many methods, in Figure 4.6 its public interface consists of a single method, prepare_bicycle. Because Mechanic promises that its public interface is stable and unchanging, having a small public interface means that there are few methods for others to depend on. This reduces the likelihood of Mechanic someday changing its public interface, breaking its promise, and forcing changes on many other classes.

This change of message patterns is a great improvement to the maintainability of the code but Trip still knows a lot about Mechanic. The code would be more flexible and more maintainable if Trip could accomplish its goals while knowing even less.

Seeking Context Independence

The things that Trip knows about other objects make up its *context*. Think of it this way: Trip *has* a single responsibility but it *expects* a context. In Figure 4.6 Trip expects to be holding onto a Mechanic object that can respond to the prepare_bicycle message.

Context is a coat that Trip wears everywhere; any use of Trip, be it for testing or otherwise, requires that its context be established. Preparing a trip *always* requires preparing bicycles and in doing so Trip *always* sends the prepare_bicycle message to its Mechanic. You cannot reuse Trip unless you provide a Mechanic-like object that can respond to this message.

The context that an object expects has a direct effect on how difficult it is to reuse. Objects that have a simple context are easy to use and easy to test; they expect few things from their surroundings. Objects that have a complicated context are hard to use and hard to test; they require complicated setup before they can do anything.

The best possible situation is for an object to be completely independent of its context. An object that could collaborate with others without knowing who they are or what they do could be reused in novel and unanticipated ways.

You already know the technique for collaborating with others without knowing who they are—dependency injection. The new problem here is for Trip to invoke the correct behavior from Mechanic without knowing what Mechanic does. Trip wants to collaborate with Mechanic while maintaining context independence.

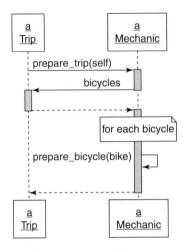

Figure 4.7   A *Trip* asks a *Mechanic* to prepare the *Trip*.

At first glance this seems impossible. Trips have bicycles, bicycles must be prepared, and mechanics prepare bicycles. Having Trip ask Mechanic to prepare a Bicycle seems inevitable.

However, it is not. The solution to this problem lies in the distinction between *what* and *how*, and arriving at a solution requires concentrating on what Trip wants.

What Trip wants is to be prepared. The knowledge that it must be prepared is completely and legitimately within the realm of Trip's responsibilities. However, the fact that *bicycles* need to be prepared may belong to the province of Mechanic. The need for bicycle preparation is more how a Trip gets prepared than what a Trip wants.

Figure 4.7 illustrates a third alternative sequence diagram for Trip preparation. In this example, Trip merely tells Mechanic what it wants, that is, to be prepared, and passes itself along as an argument.

In this sequence diagram, Trip knows nothing about Mechanic but still manages to collaborate with it to get bicycles ready. Trip tells Mechanic what it wants, passes self along as an argument, and Mechanic immediately calls back to Trip to get the list of the Bicycles that need preparing.

In Figure 4.7:

- The public interface for Trip includes bicycles.

- The public interface for Mechanic includes prepare_trip and perhaps prepare_bicycle.

- `Trip` expects to be holding onto an object that can respond to `prepare_trip`.

- `Mechanic` expects the argument passed along with `prepare_trip` to respond to `bicycles`.

All of the knowledge about how mechanics prepare trips is now isolated inside of `Mechanic` and the context of `Trip` has been reduced. Both of the objects are now easier to change, to test, and to reuse.

Trusting Other Objects

The designs illustrated by Figures 4.5 through 4.7 represent a movement towards increasingly *object*-oriented code and as such they mirror the stages of development of the novice designer.

Figure 4.5 is quite procedural. A `Trip` tells a `Mechanic` how to prepare a `Bicycle`, almost as if `Trip` were the main program and `Mechanic` a bunch of callable functions. In this design, `Trip` is the only object that knows exactly how to prepare a bike; getting a bike prepared requires using a `Trip` or duplicating the code. `Trip`'s context is large, as is `Mechanic`'s public interface. These two classes are not islands with bridges between them, they are instead a single, woven cloth.

Many new object-oriented programmers start out working just this way, writing procedural code. It's inevitable; this style closely mirrors the best practices of their former procedural languages. Unfortunately, coding in a procedural style defeats the purpose of object orientation. It reintroduces the exact maintenance issues that OOP is designed to avoid.

Figure 4.6 is more object-oriented. Here, a `Trip` *asks* a `Mechanic` to prepare a `Bicycle`. `Trip`'s context is reduced, and `Mechanic`'s public interface is smaller. Additionally, `Mechanic`'s public interface is now something that any object may profitably use; you don't need a `Trip` to prepare a bike. These objects now communicate in a few well-defined ways; they are less coupled and more easily reusable.

This style of coding places the responsibilities in the correct objects, a great improvement, but continues to require that `Trip` have more context than is necessary. `Trip` still knows that it holds onto an object that can respond to `prepare_bicycle`, and it must *always* have this object.

Figure 4.7 is far more object-oriented. In this example, `Trip` doesn't know or care that it has a `Mechanic` and it doesn't have any idea what the `Mechanic` will do. `Trip` merely holds onto an object to which it will send `prepare_trip`; it trusts the receiver of this message to behave appropriately.

Expanding on this idea, `Trip` could place a number of such objects into an array and send each the `prepare_trip` message, trusting every preparer to do whatever it does because of the kind of thing that it is. Depending on how `Trip` was being used, it might have many preparers or it might have few. This pattern allows you to add newly introduced preparers to `Trip` without changing any of its code, that is, you can *extend* `Trip` without *modifying* it.

If objects were human and could describe their own relationships, in Figure 4.5 `Trip` would be telling `Mechanic`: "I know what I want and I know how you do it;" in Figure 4.6: "I know what I want and I know what you do" and in Figure 4.7: "I know what I want and *I trust you to do your part.*"

This blind trust is a keystone of object-oriented design. It allows objects to collaborate without binding themselves to context and is necessary in any application that expects to grow and change.

Using Messages to Discover Objects

Armed with knowledge about the distinction between *what* and *how*, and the importance of context and trust, it's time to return to the original design problem from Figures 4.3 and 4.4.

Remember that the use case for that problem stated: A customer, in order to choose a trip, would like to see a list of available trips of appropriate difficulty, on a specific date, where rental bicycles are available.

Figure 4.3 was a literal translation of this use case, one in which `Trip` had too much responsibility. Figure 4.4 was an attempt to move the responsibility for finding available bicycles from `Trip` to `Bicycle`, but in doing so it placed an obligation on `Customer` to know far too much about what makes a trip "suitable."

Neither of these designs is very reusable or tolerant of change. These problems are revealed, inescapably, in the sequence diagrams. Both designs contain a violation of the single responsibility principle. In Figure 4.3, `Trip` knows too much. In Figure 4.4, `Customer` knows too much, tells other objects how to behave, and requires too much context.

It is completely reasonable that `Customer` would send the `suitable_trips` message. That message repeats in both sequence diagrams because it feels innately correct. It is exactly *what* `Customer` wants. The problem is not with the sender, it is with the receiver. You have not yet identified an object whose responsibility it is to implement this method.

This application needs an object to embody the rules at the intersection of `Customer`, `Trip` and `Bicycle`. The `suitable_trips` method will be part of *its* public interface.

The realization that you need an as yet undefined object is one that you can arrive at via many routes. The advantage of discovering this missing object via sequence diagrams is that the cost of being wrong is very low and the impediments to changing your mind are extremely few. The sequence diagrams are experimental and will be discarded; your lack of attachment to them is a feature. They do not reflect your ultimate design, but instead they create an intention that is the starting point for your design.

Regardless of how you reach this point it is now clear that you need a new object, one that you discovered because of your need to send it a message.

Perhaps the application should contain a `TripFinder` class. Figure 4.8 shows a sequence diagram where a `TripFinder` is responsible for finding suitable trips.

`TripFinder` contains all knowledge of what makes a trip suitable. It knows the rules; its job is to do whatever is necessary to respond to this message. It provides a

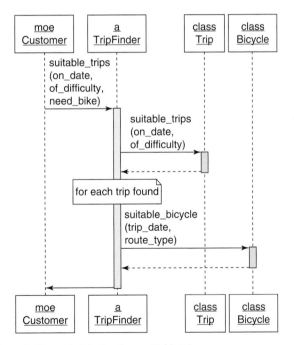

Figure 4.8   Moe asks the `TripFinder` for a suitable trip.

consistent public interface while hiding messy and changeable internal implementation details.

Moving this method into `TripFinder` makes the behavior available to any other object. In the unknown future perhaps other touring companies will use `TripFinder` to locate suitable trips via a Web service. Now that this behavior has been extracted from `Customer`, it can be used, in isolation, by any other object.

Creating a Message-Based Application

This section used sequence diagrams to explore design, define public interfaces, and discover objects.

Sequence diagrams are powerfully useful in a transient way; they make otherwise impossibly convoluted conversations comprehensible. Flip back through the last several pages and imagine attempting this discussion without them.

Useful as they are, they are a tool, nothing more. They help keep the focus on messages and allow you to form a rational intention about the first thing to assert in a test. Switching your attention from objects to messages allows you to concentrate on designing an application built upon public interfaces.

Writing Code That Puts Its Best (Inter)Face Forward

The clarity of your interfaces reveals your design skills and reflects your self-discipline. Because design skills are always improving but never perfected, and because even today's beautiful design may look ugly in light of tomorrow's requirement, it is difficult to create perfect interfaces.

This, however, should not deter you from trying. Interfaces evolve and to do so they must first be born. It is more important that a well-defined interface exist than that it be perfect.

Think about interfaces. Create them intentionally. It is your interfaces, more than all of your tests and any of your code, that define your application and determine its future.

The following section contains rules-of-thumb for creating interfaces.

Create Explicit Interfaces

Your goal is to write code that works today, that can easily be reused, and that can be adapted for unexpected use in the future. Other people will invoke your methods; it is your obligation to communicate which ones are dependable.

Every time you create a class, declare its interfaces. Methods in the *public* interface should

- Be explicitly identified as such
- Be more about *what* than *how*
- Have names that, insofar as you can anticipate, will not change
- Take a hash as an options parameter

Be just as intentional about the private interface; make it inescapably obvious. Tests, because they serve as documentation, can support this endeavor. Either do not test private methods or, if you must, segregate those tests from the tests of public methods. Do not allow your tests to fool others into unintentionally depending on the changeable, private interface.

Ruby provides three relevant keywords: `public`, `protected`, and `private`. Use of these keywords serves two distinct purposes. First, they indicate which methods are stable and which are unstable. Second, they control how visible a method is to other parts of your application. These two purposes are very different. Conveying information that a method is stable or unstable is one thing; attempting to control how others use it is quite another.

Public, Protected, and Private Keywords

The `private` keyword denotes the least stable kind of method and provides the most restricted visibility. Private methods must be called with an implicit receiver, or, inversely, may never be called with an explicit receiver.

If class `Trip` contains private method `fun_factor`, you may not send `self.fun_factor` from within `Trip` or `a_trip.fun_factor` from another object. However, you may send `fun_factor`, defaulting to self (the implicit receiver) from within instances of `Trip` and its subclasses.

The `protected` keyword also indicates an unstable method, but one with slightly different visibility restrictions. Protected methods allow explicit receivers as long as the receiver is `self` or an instance of the same class or subclass of `self`.

Thus, if `Trip`'s `fun_factor` method is `protected`, you may always send `self.fun_factor`. Additionally, you may send `a_trip.fun_factor`, but only from within a class where `self` is the same kind of thing (class or subclass) as `a_trip`.

The `public` keyword indicates that a method is stable; public methods are visible everywhere.

To further complicate matters, Ruby not only provides these keywords but also supplies various mechanisms for circumventing the visibility restrictions that `private` and `protected` impose. Users of a class can redefine any method to `public` regardless of its initial declaration. The `private` and `protected` keywords are more like flexible barriers than concrete restrictions. Anyone can get by them; it's simply a matter of expending the effort.

Therefore, any notion that you can prevent method access by using these keywords is an illusion. The keywords don't deny access, they just make it a bit harder. Using them sends two messages:

- You believe that you have better information *today* than programmers will have *in the future*.

- You believe that those future programmers need to be prevented from accidentally using a method that you currently consider unstable.

These beliefs may be correct but the future is a long way off and one can never be certain. The most apparently stable methods may change regularly and the most initially unstable may survive the test of time. If the illusion of control is a comfort, feel free to use the keywords. However, many perfectly competent Ruby programmers omit them and instead use comments or a special method naming convention (Ruby on Rails, for example, adds a leading '_' to private methods) to indicate the *public* and *private* parts of interfaces.

These strategies are perfectly acceptable and sometimes even preferable. They supply information about method stability without imposing visibility restrictions. Use of them trusts future programmers to make good choices about which methods to depend upon based on the increased information they have at that time.

Regardless of how you choose to do so, as long as you find some way to convey this information you have fulfilled your obligations to the future.

Honor the Public Interfaces of Others

Do your best to interact with other classes using only their public interfaces. Assume that the authors of those classes were just as intentional as you are now and they are trying desperately, across time and space, to communicate which methods are dependable. The public/private distinctions they made are intended to help *you* and it's best to heed them.

If your design forces the use of a private method in another class, first rethink your design. It's possible that a committed effort will unearth an alternative; you should try very hard to find one.

When you depend on a private interface you increase the risk of being forced to change. When that private interface is part of an external framework that undergoes periodic releases, this dependency is like a time bomb that will go off at the worst possible moment. Inevitably, the person who created the dependency leaves for greener pastures, the external framework gets updated, the private method being depended upon changes, and the application breaks in a way that baffles current maintainers.

A dependency on a private method of an external framework is a form of technical debt. Avoid these dependencies.

Exercise Caution When Depending on Private Interfaces

Despite your best efforts you may find that you *must* depend on a private interface. This is a dangerous dependency that should be isolated using the techniques described in Chapter 3. Even if you cannot avoid using a private method, you can prevent the method from being referenced in many places in your application. Depending on a private interface increases risk; keep this risk to a minimum by isolating the dependency.

Minimize Context

Construct public interfaces with an eye toward minimizing the context they require from others. Keep the *what* versus *how* distinction in mind; create public methods that allow senders to get what they want without knowing how your class implements its behavior.

Conversely, do not succumb to a class that has an ill-defined or absent public interface. When faced with a situation like that of the Mechanic class in Figure 4.5, do not give up and tell it how to behave by invoking all of its methods. Even if the original author did not define a public interface it is not too late to create one for yourself.

Depending on how often you plan to use this new public interface, it can be a new method that you define and place in the Mechanic class, a new wrapper class that you create and use instead of Mechanic, or a single wrapping method that you place in your own class. Do what best suits your needs, but create some kind of defined public interface and use it. This reduces your class's context, making it easier to reuse and simpler to test.

The Law of Demeter

Having read about responsibilities, dependencies, and interfaces you are now equipped to explore the Law of Demeter.

The Law of Demeter (LoD) is a set of coding rules that results in loosely coupled objects. Loose coupling is nearly always a virtue but is just one component of design and must be balanced against competing needs. Some Demeter violations are harmless, but others expose a failure to correctly identify and define public interfaces.

Defining Demeter

Demeter restricts the set of objects to which a method may *send* messages; it prohibits routing a message to a third object via a second object of a different type. Demeter is often paraphrased as "only talk to your immediate neighbors" or "use only one dot." Imagine that Trip's `depart` method contains each of the following lines of code:

```
customer.bicycle.wheel.tire

customer.bicycle.wheel.rotate

hash.keys.sort.join(', ')
```

Each line is a message chain containing a number of dots (periods). These chains are colloquially referred to as *train wrecks*; each method name represents a train car and the dots are the connections between them. These trains are an indication that you might be violating Demeter.

Consequences of Violations

Demeter became a "law" because a human being decided so; don't be fooled by its grandiose name. As a law it's more like "floss your teeth every day," than it is like gravity. You might prefer not to confess to your dentist but occasional violations will not collapse the universe.

Chapter 2 stated that code should be *transparent, reasonable, usable* and *exemplary*. Some of the message chains above fail when judged against TRUE:

- If `wheel` changes `tire` or `rotate`, `depart` may have to change. `Trip` has nothing to do with `wheel` yet changes to `wheel` might force changes in `Trip`. This unnecessarily raises the cost of change; the code is not *reasonable*.

- Changing `tire` or `rotate` may break something in `depart`. Because `Trip` is distant and apparently unrelated, the failure will be completely unexpected. This code is not *transparent*.

- `Trip` cannot be reused unless it has access to a `customer` with a `bicycle` that has a `wheel` and a `tire`. It requires a lot of context and is not easily *usable*.

- This pattern of messages will be replicated by others, producing more code with similar problems. This style of code, unfortunately, breeds itself. It is not *exemplary*.

The first two message chains are nearly identical, differing only in that one retrieves a distant attribute (`tire`) and the other invokes distant behavior (`rotate`). Even experienced designers argue about how firmly Demeter applies to message chains that return *attributes*. It may be cheapest, *in your specific case*, to reach through intermediate objects to retrieve distant attributes. Balance the likelihood and cost of change against the cost of removing the violation. If, for example, you are printing a report of a set of related objects, the most rational strategy may be to explicitly specify the intermediate objects and to change the report if it becomes necessary. Because the risk incurred by Demeter violations is low for stable attributes, this may be the most cost-efficient strategy.

This tradeoff is permitted as long as you are not changing the value of the attribute you retrieve. If `depart` sends `customer.bicycle.wheel.tire` with the intent of altering the result, it is not just retrieving an attribute, it is implementing behavior that belongs in `Wheel`. In this case, `customer.bicycle.wheel.tire` becomes just like `customer.bicycle.wheel.rotate`; it's a chain that reaches across many objects to get to distant behavior. The inherent cost of this coding style is high; this violation should be removed.

The third message chain, `hash.keys.sort.join` is perfectly reasonable and, despite the abundance of dots, may not be a Demeter violation at all. Instead of evaluating this phrase by counting the "dots," evaluate it by checking the types of the intermediate objects.

`hash.keys` returns an `Enumerable`

`hash.keys.sort` also returns an `Enumerable`

`hash.keys.sort.join` returns a `String`

By this logic, there is a slight Demeter violation. However, if you can bring yourself to accept that `hash.keys.sort.join` actually returns an `Enumerable` of `Strings`, all of the intermediate objects have the same type and there is no Demeter violation. If you remove the dots from *this* line of code, your costs may well go up instead of down.

As you can see, Demeter is more subtle than first appears. Its fixed rules are not an end in themselves; like every design principle, it exists *in service* of your overall goals. Certain "violations" of Demeter reduce your application's flexibility and maintainability, while others make perfect sense.

Avoiding Violations

One common way to remove "train wrecks" from code is to use delegation to avoid the "dots." In object-oriented terms, to *delegate* a message is to pass it on to another object, often via a wrapper method. The wrapper method encapsulates, or hides, knowledge that would otherwise be embodied in the message chain.

There are a number of ways to accomplish delegation. Ruby contains `delegate.rb` and `forwardable.rb` and the Ruby on Rails framework includes the `delegate` method. Each of these exists to make it easy for an object to automatically intercept a message sent to *self* and to instead send it somewhere else.

Delegation is tempting as a solution to the Demeter problem because it removes the visible evidence of violations. This technique is sometimes useful, but beware, it can result in code that obeys the letter of the law while ignoring its spirit. Using delegation to hide tight coupling is not the same as decoupling the code.

Listening to Demeter

Demeter is trying to tell you something and it isn't "use more delegation."

Message chains like `customer.bicycle.wheel.rotate` occur when your design thoughts are unduly influenced by objects you already know. Your familiarity with the public interfaces of known objects may lead you to string together long message chains to get at distant behavior.

Reaching across disparate objects to invoke distant behavior is tantamount to saying, "there's some behavior way over there that I need right here and *I know how to go get it.*" The code knows not only *what* it wants (to rotate) but *how* to navigate through a bunch of intermediate objects to reach the desired behavior. Just as `Trip`, earlier, knew how `Mechanic` should prepare a bike and so was tightly coupled to `Mechanic`, here the `depart` method knows how to navigate through a series of objects to make a wheel rotate and therefore is tightly coupled to your overall object structure.

This coupling causes all kinds of problems. The most obvious is that it raises the risk that `Trip` will be forced to change because of an unrelated change somewhere in the message chain. However, there's another problem here that is even more serious.

When the `depart` method knows this chain of objects, it binds itself to a very specific implementation and it cannot be reused in any other context. `Customers` must always have `Bicycles`, which in turn must have `Wheels` that `rotate`.

Consider what this message chain would look like if you had started out by deciding *what* depart wants from `customer`. From a message-based point of view, the answer is obvious:

```
customer.ride
```

The `ride` method of customer hides implementation details from `Trip` and reduces both its context and its dependencies, significantly improving the design. When FastFeet changes and begins leading hiking trips it's much easier to generalize from `customer.ride` to `customer.depart` or `customer.go` than to disentangle the tentacles of this message chain from your application.

The train wrecks of Demeter violations are clues that there are objects whose public interfaces are lacking. Listening to Demeter means paying attention to your point of view. If you shift to a message-based perspective, the messages you find will become public interfaces in the objects they lead you to discover. However, if you are bound by the shackles of existing domain objects, you'll end up assembling their existing public interfaces into long message chains and thus will miss the opportunity to find and construct flexible public interfaces.

Summary

Object-oriented applications are defined by the messages that pass between objects. This message passing takes place along "public" interfaces; well-defined public interfaces consist of stable methods that expose the responsibilities of their underlying classes and provide maximal benefit at minimal cost.

Focusing on messages reveals objects that might otherwise be overlooked. When messages are *trusting* and ask for what the sender wants instead of telling the receiver how to behave, objects naturally evolve public interfaces that are flexible and reusable in novel and unexpected ways.

CHAPTER 5

Reducing Costs with Duck Typing

The purpose of object-oriented design is to reduce the cost of change. Now that you know messages are at the design center of your application, and now that you are committed to the construction of rigorously defined public interfaces, you can combine these two ideas into a powerful design technique that further reduces your costs.

This technique is known as *duck typing*. Duck types are public interfaces that are not tied to any specific class. These across-class interfaces add enormous flexibility to your application by replacing costly dependencies on class with more forgiving dependencies on messages.

Duck typed objects are chameleons that are defined more by their behavior than by their class. This is how the technique gets its name; if an object quacks like a duck and walks like a duck, then its class is immaterial, it's a duck.

This chapter shows you how to recognize and exploit duck types to make your application more flexible and easier to change.

Understanding Duck Typing

Programming languages use the term "type" to describe the category of the contents of a variable. Procedural languages provide a small, fixed number of types, generally used to describe kinds of *data*. Even the humblest language defines types to hold strings, numbers, and arrays.

It is knowledge of the category of the contents of a variable, or its type, that allows an application to have an expectation about how those contents will behave. Applications quite reasonably assume that numbers can be used in mathematical expressions, strings concatenated, and arrays indexed.

In Ruby these expectations about the behavior of an object come in the form of beliefs about its public interface. If one object knows another's type, it knows to which messages that object can respond.

An instance of the Mechanic class contains, obviously, the complete public interface of Mechanic. It is blindingly apparent that any object holding onto an instance of Mechanic can treat the instance as if it *is* a Mechanic; the object, by its very nature, implements the Mechanic class's public interface.

However, you are not limited to expecting an object to respond to just *one* interface. A Ruby object is like a partygoer at a masquerade ball that changes masks to suit the theme. It can expose a different face to every viewer; it can implement many different interfaces.

Just as beauty is in the physical world, within your application an object's type is in the eye of the beholder. Users of an object need not, and should not, be concerned about its class. Class is just one way for an object to acquire a public interface; the public interface an object obtains by way of its class may be one of several that it contains. Applications may define many public interfaces that are not related to one specific class; these interfaces cut across class. Users of any object can blithely expect it to act like any, or all, of the public interfaces it implements. It's not what an object *is* that matters, it's what it *does*.

If every object trusts all others to be what it expects at any given moment, and any object can be any kind of thing, the design possibilities are infinite. These possibilities can be used to create flexible designs that are marvels of structured creativity or, alternatively, to construct terrifying designs that are incomprehensibly chaotic.

Using this flexibility wisely requires that you recognize these across-class types and construct their public interfaces as intentionally and as diligently as you did those of within-class types back in Chapter 4, Creating Flexible Interfaces. Across-class types, duck types, have public interfaces that represent a contract that must be explicit and well-documented.

The best way to explain duck types is to explore the consequences of not using them. This section contains an example that goes through several refactorings, solving a messy design problem by finding and implementing a duck type.

Overlooking the Duck

In the following code Trip's prepare method sends message prepare_bicycles to
the object contained in its mechanic parameter. Notice that the Mechanic class is
not referenced; even though the parameter name is mechanic, the object it contains
could be of any class.

```ruby
1  class Trip
2    attr_reader :bicycles, :customers, :vehicle
3
4    # this 'mechanic' argument could be of any class
5    def prepare(mechanic)
6      mechanic.prepare_bicycles(bicycles)
7    end
8
9    # ...
10 end
11
12 # if you happen to pass an instance of *this* class,
13 # it works
14 class Mechanic
15   def prepare_bicycles(bicycles)
16     bicycles.each {|bicycle| prepare_bicycle(bicycle)}
17   end
18
19   def prepare_bicycle(bicycle)
20     #...
21   end
22 end
```

Figure 5.1 contains the corresponding sequence diagram, where an outside object gets
everything started by sending prepare to Trip, passing along an argument.

The prepare method has no explicit dependency on the Mechanic class but it does
depend on receiving an object that can respond to prepare_bicycles. This dependency is so fundamental that it's easy to miss or to discount, but nonetheless, it exists.
Trip's prepare method firmly believes that its argument contains a preparer of bicycles.

Compounding the Problem

You may already have noticed that this example is like the sequence diagram in Figure 4.6
of Chapter 4. The next refactoring there improved the design by pushing knowledge

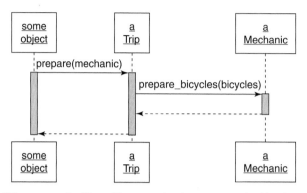

Figure 5.1   Trip prepares itself by asking a mechanic to prepare the bicycles.

of how a `Trip` gets prepared into `Mechanic`. The next example here, alas, is no improvement at all.

Imagine that requirements change. In addition to a mechanic, trip preparation now involves a trip coordinator and a driver. Following the established pattern of the code, you create new `TripCoordinator` and `Driver` classes and give them the behavior for which they are responsible. You also change `Trip`'s prepare method to invoke the correct behavior from each of its arguments.

The following code illustrates the change. The new `TripCoordinator` and `Driver` classes are simple and inoffensive but `Trip`'s prepare method is now a cause for alarm. It refers to three different classes by name and knows specific methods implemented in each. Risks have dramatically gone up. `Trip`'s prepare method might be forced to change because of a change elsewhere and it might unexpectedly break as the result of a distant, unrelated change.

```
 1  # Trip preparation becomes more complicated
 2  class Trip
 3    attr_reader :bicycles, :customers, :vehicle
 4
 5    def prepare(preparers)
 6      preparers.each {|preparer|
 7        case preparer
 8        when Mechanic
 9          preparer.prepare_bicycles(bicycles)
10        when TripCoordinator
11          preparer.buy_food(customers)
12        when Driver
```

```
13          preparer.gas_up(vehicle)
14          preparer.fill_water_tank(vehicle)
15        end
16      }
17    end
18 end
19
20 # when you introduce TripCoordinator and Driver
21 class TripCoordinator
22   def buy_food(customers)
23     # ...
24   end
25 end
26
27 class Driver
28   def gas_up(vehicle)
29     #...
30   end
31
32   def fill_water_tank(vehicle)
33     #...
34   end
35 end
```

This code is the first step in a process that will paint you into a corner with no way out. Code like this gets written when programmers are blinded by existing classes and neglect to notice that they have overlooked important messages; this dependent-laden code is a natural outgrowth of a class-based perspective.

The roots of the problem are innocent enough. It's easy to fall into the trap of thinking of the original prepare method as expecting an actual instance of Mechanic. Your technical brain surely recognizes that prepare's argument can legally be of any class, but that doesn't save you; in your heart of hearts you think of the argument as being a Mechanic.

Because you know that Mechanic understands prepare_bicycle and are confident that you are passing a Mechanic, initially all is well. This perspective works fine until something changes and instances of classes other than Mechanic begin to appear on the argument list. When that happens, prepare must suddenly deal with objects that do not understand prepare_bicycle.

If your design imagination is constrained by class and you find yourself unexpectedly dealing with objects that don't understand the message you are sending, your tendency is to go hunt for messages that these new objects *do* understand. Because the new arguments are instances of `TripCoordinator` and `Driver`, you naturally examine the public interfaces of those classes and find `buy_food`, `gas_up` and `fill_water_tank`. This is the behavior that `prepare` wants.

The most obvious way to invoke this behavior is to send these very messages, but now you're stuck. Every one of your arguments is of a different class and implements different methods; you must determine each argument's class to know which message to send. Adding a `case` statement that switches on class solves the problem of sending the correct message to the correct object but causes an explosion of dependencies.

Count the number of new dependencies in the `prepare` method. It relies on specific classes, no others will do. It relies on the explicit names of those classes. It knows the names of the messages that each class understands, along with the arguments that those messages require. All of this knowledge increases risk; many distant changes will now have side effects on this code.

To make matters worse, this style of code propagates itself. When another new trip preparer appears, you, or the next person down the programming line, will add a new when branch to the `case` statement. Your application will accrue more and more methods like this, where the method knows many class names and sends a specific message based on class. The logical endpoint of this programming style is a stiff and inflexible application, where it eventually becomes easier to rewrite everything than to change anything.

Figure 5.2 shows the new sequence diagram. Every sequence diagram thus far has been simpler than its corresponding code, but this new diagram looks frighteningly complicated. This complexity is a warning. Sequence diagrams should always be simpler than the code they represent; when they are not, something is wrong with the design.

Finding the Duck

The key to removing the dependencies is to recognize that because `Trip`'s `prepare` method serves a single purpose, its arguments arrive wishing to collaborate to accomplish a single goal. Every argument is here for the same reason and that reason is unrelated to the argument's underlying class.

Avoid getting sidetracked by your knowledge of what each argument's class already does; think instead about what `prepare` needs. Considered from `prepare`'s

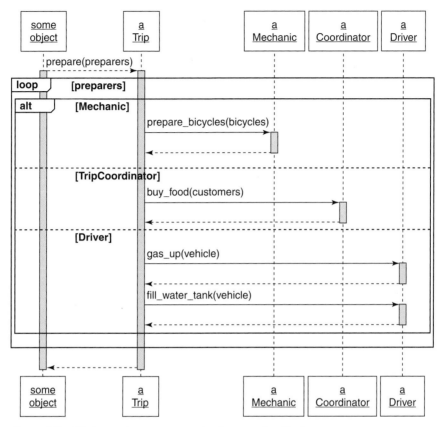

Figure 5.2 Trip knows too many concrete classes and methods.

point of view, the problem is straightforward. The `prepare` method wants to prepare the trip. Its arguments arrive ready to collaborate in trip preparation. The design would be simpler if `prepare` just trusted them to do so.

Figure 5.3 illustrates this idea. Here the `prepare` method doesn't have a preordained expectation about the class of its arguments, instead it expects each to be a "Preparer."

This expectation neatly turns the tables. You've pried yourself loose from existing classes and invented a duck type. The next step is to ask what message the `prepare` method can fruitfully send each `Preparer`. From this point of view, the answer is obvious: `prepare_trip`.

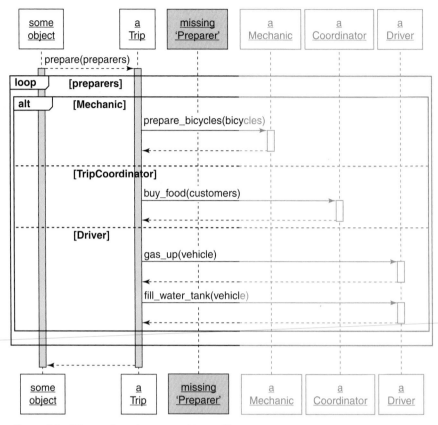

Figure 5.3   Trip needs each argument to act like a preparer.

Figure 5.4 introduces the new message. Trip's `prepare` method now expects its arguments to be `Preparers` that can respond to `prepare_trip`.

What kind of thing is `Preparer`? At this point it has no concrete existence; it's an abstraction, an agreement about the public interface on an idea. It's a figment of design.

Objects that implement `prepare_trip` *are* `Preparers` and, conversely, objects that interact with `Preparers` only need trust them to implement the `Preparer` interface. Once you see this underlying abstraction, it's easy to fix the code. `Mechanic`, `TripCoordinator` and `Driver` should behave like `Preparers`; they should implement `prepare_trip`.

Here's the code for the new design. The `prepare` method now expects its arguments to be `Preparers` and each argument's class implements the new interface.

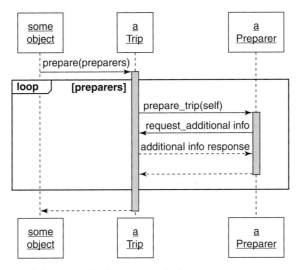

Figure 5.4   Trip collaborates with the preparer duck.

```ruby
1  # Trip preparation becomes easier
2  class Trip
3    attr_reader :bicycles, :customers, :vehicle
4
5    def prepare(preparers)
6      preparers.each {|preparer|
7        preparer.prepare_trip(self)}
8    end
9  end
10
11 # when every preparer is a Duck
12 # that responds to 'prepare_trip'
13 class Mechanic
14   def prepare_trip(trip)
15     trip.bicycles.each {|bicycle|
16       prepare_bicycle(bicycle)}
17   end
18
19   # ...
20 end
21
22 class TripCoordinator
23   def prepare_trip(trip)
```

```
24        buy_food(trip.customers)
25    end
26
27    # . . .
28 end
29
30 class Driver
31    def prepare_trip(trip)
32        vehicle = trip.vehicle
33        gas_up(vehicle)
34        fill_water_tank(vehicle)
35    end
36    # . . .
37 end
```

The `prepare` method can now accept new `Preparers` without being forced to change, and it's easy to create additional `Preparers` if the need arises.

Consequences of Duck Typing

This new implementation has a pleasing symmetry that suggests a rightness about the design, but the consequences of introducing a duck type go deeper.

In the initial example, the `prepare` method depends on a concrete class. In this most recent example, `prepare` depends on a duck type. The path between these examples leads through a thicket of complicated, dependent-laden code.

The concreteness of the first example makes it simple to understand but dangerous to extend. The final, duck typed, alternative is more abstract; it places slightly greater demands on your understanding but in return offers ease of extension. Now that you have discovered the duck, you can elicit new behavior from your application without changing any existing code; you simply turn another object into a `Preparer` and pass it into `Trip`'s `prepare` method.

This tension between the costs of concretion and the costs of abstraction is fundamental to object-oriented design. Concrete code is easy to understand but costly to extend. Abstract code may initially seem more obscure but, once understood, is far easier to change. Use of a duck type moves your code along the scale from more concrete to more abstract, making the code easier to extend but casting a veil over the underlying class of the duck.

The ability to tolerate ambiguity about the class of an object is the hallmark of a confident designer. Once you begin to treat your objects as if they are defined by their behavior rather than by their class, you enter into a new realm of expressive flexible design.

Polymorphism

The term *polymorphism* is commonly used in object-oriented programming but its use in everyday speech is rare enough to warrant a definition.

Polymorphism expresses a very specific concept and can be used, depending on your inclinations, either to communicate or to intimidate. Either way, it's important to have a clear understanding of its meaning.

First, a general definition: *Morph* is the Greek word for form, *morphism* is the state of having a form, and *polymorphism* is the state of having many forms. Biologists use this word. Darwin's famous finches are polymorphic; a single species has many forms.

Polymorphism in OOP refers to the ability of many different objects to respond to the same message. Senders of the message need not care about the class of the receiver; receivers supply their own specific version of the behavior.

A single message thus has many (poly) forms (morphs).

There are a number of ways to achieve polymorphism; duck typing, as you have surely guessed, is one. Inheritance and behavior sharing (via Ruby modules) are others, but those are topics for the next chapters.

Polymorphic methods honor an implicit bargain; they agree to be interchangeable *from the sender's point of view*. Any object implementing a polymorphic method can be substituted for any other; the sender of the message need not know or care about this substitution.

This substitutability doesn't happen by magic. When you use polymorphism it's up to you to make sure all of your objects are well-behaved. This idea is covered in Chapter 7, Sharing Role Behavior with Modules.

Writing Code That Relies on Ducks

Using duck typing relies on your ability to recognize the places where your application would benefit from across-class interfaces. It is relatively easy to implement a duck type; your design challenge is to notice that you need one and to abstract its interface.

This section contains patterns that reveal paths you can follow to discover ducks.

Recognizing Hidden Ducks

Many times unacknowledged duck types already exist, lurking within existing code. Several common coding patterns indicate the presence of a hidden duck. You can replace the following with ducks:

- Case statements that switch on class

- kind_of? and is_a?

- responds_to?

Case Statements That Switch on Class

The most common, obvious pattern that indicates an undiscovered duck is the example you've already seen; a case statement that switches on the class names of domain objects of your application. The following prepare method (same as above) should grab your attention as if it were playing trumpets.

```
 1 class Trip
 2   attr_reader :bicycles, :customers, :vehicle
 3
 4   def prepare(preparers)
 5     preparers.each {|preparer|
 6       case preparer
 7       when Mechanic
 8         preparer.prepare_bicycles(bicycles)
 9       when TripCoordinator
10         preparer.buy_food(customers)
11       when Driver
12         preparer.gas_up(vehicle)
13         preparer.fill_water_tank(vehicle)
14       end
15     }
16   end
17 end
```

When you see this pattern you know that all of the preparers must share something in common; they arrive here because of that common thing. Examine the code and ask yourself, "What is it that prepare wants from each of its arguments?"

The answer to that question suggests the message you should send; this message begins to define the underlying duck type.

Here the prepare method wants its arguments to prepare the trip. Thus, prepare_trip becomes a method in the public interface of the new Preparer duck.

kind_of? and is_a?

There are various ways to check the class of an object. The case statement above is one of them. The kind_of? and is_a? messages (they are synonymous) also check class. Rewriting the previous example in the following way does nothing to improve the code.

```
1   if preparer.kind_of?(Mechanic)
2     preparer.prepare_bicycles(bicycle)
3   elsif preparer.kind_of?(TripCoordinator)
4     preparer.buy_food(customers)
5   elsif preparer.kind_of?(Driver)
6     preparer.gas_up(vehicle)
7     preparer.fill_water_tank(vehicle)
8   end
```

Using kind_of? is no different than using a case statement that switches on class; they are the same thing, they cause exactly the same problems, and they should be corrected using the same techniques.

responds_to?

Programmers who understand that they should not depend on class names but who haven't yet made the leap to duck types are tempted to replace kind_of? with responds_to?. For example:

```
1   if preparer.responds_to?(:prepare_bicycles)
2     preparer.prepare_bicycles(bicycle)
3   elsif preparer.responds_to?(:buy_food)
4     preparer.buy_food(customers)
5   elsif preparer.responds_to?(:gas_up)
6     preparer.gas_up(vehicle)
7     preparer.fill_water_tank(vehicle)
8   end
```

While this slightly decreases the number of dependencies, this code still has too many. The class names are gone but the code is still very bound to class. What object will know prepare_bicycles other than Mechanic? Don't be fooled by the removal of explicit class references. This example still expects very specific classes.

Even if you are in a situation where more than one class implements `prepare_bicycles` or `buy_food`, this code pattern still contains unnecessary dependencies; it controls rather than trusts other objects.

Placing Trust in Your Ducks

Use of `kind_of?`, `is_a?`, `responds_to?`, and `case` statements that switch on your classes indicate the presence of an unidentified duck. In each case the code is effectively saying "I know who you are and because of that *I know what you do.*" This knowledge exposes a lack of trust in collaborating objects and acts as a millstone around your object's neck. It introduces dependencies that make code difficult to change.

Just as in Demeter violations, this style of code is an indication that you are missing an object, one whose public interface you have not yet discovered. The fact that the missing object is a duck type instead of a concrete class matters not at all; it's the interface that matters, not the class of the object that implements it.

Flexible applications are built on objects that operate on trust; it is your job to make your objects trustworthy. When you see these code patterns, concentrate on the offending code's expectations and use those expectations to find the duck type. Once you have a duck type in mind, define its interface, implement that interface where necessary, and then trust those implementers to behave correctly.

Documenting Duck Types

The simplest kind of duck type is one that exists merely as an agreement about its public interface. This chapter's example code implements that kind of duck, where several different classes implement `prepare_trip` and can thus be treated like `Preparers`.

The `Preparer` duck type and its public interface are a concrete part of the design but a virtual part of the code. `Preparers` are abstract; this gives them strength as a design tool but this very abstraction makes the duck type less than obvious in the code.

When you create duck types you must both document *and* test their public interfaces. Fortunately, good tests are the best documentation, so you are already halfway done; you need only write the tests.

See Chapter 9, Designing Cost-Effective Tests, for more on testing duck types.

Sharing Code Between Ducks

In this chapter, `Preparer` ducks provide class-specific versions of the behavior required by their interface. `Mechanic`, `Driver` and `TripCoordinator` each implement method `prepare_trip`. This method signature is the only thing they have in common. They share only the interface, not the implementation.

Once you start using duck types, however, you'll find that classes that implement them often need to share some behavior in common. Writing ducks that share code is one of the topics covered in Chapter 7.

Choosing Your Ducks Wisely

Every example thus far unequivocally declares that you should not use `kind_of?` or `responds_to?` to decide what message to send an object, yet you don't have to look far to find reams of well-received code that do exactly that.

The following code is an example from the Ruby on Rails framework (active_record/relations/finder_methods.rb). This example patently uses class to decide how to deal with its input, a technique that is in direct opposition to the guidelines stated above. The `first` method below clearly decides how to behave based on the class of its `args` argument.

If sending a message based on the class of the receiving object is the death knell for your application, why is this code acceptable?

```
1  # A convenience wrapper for <tt>find(:first, *args)</tt>.
2  # You can pass in all the same arguments to this
3  # method as you can to <tt>find(:first)</tt>.
4  def first(*args)
5    if args.any?
6      if args.first.kind_of?(Integer) ||
7          (loaded? && !args.first.kind_of?(Hash))
8        to_a.first(*args)
9      else
10       apply_finder_options(args.first).first
11     end
12   else
13     find_first
14   end
15 end
```

The major difference between this example and the previous ones is the stability of the classes that are being checked. When `first` depends on `Integer` and `Hash`, it is depending on core Ruby classes that are far more stable than it is. The likelihood of `Integer` or `Hash` changing in such a way as to force `first` to change is vanishingly small. This dependency is safe. There probably *is* a duck type hidden somewhere in this code but it will likely not reduce your overall application costs to find and implement it.

From this example you can see that the decision to create a new duck type relies on judgment. The purpose of design is to lower costs; bring this measuring stick to every situation. If creating a duck type would reduce unstable dependencies, do so. Use your best judgment.

The above example's underlying duck spans `Integer` and `Hash` and therefore its implementation would require making changes to Ruby base classes. Changing base classes is known as *monkey patching* and is a delightful feature of Ruby but can be perilous in untutored hands.

Implementing duck types across your own classes is one thing, changing Ruby base classes to introduce new duck types is quite another. The tradeoffs are different; the risks are greater. Neither of these considerations should prevent you from monkey patching Ruby at need; however, you must be able to eloquently defend this design decision. The standard of proof is high.

Conquering a Fear of Duck Typing

This chapter has thus far delicately sidestepped the dynamic versus static typing battlefield, but the issue can no longer be avoided. If you have a statically typed programming background and find the idea of duck typing alarming, this section is for you.

If you are unfamiliar with the argument, are happily using Ruby, and were convinced by the prior discourse on duck typing, you can skim this section without fear of missing important new concepts. You might, however, find what follows useful if you need to fend off arguments made by your more statically typed friends.

Subverting Duck Types with Static Typing

Early in this chapter, *type* was defined as the category of the contents of a variable. Programming languages are either *statically* or *dynamically* typed. Most (though not all) statically typed languages require that you explicitly declare the type of each variable and every method parameter. Dynamically typed languages omit this requirement; they allow you to put any value in any variable and pass any argument to any method, without further declaration. Ruby, obviously, is dynamically typed.

Relying on dynamic typing makes some people uncomfortable. For some, this discomfort is caused by a lack of experience, for others, by a belief that static typing is more reliable.

The lack-of-experience problem cures itself, but the belief that static typing is fundamentally preferable often persists because it is self-reinforcing. Programmers who fear dynamic typing tend to check the classes of objects in their code; these very checks subvert the power of dynamic typing, making it impossible to use duck types.

Methods that cannot behave correctly unless they know the classes of their arguments will fail (with type errors) when new classes appear. Programmers who believe in static typing take these failures as proof that more type checking is needed. When more checks are added, the code becomes less flexible and even more dependent on class. The new dependencies cause additional type failures, and the programmer responds to these failures by adding yet more type checking. Anyone caught in this loop will naturally have a hard time believing that the solution to their type problem is to remove type checking altogether.

Duck typing provides a way out of this trap. It removes the dependencies on class and thus avoids the subsequent type failures. It reveals stable abstractions on which your code can safely depend.

Static versus Dynamic Typing

This section compares dynamic and static typing, hoping to allay any fears that keep you from being fully committed to dynamic types.

Static and dynamic typing both make promises and each has costs and benefits. Static typing aficionados cite the following qualities:

- The compiler unearths type errors at compile time.

- Visible type information serves as documentation.

- Compiled code is optimized to run quickly.

These qualities represent strengths in a programming language only if you accept this set of corresponding assumptions:

- Runtime type errors will occur unless the compiler performs type checks.

- Programmers will not otherwise understand the code; they cannot infer an object's type from its context.

- The application will run too slowly without these optimizations.

Dynamic typing proponents list these qualities:

- Code is interpreted and can be dynamically loaded; there is no compile/make cycle.

- Source code does not include explicit type information.

- Metaprogramming is easier.

These qualities are strengths if you accept this set of assumptions:

- Overall application development is faster without a compile/make cycle.

- Programmers find the code easier to understand when it does not contain type declarations; they can infer an object's type from its context.

- Metaprogramming is a desirable language feature.

Embracing Dynamic Typing

Some of these qualities and assumptions are based on empirical facts and are easy to evaluate. There is no doubt that, for certain applications, well-optimized statically typed code will outperform a dynamically typed implementation. When a dynamically typed application cannot be tuned to run quickly enough, static typing is the alternative. If you must, you must.

Arguments about the value of type declarations as documentation are more subjective. Those experienced with dynamic typing find type declarations distracting. Those used to static typing may be disoriented by lack of type information. If you are coming from a statically typed language, like Java or C++, and feel unmoored by the lack of explicit type declarations in Ruby, hang in there. There's lots of anecdotal evidence to suggest that, once accustomed to it, you'll find this less verbose syntax easier to read, write, and understand.

Metaprogramming (i.e., writing code that writes code) is a topic that programmers tend to feel strongly about and the side of the argument they support is related to their past experience. If you have solved a massive problem with a simple, elegant piece of metaprogramming, you become an advocate for life. On the other hand, if you've faced the daunting task of debugging an overly clever, completely obscure, and possibly unnecessary bit of metaprogramming, you may perceive it as a tool for programmers to inflict pain upon one another and wish to banish it forever.

Metaprogramming is a scalpel; though dangerous in the wrong hands, it's a tool no good programmer should willingly be without. It confers great power and requires

Figure 5.5   Sharp instruments: useful, but not for everyone.

great responsibility. The fact that some people cannot be trusted with knives does not mean sharp instruments should be taken from the hands of all. Metaprogramming, used wisely, has great value; ease of metaprogramming is a strong argument in favor of dynamic typing.

The two remaining qualities are static typing's compile time type checking and dynamic typing's lack of a compile/make cycle. Static typing advocates assert that preventing unexpected type errors at runtime is so necessary and so valuable that its benefit trumps the greater programming efficiency that is gained by removing the compiler.

This argument rests on static typing's premise that:

- The compiler truly *can* save you from accidental type errors.

- Without the compiler's help, these type errors *will* occur.

If you have spent years programming in a statically typed language you may accept these assertions as gospel. However, dynamic typing is here to shake the foundations of your belief. To these arguments dynamic typing says "It can't" and "They won't."

The compiler *cannot* save you from accidental type errors. Any language that allows casting a variable to a new type is vulnerable. Once you start casting, all bets are off; the compiler excuses itself and you are left to rely on your own wits to prevent type errors. The code is only as good as your tests; runtime failures can still occur. The notion that static typing provides safety, comforting though it may be, is an illusion.

Furthermore, it doesn't actually matter whether the compiler can save you or not; you don't need saving. In the real world, compiler preventable runtime type errors *almost never occur*. It just doesn't happen.

This is not to suggest that you'll never experience a runtime type error. Few programmers make it through life without sending a message to an uninitialized variable or assuming an array has elements when it is actually empty. However, discovering at runtime that `nil` doesn't understand the message it received is not something the compiler could have prevented. These errors are equally likely in both type systems.

Dynamic typing allows you to trade compile time type checking, a serious restriction that has high cost and provides little value, for the huge gains in efficiency provided by removing the compile/make cycle. This trade is a bargain. Take it.

Duck typing is built on dynamic typing; to use duck typing you must *embrace* this dynamism.

Summary

Messages are at the center of object-oriented applications and they pass among objects along public interfaces. Duck typing detaches these public interfaces from specific classes, creating virtual types that are defined by what they do instead of by who they are.

Duck typing reveals underlying abstractions that might otherwise be invisible. Depending on these abstractions reduces risk and increases flexibility, making your application cheaper to maintain and easier to change.

Chapter 6

Acquiring Behavior Through Inheritance

Well-designed applications are constructed of reusable code. Small, trustworthy self-contained objects with minimal context, clear interfaces, and injected dependencies are inherently reusable. This book has, up to now, concentrated on creating objects with exactly these qualities.

Most object-oriented languages, however, have another code sharing technique, one built into the very syntax of the language: *inheritance.* This chapter offers a detailed example of how to write code that properly uses inheritance. Its goal is to teach you to build a technically sound inheritance hierarchy; its purpose is to prepare you to decide if you should.

Once you understand how to use classical inheritance, the concepts are easily transferred to other inheritance mechanisms. Inheritance is thus a topic for two chapters. This chapter contains a tutorial that illustrates how to write inheritable code. Chapter 7, Sharing Role Behavior with Modules, expands these techniques to the problem of sharing code via Ruby modules.

Understanding Classical Inheritance

The idea of inheritance may seem complicated but as with all complexity, there's a simplifying abstraction. Inheritance is, at its core, a mechanism for *automatic message delegation.* It defines a forwarding path for not-understood messages. It creates

105

relationships such that, if one object cannot respond to a received message, it delegates that message to another. You don't have to write code to explicitly delegate the message, instead you define an inheritance relationship between two objects and the forwarding happens automatically.

In classical inheritance these relationships are defined by creating subclasses. Messages are forwarded from subclass to superclass; the shared code is defined in the class hierarchy.

The term *classical* is a play on the word *class*, not a nod to an archaic technique, and it serves to distinguish this superclass/subclass mechanism from other inheritance techniques. JavaScript, for example, has prototypical inheritance and Ruby has *modules* (more on modules in the next chapter), both of which also provide a way to share code via automatic delegation of messages.

The uses and misuses of inheritance are best understood by example, and this chapter's example provides a thorough grounding in the techniques of classical inheritance. The example begins with a single class and goes through a number of refactorings to reach a satisfactory set of subclasses. Each step is small and easily understood but it takes a whole chapter's worth of code to illustrate all of the ideas.

Recognizing Where to Use Inheritance

The first challenge is recognizing where inheritance would be useful. This section illustrates how to know when you have the problem that inheritance solves.

Assume that FastFeet leads road bike trips. Road bicycles are lightweight, curved handlebar (drop bar), skinny tired bikes that are meant for paved roads. Figure 6.1 shows a road bike.

Mechanics are responsible for keeping bicycles running (no matter how much abuse customers heap upon them), and they take an assortment of spare parts on every trip. The spares they need depend on which bicycles they take.

Starting with a Concrete Class

FastFeet's application already has a `Bicycle` class, shown below. Every road bike that's going on a trip is represented by an instance of this class.

Bikes have an overall size, a handlebar tape color, a tire size, and a chain type. Tires and chains are integral parts and so spares must always be taken. Handlebar tape may seem less necessary, but in real life it is just as required. No self-respecting cyclist would tolerate dirty or torn bar tape; mechanics must carry spare tape in the correct, matching color.

Figure 6.1   A lightweight, drop-bar, skinny tired road bike.

```ruby
 1  class Bicycle
 2    attr_reader :size, :tape_color
 3
 4    def initialize(args)
 5      @size       = args[:size]
 6      @tape_color = args[:tape_color]
 7    end
 8
 9    # every bike has the same defaults for
10    # tire and chain size
11    def spares
12      { chain:        '10-speed',
13        tire_size:    '23',
14        tape_color:   tape_color}
15    end
16
17    # Many other methods...
18  end
19
20  bike = Bicycle.new(
21          size:        'M',
22          tape_color:  'red' )
```

```
23
24 bike.size      # -> 'M'
25 bike.spares
26 # -> {:tire_size    => "23",
27 #      :chain        => "10-speed",
28 #      :tape_color   => "red"}
```

Bicycle instances can respond to the spares, size, and tape_color messages and a Mechanic can figure out what spare parts to take by asking each Bicycle for its spares. Despite the fact that the spares method commits the sin of embedding default strings directly inside itself, the above code is fairly reasonable. This model of a bicycle is obviously missing a few bolts and is not something you could actually *ride*, but it will do for this chapter's example.

This class works just fine until something changes. Imagine that FastFeet begins to lead mountain bike trips.

Mountain bikes and road bikes are much alike but there are clear differences between them. Mountain bikes are meant to be ridden on dirt paths instead of paved roads. They have sturdy frames, fat tires, straight-bar handlebars (with rubber hand grips instead of tape), and suspension. The bicycle in Figure 6.2 has front suspension only, but some mountain bikes also have rear, or "full" suspension.

Figure 6.2   A beefy, straight-bar, front-suspension, fat-tired mountain bike.

Your design task is to add support for mountain bikes to FastFeet's application.

Much of the behavior that you need already exists; mountain bikes are definitely bicycles. They have an overall bike size and a chain and tire size. The only differences between road and mountain bikes are that road bikes need handlebar tape and mountain bikes have suspension.

Embedding Multiple Types

When a preexisting concrete class contains most of the behavior you need, it's tempting to solve this problem by adding code to that class. This next example does just that, it changes the existing `Bicycle` class so that `spares` works for both road and mountain bikes.

As you see below, three new variables have been added, along with their corresponding accessors. The new `front_shock` and `rear_shock` variables hold mountain bike specific parts. The new `style` variable determines which parts appear on the spares list. Each of these new variables is handled properly by the `initialize` method.

The code to add these three variables is simple, even mundane; the change to `spares` proves more interesting. The `spares` method now contains an `if` statement that checks the contents of the variable `style`. This `style` variable acts to divide instances of `Bicycle` into two different categories—those whose `style` is `:road` and those whose `style` is anything else.

If any alarms are going off as you review this code, please be reassured, they will soon be silenced. This example is simply a detour that illustrates an *antipattern*, that is, a common pattern that appears to be beneficial but is actually detrimental, and for which there is a well-known alternative.

> **Note**
>
> In case you're confused by the tire sizes below, know that bicycle tire sizing is, by tradition, inconsistent. Road bikes originated in Europe and use metric sizing; a 23-millimeter tire is slightly less than an inch wide. Mountain bikes originated in the United States and give tire sizes in inches. In the example below, the 2.1-inch mountain bike tire is more than twice as wide as the 23 mm road bike tire.

```
1  class Bicycle
2    attr_reader :style, :size, :tape_color,
3                :front_shock, :rear_shock
4
5    def initialize(args)
6      @style       = args[:style]
7      @size        = args[:size]
8      @tape_color  = args[:tape_color]
9      @front_shock = args[:front_shock]
10     @rear_shock  = args[:rear_shock]
11   end
12
13   # checking "style" starts down a slippery slope
14   def spares
15     if style == :road
16       { chain:        '10-speed',
17         tire_size:    '23',          # milimeters
18         tape_color:   tape_color }
19     else
20       { chain:        '10-speed',
21         tire_size:    '2.1',         # inches
22         rear_shock:   rear_shock }
23     end
24   end
25 end
26
27 bike = Bicycle.new(
28         style:        :mountain,
29         size:         'S',
30         front_shock:  'Manitou',
31         rear_shock:   'Fox')
32
33 bike.spares
34 # -> {:tire_size    => "2.1",
35 #     :chain        => "10-speed",
36 #     :rear_shock   => 'Fox'}
```

This code makes decisions about spare parts based on the value held in `style`; structuring the code this way has many negative consequences. If you add a new `style` you must change the `if` statement. If you write careless code where the last option is the default (as does the code above) an unexpected `style` will do *something* but perhaps not what you expect. Also, the `spares` method started out containing embedded default strings, some of these strings are now duplicated on each side of the `if` statement.

`Bicycle` has an implied public interface that includes `spares`, `size`, and all the individual parts. The `size` method still works, `spares` generally works, but the parts methods are now unreliable. It's impossible to predict, for any specific instance of `Bicycle`, whether a specific part has been initialized. Objects holding onto an instance of `Bicycle` may, for example, be tempted to check `style` before sending it `tape_color` or `rear_shock`.

The code wasn't great to begin with; this change did nothing to improve it.

The initial `Bicycle` class was imperfect but its imperfections were hidden—encapsulated within the class. These new flaws have broader consequences. `Bicycle` now has more than one responsibility, contains things that might change for different reasons, and cannot be reused as is.

This pattern of coding will lead to grief but is not without value. It vividly illustrates an antipattern that, once noticed, suggests a better design.

This code contains an `if` statement that checks *an attribute that holds the category of self* to determine what message to send to *self*. This should bring back memories of a pattern discussed in the previous chapter on duck typing, where you saw an `if` statement that checked the *class of an object* to determine what message to send to *that object*.

In both of these patterns an object decides what message to send based on a category of the receiver. You can think of *the class of an object* as merely a specific case of *an attribute that holds the category of self*; considered this way, these patterns are the same. In each case if the sender could talk it would be saying "I know *who you are* and because of that I know *what you do*." This knowledge is a dependency that raises the cost of change.

Be on the lookout for this pattern. While sometimes innocent and occasionally defensible, its presence might be exposing a costly flaw in your design. Chapter 5, Reducing Costs with Duck Typing, used this pattern to discover a missing duck type; here the pattern indicates a missing subtype, better known as a subclass.

Finding the Embedded Types

The `if` statement in the `spares` method above switches on a variable named `style`, but it would have been just as natural to call that variable `type` or `category`. Variables with these kinds of names are your cue to notice the underlying pattern. *Type* and *category* are words perilously similar to those you would use when describing a class. After all, what is a class if not a category or type?

The `style` variable effectively divides instances of `Bicycle` into two different kinds of things. These two things share a great deal of behavior but differ along the `style` dimension. Some of `Bicycle`'s behavior applies to all bicycles, some only to road bikes, and some only to mountain bikes. This single class contains several different, but related, types.

This is the exact problem that inheritance solves; that of highly related types that share common behavior but differ along some dimension.

Choosing Inheritance

Before proceeding to the next example it's worth examining inheritance in more detail. Inheritance may seem like a mysterious art but, like most design ideas, it's simple when looked from the right perspective.

It goes without saying that objects receive messages. No matter how complicated the code, the receiving object ultimately handles any message in one of two ways. It either responds directly or it passes the message on to some other object for a response.

Inheritance provides a way to define two objects as having a relationship such that when the first receives a message that it does not understand, it *automatically* forwards, or delegates, the message to the second. It's as simple as that.

The word *inheritance* suggests a biological family tree where a few progenitors sit at the top and descendents branch off below. This family tree image is, however, a bit misleading. In many parts of the biological world it's common for descendents to have two ancestors. You, for example, quite likely have two parents. Languages that allow objects to have multiple parents are described as having *multiple inheritance* and the designers of these languages face interesting challenges. When an object with multiple parents receives a message that it does not understand, to which parent ought it forward that message? If more than one of its parents implements the message, which implementation has priority? As you might guess, things get complicated quickly.

Many object-oriented languages sidestep these complications by providing *single inheritance*, whereby a subclass is allowed only one parent superclass. Ruby does this; it has single inheritance. A superclass may have many subclasses, but each subclass is permitted only one superclass.

Message forwarding via classical inheritance takes place between *classes*. Because duck types cut across classes, they do not use classical inheritance to share common behavior. Duck types share code via Ruby modules (more on modules in the next chapter).

Even if you have never explicitly created a class hierarchy of your own, you use inheritance. When you define a new class but do not specify its superclass, Ruby automatically sets your new class's superclass to Object. Every class you create is, by definition, a subclass of something.

You also already benefit from automatic delegation of messages to superclasses. When an object receives a message it does not understand, Ruby automatically forwards that message up the superclass chain in search of a matching method implementation. A simple example is illustrated in Figure 6.3, which shows how Ruby objects respond to the nil? message.

Remember that in Ruby, nil is an instance of class NilClass; it's an object like any other. Ruby contains two implementations of nil?, one in NilClass, and the other in Object. The implementation in NilClass unconditionally returns true, the one in Object, false.

When you send nil? to an instance of NilClass, it, obviously, answers true. When you send nil? to anything else, the message travels up the hierarchy from one superclass to the next until it reaches Object, where it invokes the implementation that answers false. Thus, nil reports that it *is* nil and all other objects report that they are not. This elegantly simple solution illustrates the power and usefulness of inheritance.

The fact that unknown messages get delegated up the superclass hierarchy implies that subclasses are everything their superclasses are, plus *more*. An instance of String *is* a String, but it's also an Object. Every String is assumed to contain

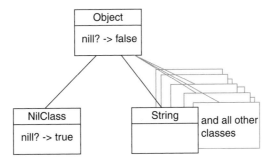

When an instance of NilClass receives the nil? message, its implementation returns true.

When instance of other classes receive the nil? message, the message automatically travels up the superclass hierarchy to object, whose implementation returns false.

Figure 6.3 *NilClass* answers true to *nil?*, string (and all others) answer false.

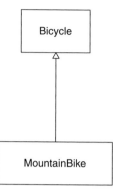

Figure 6.4   MountainBike is a subclass of bicycle.

`Object`'s entire public interface and must respond appropriately to any message defined in that interface. Subclasses are thus specializations of their superclasses.

The current `Bicycle` example embeds multiple types inside the class. It's time to abandon this code and revert to the original version of `Bicycle`. Perhaps mountain bikes are a specialization of `Bicycle`; perhaps this design problem can be solved using inheritance.

Drawing Inheritance Relationships

Just as you used UML sequence diagrams to communicate message passing in Chapter 4, Creating Flexible Interfaces, you can use UML class diagrams to illustrate class relationships.

Figure 6.4 contains a class diagram. The boxes represent classes. The connecting line indicates that the classes are related. The hollow triangle means that the relationship is inheritance. The pointed end of the triangle is attached to the box containing the superclass. Thus, the figure shows `Bicycle` as a superclass of `MountainBike`.

Misapplying Inheritance

Under the premise that the journey is more useful than the destination, and that experiencing common mistakes by proxy is less painful than experiencing them in person, this next section continues to show code that is unworthy of emulation. The code illustrates common difficulties encountered by novices. If you are practiced at using inheritance and are comfortable with these techniques, feel free to skim. However, if you are new to inheritance, or you find that all of your attempts go awry, then follow along carefully.

The following is a first attempt at a `MountainBike` subclass. This new subclass is a direct descendent of the original `Bicycle` class. It implements two methods, `initialize` and `spares`. Both of these methods are already implemented in `Bicycle`, therefore, they are said to be *overridden* by `MountainBike`.

In the following code each of the overridden methods sends `super`.

```ruby
1  class MountainBike < Bicycle
2    attr_reader :front_shock, :rear_shock
3
4    def initialize(args)
5      @front_shock = args[:front_shock]
6      @rear_shock  = args[:rear_shock]
7      super(args)
8    end
9
10   def spares
11     super.merge(rear_shock: rear_shock)
12   end
13 end
```

Sending `super` in any method passes that message up the superclass chain. Thus, for example, the send of `super` in `MountainBike`'s `initialize` method (line 7 above) invokes the `initialize` method of its superclass, `Bicycle`.

Jamming the new `MountainBike` class directly under the existing `Bicycle` class was blindly optimistic, and, predictably, running the code exposes several flaws. Instances of `MountainBike` have some behavior that just doesn't make sense. The following example shows what happens if you ask a `MountainBike` for its `size` and `spares`. It reports its size correctly but says that it has skinny tires and implies that it needs handlebar tape, both of which are incorrect.

```ruby
1  mountain_bike = MountainBike.new(
2                    size:          'S',
3                    front_shock:   'Manitou',
4                    rear_shock:    'Fox')
5
6  mountain_bike.size # -> 'S'
7
8  mountain_bike.spares
9  # -> {:tire_size   => "23",          <- wrong!
10 #      :chain       => "10-speed",
```

```
11 #     :tape_color  => nil,         <- not applicable
12 #     :front_shock => 'Manitou',
13 #     :rear_shock  => "Fox"}
```

It comes as no surprise that instances of MountainBike contain a confusing mishmash of road and mountain bike behavior. The Bicycle class is a concrete class that was not written to be subclassed. It combines behavior that is general to all bicycles with behavior that is specific to road bikes. When you slam MountainBike under Bicycle, you inherit all of this behavior—the general and the specific, whether it applies or not.

Figure 6.5 takes serious liberties with class diagrams to illustrate this idea. It shows road bike behavior embedded inside of Bicycle. The way this code is arranged causes MountainBike to inherit behavior that it does not want or need.

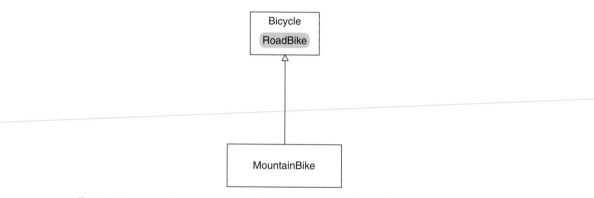

Figure 6.5   *Bicycle* combines general bicycle behavior with specific road bike behavior.

The Bicycle class contains behavior that is appropriate for both a peer and a parent of MountainBike. Some of the behavior in Bicycle is correct for MountainBike, some is wrong, and some doesn't even apply. As written, Bicycle should not act as the superclass of MountainBike.

Because design is evolutionary, this situation arises all the time. The problem here started with the names of these classes.

Finding the Abstraction

In the beginning, there was one idea, a bicycle, and it was modeled as a single class, Bicycle. The original designer chose a generic name for an object that was actually slightly more specialized. The existing Bicycle class doesn't represent just *any* kind of bicycle, it represents a specific kind—a road bike.

This naming choice is perfectly appropriate in an application where every `Bicycle` *is* a road bike. When there's only one kind of bike, choosing `RoadBike` for the class name is unnecessary, perhaps even overly specific. Even if you suspect that you will someday have mountain bikes, `Bicycle` is a fine choice for the first class name, and is sufficient unto the day.

However, now that `MountainBike` exists, `Bicycle`'s name is misleading. These two class names *imply* inheritance; you immediately expect `MountainBike` to be a specialization of `Bicycle`. It's natural to write code that creates `MountainBike` as a subclass of `Bicycle`. This is the right structure, the class names are correct, but the code in `Bicycle` is now very wrong.

Subclasses are *specializations* of their superclasses. A `MountainBike` should be everything a `Bicycle` is, plus more. Any object that expects a `Bicycle` should be able to interact with a `MountainBike` in blissful ignorance of its actual class.

These are the rules of inheritance; break them at your peril. For inheritance to work, two things must always be true. First, the objects that you are modeling must truly have a generalization–specialization relationship. Second, you must use the correct coding techniques.

It makes perfect sense to model mountain bike as a specialization of bicycle; the relationship is correct. However, the code above is a mess and if propagated will lead to disaster. The current `Bicycle` class intermingles general bicycle code with specific road bike code. It's time to separate these two things, to move the road bike code out of `Bicycle` and into a separate `RoadBike` subclass.

Creating an Abstract Superclass

Figure 6.6 shows a new class diagram where `Bicycle` is the superclass of both `MountainBike` and `RoadBike`. This is your goal; it's the inheritance structure you intend to create. `Bicycle` will contain the common behavior, and `MountainBike` and `RoadBike` will add specializations. `Bicycle`'s public interface should include `spares` and `size`, and the interfaces of its subclasses will add their individual parts.

`Bicycle` now represents an *abstract* class. Chapter 3, Managing Dependencies, defined abstract as being disassociated from any specific instance, and that definition still holds true. This new version of `Bicycle` will not define a complete bike, just the bits that all bicycles share. You can expect to create instances of `MountainBike` and `RoadBike`, but `Bicycle` is not a class to which you would ever send the new message. It wouldn't make sense; `Bicycle` no longer represents a whole bike.

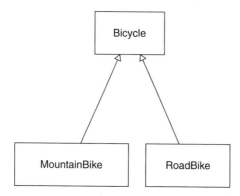

Figure 6.6 *Bicycle* as the superclass of *MountainBike* and *RoadBike*.

Some object-oriented programming languages have syntax that allows you to explicitly declare classes as abstract. Java, for example, has the `abstract` keyword. The Java compiler itself prevents creation of instances of classes to which this keyword has been applied. Ruby, in line with its trusting nature, contains no such keyword and enforces no such restriction. Only good sense prevents other programmers from creating instances of `Bicycle`; in real life, this works remarkably well.

Abstract classes exist to be subclassed. This is their sole purpose. They provide a common repository for behavior that is shared across a set of subclasses—subclasses that in turn supply specializations.

It almost never makes sense to create an abstract superclass with only one subclass. Even though the original `Bicycle` class contains general and specific behavior and it's possible to imagine modeling it as two classes from the very beginning, do not. Regardless of how strongly you anticipate having other kinds of bikes, that day may never come. Until you have a specific requirement that forces you to deal with other bikes, the current `Bicycle` class is good enough.

Even though you now have a requirement for two kinds of bikes, this *still* may not be the right moment to commit to inheritance. Creating a hierarchy has costs; the best way to minimize these costs is to maximize your chance of getting the abstraction right before allowing subclasses to depend on it. While the two bikes you know about supply a fair amount of information about the common abstraction, three bikes would supply a great deal more. If you could put this decision off until FastFeet asked for a third kind of bike, your odds of finding the right abstraction would improve dramatically.

A decision to put off the creation of the `Bicycle` hierarchy commits you to writing `MountainBike` and `RoadBike` classes that duplicate a great deal of code. A decision to proceed with the hierarchy accepts the risk that you may not yet have enough information to identify the correct abstraction. Your choice about whether to wait or to proceed hinges on how soon you expect a third bike to appear versus how much you expect the duplication to cost. If a third bike is imminent, it may be best to duplicate the code and wait for better information. However, if the duplicated code would need to change every day, it may be cheaper to go ahead and create the hierarchy. You should wait, if you can, but don't fear to move forward based on two concrete cases if this seems best.

For now, assume you have good reason to create a `Bicycle` hierarchy even though you only know about two bikes. The first step in creating the new hierarchy is to make a class structure that mirrors Figure 6.6. Ignoring the rightness of the code for a moment, the simplest way to make this change is to rename `Bicycle` to `RoadBike` and to create a new, empty `Bicycle` class. The following example does just that.

```
1  class Bicycle
2    # This class is now empty.
3    # All code has been moved to RoadBike.
4  end
5
6  class RoadBike < Bicycle
7    # Now a subclass of Bicycle.
8    # Contains all code from the old Bicycle class.
9  end
10
11 class MountainBike < Bicycle
12   # Still a subclass of Bicycle (which is now empty).
13   # Code has not changed.
14 end
```

The new `RoadBike` class is defined as a subclass of `Bicycle`. The existing `MountainBike` class already subclassed `Bicycle`. Its code did not change, but its behavior certainly has because its superclass is now empty. Code that `MountainBike` depends on has been removed from its parent and placed in a peer.

This code rearrangement merely moved the problem, as illustrated in Figure 6.7. Now, instead of containing too much behavior, `Bicycle` contains none at all. The common behavior needed by all bicycles is stuck down inside of `RoadBike` and is therefore inaccessible to `MountainBike`.

This rearrangement improves your lot because it's easier to promote code up to a superclass than to demote it down to a subclass. The reasons for this are not yet obvious but will become so as the example proceeds.

The next few iterations concentrate on achieving this new class structure by moving common behavior into `Bicycle` and using that behavior effectively in the subclasses.

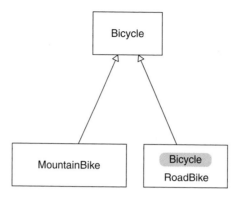

Figure 6.7   Now *RoadBike* contains all the common behavior.

RoadBike still contains everything it needs and thus it still works, but MountainBike is now seriously broken. As an example, here's what happens if you create instances of each subclass and ask them for size. RoadBike returns the correct response, MountainBike just blows up.

```
 1  road_bike = RoadBike.new(
 2                size:        'M',
 3                tape_color:  'red' )
 4
 5  road_bike.size   # => "M"
 6
 7  mountain_bike = MountainBike.new(
 8                size:         'S',
 9                front_shock:  'Manitou',
10                rear_shock:   'Fox')
11
12  mountain_bike.size
13  # NoMethodError: undefined method 'size'
```

It's obvious why this error occurs; neither MountainBike nor any of its superclasses implement size.

Promoting Abstract Behavior

The size and spares methods are common to all bicycles. This behavior belongs in Bicycle's public interface. Both methods are currently stuck down in RoadBike; the task here is to move them up to `Bicycle` so the behavior can be shared. Because the code dealing with `size` is simplest it's the most natural place to start.

Promoting `size` behavior to the superclass requires three changes as shown in the example below. The attribute reader and initialization code move from `RoadBike` to `Bicycle` (lines 2 and 5), and `RoadBike`'s `initialize` method adds a send of `super` (line 14).

```ruby
1  class Bicycle
2    attr_reader :size      # <- promoted from RoadBike
3
4    def initialize(args={})
5      @size = args[:size] # <- promoted from RoadBike
6    end
7  end
8
9  class RoadBike < Bicycle
10   attr_reader :tape_color
11
12   def initialize(args)
13     @tape_color = args[:tape_color]
14     super(args)  # <- RoadBike now MUST send 'super'
15   end
16   # ...
17 end
```

`RoadBike` now inherits the `size` method from `Bicycle`. When a `RoadBike` receives `size`, Ruby itself delegates the message up the superclass chain, searching for an implementation and finding the one in `Bicycle`. This message delegation happens automatically because `RoadBike` is a subclass of `Bicycle`.

Sharing the initialization code that sets the `@size` variable, however, requires a bit more from you. This variable is set in `Bicycle`'s `initialize` method, a method that `RoadBike` also implements, or overrides.

When `RoadBike` overrides `initialize`, it provides a receiver for this message, one that perfectly satisfies Ruby and prevents the message's automatic delegation to `Bicycle`. If both `initialize` methods need to be run, `RoadBike` is now obligated to do the delegation itself; it must send `super` to explicitly pass this message on to `Bicycle`, as it did in line 14 above.

Before this change, `RoadBike` responded correctly to `size` but `MountainBike` did not. The behavior they share in common in now defined in `Bicycle`, their common superclass. The magic of inheritance is such that both now respond correctly to `size` as shown below.

```
 1 road_bike = RoadBike.new(
 2              size:        'M',
 3              tape_color: 'red' )
 4
 5 road_bike.size   # -> ""M""
 6
 7 mountain_bike = MountainBike.new(
 8              size:         'S',
 9              front_shock: 'Manitou',
10              rear_shock:  'Fox')
11
12 mountain_bike.size # -> 'S'
```

The alert reader will notice the code that handles bicycle size has been moved twice. It was in the original `Bicycle` class, got moved *down* to `RoadBike`, and now has been promoted back *up* to `Bicycle`. The code has not changed; it has just been moved twice.

You might be tempted to skip the middleman and just leave this bit of code in `Bicycle` to begin with, but this push-everything-down-and-then-pull-some-things-up strategy is an important part of this refactoring. Many of the difficulties of inheritance are caused by a failure to rigorously separate the concrete from the abstract. `Bicycle`'s original code intermingled the two. If you begin this refactoring with that first version of `Bicycle`, attempting to isolate the concrete code and push it *down* to `RoadBike`, any failure on your part will leave dangerous remnants of concreteness in the superclass. However, if you start by moving every bit of the `Bicycle` code to `RoadBike`, you can then carefully identify and promote the abstract parts without fear of leaving concrete artifacts.

When deciding between refactoring strategies, indeed, when deciding between design strategies in general, it's useful to ask the question: "What will happen if I'm wrong?" In this case, if you create an empty superclass and push the abstract bits of code up into it, the worst that can happen is that you will fail to find and promote the entire abstraction.

This "promotion" failure creates a simple problem, one that is easily found and easily fixed. When a bit of the abstraction gets left behind, the oversight becomes visible as soon as another subclass needs the same behavior. In order to give all subclasses access to the behavior you'll be forced to either duplicate the code (in each subclass) or promote it (to the common superclass). Because even the most junior programmers have been taught not to duplicate code, this problem gets noticed no matter who works on the application in the future. The natural course of events is such that the abstraction gets identified and promoted, and the code improves. Promotion failures thus have low consequences.

However, if you attempt this refactoring from the opposite direction, trying to convert an existing class from concrete to abstract by pushing just the concrete parts *down* into a new subclass, you might accidentally leave remnants of concrete behavior behind. By definition this leftover concrete behavior does not apply to every possible new subclass. Subclasses thus begin to violate the basic rule of inheritance; they are not truly specializations of their superclasses. The hierarchy becomes untrustworthy.

Untrustworthy hierarchies force objects that interact with them to know their quirks. Inexperienced programmers do not understand and cannot fix a faulty hierarchy; when asked to use one they will embed knowledge of its quirks into their own code, often by explicitly checking the classes of objects. Knowledge of the structure of the hierarchy leaks into the rest of the application, creating dependencies that raise the cost of change. This is not a problem you want to leave behind. The consequences of a demotion failure can be widespread and severe.

The general rule for refactoring into a new inheritance hierarchy is to arrange code so that you can promote abstractions rather than demote concretions.

In light of this discussion, the question posed a few paragraphs ago might more usefully be phrased: "What will happen *when* I'm wrong?" Every decision you make includes two costs: one to implement it and another to change it when you discover that you were wrong. Taking both costs into account when choosing among alternatives motivates you to make conservative choices that minimize the cost of change.

With this in mind, turn your attention to spares.

Separating Abstract from Concrete

RoadBike and MountainBike both implement a version of spares. RoadBike's definition (repeated below) is the original one that was copied from the concrete Bicycle class. It is self-contained and thus still works.

```
1 class RoadBike < Bicycle
2   # ...
3   def spares
4     { chain:        '10-speed',
5       tire_size:    '23',
6       tape_color:   tape_color}
7   end
8 end
```

The `spares` definition in `MountainBike` (also repeated below) is leftover from the first attempt at subclassing. This method sends `super`, expecting a superclass to also implement `spares`.

```
1 class MountainBike < Bicycle
2   # ...
3   def spares
4     super.merge({rear_shock:  rear_shock})
5   end
6 end
```

`Bicycle`, however, does not yet implement the `spares` method, so sending `spares` to a `MountainBike` results in the following `NoMethodError` exception:

```
1 mountain_bike.spares
2 # NoMethodError: super: no superclass method 'spares'
```

Fixing this problem obviously requires adding a `spares` method to `Bicycle`, but doing so is not as simple as promoting the existing code from `RoadBike`.

RoadBike's `spares` implementation knows far too much. The `chain` and `tire_size` attributes are common to all bicycles, but `tape_color` should be known only to road bikes. The hard-coded `chain` and `tire_size` values are not the correct defaults for every possible subclass. This method has many problems and cannot be promoted as is.

It mixes a bunch of different things. When this awkward mix was hidden inside a single method of a single class it was survivable, even (depending on your tolerance) ignorable, but now that you would like to share only part of this behavior, you must untangle the mess and separate the abstract parts from the concrete parts. The abstractions will be promoted up to `Bicycle`, the concrete parts will remain in `RoadBike`.

Put away thoughts of the overall `spares` method for a moment and concentrate on promoting just the pieces that all bicycles share, `chain` and `tire_size`. They are attributes, like `size`, and should be represented by accessors and setters instead of hard-coded values. Here are the requirements:

- Bicycles have a chain and a tire size.
- All bicycles share the same default for chain.

- Subclasses provide their own default for tire size.

- Concrete instances of subclasses are permitted to ignore defaults and supply instance-specific values.

The code for similar things should follow a similar pattern. Here's new code that handles size, chain, and tire_size in a similar way.

```
 1 class Bicycle
 2   attr_reader :size, :chain, :tire_size
 3
 4   def initialize(args={})
 5     @size      = args[:size]
 6     @chain     = args[:chain]
 7     @tire_size = args[:tire_size]
 8   end
 9   # ...
10 end
```

RoadBike and MountainBike inherit the attr_reader definitions in Bicycle and both send super in their initialize methods. All bikes now understand size, chain, and tire_size and each may supply subclass-specific values for these attributes. The first and last requirements listed above have been met.

Despite the buildup, there's nothing special about this code. Good sense suggests that it should have been written like this in the beginning; it's high time this version appeared. It is inheritable by subclasses, certainly, but nothing about the code suggests that it *expects* to be inherited.

Meeting the two requirements that deal with defaults, however, adds something interesting.

Using the Template Method Pattern

This next change alters Bicycle's initialize method to send messages to get defaults. There are two new messages, default_chain and default_tire_size, in lines 6 and 7 below.

While wrapping the defaults in methods is good practice in general, these new message sends serve a dual purpose. Bicycle's main goal in sending these messages is to give subclasses an opportunity to contribute specializations by overriding them.

This technique of defining a basic structure in the superclass and sending messages to acquire subclass-specific contributions is known as the *template method* pattern.

In the following code, `MountainBike` and `RoadBike` take advantage of only one of these opportunities for specialization. Both implement `default_tire_size`, but neither implements `default_chain`. Each subclass thus supplies its own default for tire size but inherits the common default for chain.

```ruby
 1 class Bicycle
 2   attr_reader :size, :chain, :tire_size
 3
 4   def initialize(args={})
 5     @size      = args[:size]
 6     @chain     = args[:chain]     || default_chain
 7     @tire_size = args[:tire_size] || default_tire_size
 8   end
 9
10   def default_chain         # <- common default
11     '10-speed'
12   end
13 end
14
15 class RoadBike < Bicycle
16   # ...
17   def default_tire_size     # <- subclass default
18     '23'
19   end
20 end
21
22 class MountainBike < Bicycle
23   # ...
24   def default_tire_size     # <- subclass default
25     '2.1'
26   end
27 end
```

`Bicycle` now provides structure, a common algorithm if you will, for its subclasses. Where it permits them to influence the algorithm, it sends messages. Subclasses contribute to the algorithm by implementing matching methods.

All bicycles now share the same default for chain but use different defaults for tire size, as shown below:

```ruby
 1 road_bike = RoadBike.new(
 2             size:       'M',
```

```
 3                       tape_color: 'red' )
 4
 5 road_bike.tire_size      # => '23'
 6 road_bike.chain          # => "10-speed"
 7
 8 mountain_bike = MountainBike.new(
 9                   size:         'S',
10                   front_shock:  'Manitou',
11                   rear_shock:   'Fox')
12
13 mountain_bike.tire_size # => '2.1'
14 road_bike.chain          # => "10-speed"
```

It's too early to celebrate this success, however, because there's still something wrong with the code. It contains a booby trap, awaiting the unwary.

Implementing Every Template Method

Bicycle's initialize method sends default_tire_size but Bicycle itself does not implement it. This omission can cause problems downstream. Imagine that FastFeed adds another new bicycle type, the recumbent. Recumbents are low, long bicycles that place the rider in a laid-back, reclining position; these bikes are fast and easy on the rider's back and neck.

What happens if some programmer innocently creates a new RecumbentBike subclass but neglects to supply a default_tire_size implementation? He encounters the following error.

```
1 class RecumbentBike < Bicycle
2   def default_chain
3     '9-speed'
4   end
5 end
6
7 bent = RecumbentBike.new
8 # NameError: undefined local variable or method
9 #    'default_tire_size'
```

The original designer of the hierarchy rarely encounters this problem. She *wrote* Bicycle; she understands the requirements that subclasses must meet. The existing code works. These errors occur in the future, when the application is being changed to meet a new requirement, and are encountered by other programmers, ones who understand far less about what's going on.

The root of the problem is that `Bicycle` imposes a requirement upon its subclasses that is not obvious from a glance at the code. As `Bicycle` is written, subclasses *must* implement `default_tire_size`. Innocent and well-meaning subclasses like `RecumbentBike` may fail because they do not fulfill requirements of which they are unaware.

A world of potential hurt can be assuaged, in advance, by following one simple rule. Any class that uses the template method pattern must supply an implementation for every message it sends, even if the only reasonable implementation in the sending class looks like this:

```
1 class Bicycle
2   #...
3   def default_tire_size
4     raise NotImplementedError
5   end
6 end
```

Explicitly stating that subclasses are required to implement a message provides useful documentation for those who can be relied upon to read it and useful error messages for those who cannot.

Once Bicycle provides this implementation of `default_tire_size`, creating a new `RecumbentBike` fails with the following error.

```
1 bent = RecumbentBike.new
2 # NotImplementedError: NotImplementedError
```

While it is perfectly acceptable to merely raise this error and rely on the stack trace to track down its source, you may also explicitly supply additional information, as shown in line 5 below.

```
1 class Bicycle
2   #...
3   def default_tire_size
4     raise NotImplementedError,
5           "This #{self.class} cannot respond to:"
6   end
7 end
```

This additional information makes the problem inescapably clear. As running this code shows, this `RecumbentBike` needs access to an implementation of `default_tire_size`.

```
1 bent = RecumbentBike.new
2 #   NotImplementedError:
3 #     This RecumbentBike cannot respond to:
4 #             'default_tire_size'
```

Whether encountered two minutes or two months after writing the `RecumbentBike` class, this error is unambiguous and easily corrected.

Creating code that fails with reasonable error messages takes minor effort in the present but provides value forever. Each error message is a small thing, but small things accumulate to produce big effects and it is this attention to detail that marks you as a serious programmer. Always document template method requirements by implementing matching methods that raise useful errors.

Managing Coupling Between Superclasses and Subclasses

`Bicycle` now contains most of the abstract bicycle behavior. It has code to manage overall bike size, chain, and tire size, and its structure invites subclasses to supply common defaults for these attributes. The superclass is almost complete; it's missing only an implementation of `spares`.

This `spares` superclass implementation can be written in a number of ways; the alternatives vary in how tightly they couple the subclasses and superclasses together. Managing coupling is important; tightly coupled classes stick together and may be impossible to change independently.

This section shows two different implementations of spares—an easy, obvious one and another that is slightly more sophisticated but also more robust.

Understanding Coupling

This first implementation of spares is simplest to write but produces the most tightly coupled classes.

Remember that `RoadBike`'s current implementation looks like this:

```
1  class RoadBike < Bicycle
2    # ...
3    def spares
4      { chain:        '10-speed',
5        tire_size:    '23',
6        tape_color:   tape_color}
7    end
8  end
```

This method is a mishmash of different things and the last attempt at promoting it took a detour to clean up the code. That detour extracted the hard-coded values for chain and tire into variables and messages, and promoted just those parts up the `Bicycle`. The methods that deal with chain and tire size are now available in the superclass.

MountainBike's current spares implementation looks like this:

```
1  class MountainBike < Bicycle
2    # ...
3    def spares
4      super.merge({rear_shock:   rear_shock})
5    end
6  end
```

MountainBike's spares method sends super; it expects one of its superclasses to implement spares. MountainBike merges its own spare parts hash into the result returned by super, clearly expecting that result to also be a hash.

Given that `Bicycle` can now send messages to get chain and tire size and that its spares implementation ought to return a hash, adding the following spares method meets MountainBike's needs.

```
1  class Bicycle
2    #...
3    def spares
4      { tire_size:   tire_size,
5        chain:       chain}
6    end
7  end
```

Once this method is placed in `Bicycle` all of `MountainBike` works. Bringing `RoadBike` along is merely a matter of changing its `spares` implementation to mirror `MountainBike`'s, that is, replacing the code for chain and tire size with a send to `super` and adding the road bike specializations to the resulting hash.

Assuming this final change to `MountainBike` has been made, the following listing shows all of the code written so far and completes the first implementation of this hierarchy.

Notice that the code follows a discernible pattern. Every template method sent by `Bicycle` is implemented in `Bicycle` itself, and `MountainBike` and `RoadBike` both send `super` in their `initialize` and `spares` methods.

```
1  class Bicycle
2    attr_reader :size, :chain, :tire_size
3
4    def initialize(args={})
5      @size       = args[:size]
6      @chain      = args[:chain]      || default_chain
7      @tire_size  = args[:tire_size]  || default_tire_size
8    end
9
10   def spares
11     { tire_size:  tire_size,
12       chain:      chain}
13   end
14
15   def default_chain
16     '10-speed'
17   end
18
19   def default_tire_size
20     raise NotImplementedError
21   end
22 end
23
24 class RoadBike < Bicycle
25   attr_reader :tape_color
26
27   def initialize(args)
28     @tape_color = args[:tape_color]
29     super(args)
30   end
```

```ruby
31
32   def spares
33     super.merge({ tape_color: tape_color})
34   end
35
36   def default_tire_size
37     '23'
38   end
39 end
40
41 class MountainBike < Bicycle
42   attr_reader :front_shock, :rear_shock
43
44   def initialize(args)
45     @front_shock = args[:front_shock]
46     @rear_shock =  args[:rear_shock]
47     super(args)
48   end
49
50   def spares
51     super.merge({rear_shock: rear_shock})
52   end
53
54   def default_tire_size
55     '2.1'
56   end
57 end
```

This class hierarchy works, and you might be tempted to stop right here. However, just because it works doesn't guarantee that it's good enough. It still contains a booby trap worth removing.

Notice that the `MountainBike` and `RoadBike` subclasses follow a similar pattern. They each know things about themselves (their spare parts specializations) and things about their superclass (that it implements `spares` to return a hash and that it responds to `initialize`).

Knowing things about other classes, as always, creates dependencies and dependencies couple objects together. The dependencies in the code above are also the booby traps; both are created by the sends of `super` in the subclasses.

Here's an illustration of the trap. If someone creates a new subclass and forgets to send `super` in its `initialize` method, he encounters this problem:

```ruby
 1  class RecumbentBike < Bicycle
 2    attr_reader :flag
 3
 4    def initialize(args)
 5      @flag = args[:flag]  # forgot to send 'super'
 6    end
 7
 8    def spares
 9      super.merge({flag: flag})
10    end
11
12    def default_chain
13      '9-speed'
14    end
15
16    def default_tire_size
17      '28'
18    end
19  end
20
21  bent = RecumbentBike.new(flag: 'tall and orange')
22  bent.spares
23  # -> {:tire_size => nil, <- didn't get initialized
24  #     :chain     => nil,
25  #     :flag      => "tall and orange"}
```

When RecumbentBike fails to send super during initialize it misses out on the common initialization provided by Bicycle and does not get a valid size, chain, or tire size. This error can manifest at a time and place far distant from its cause, making it very hard to debug.

A similarly devilish problem occurs if RecumbentBike forgets to send super in its spares method. Nothing blows up, instead the spares hash is just wrong and this wrongness may not become apparent until a Mechanic is standing by the road with a broken bike, searching the spare parts bin in vain.

Any programmer can forget to send super and therefore cause these errors, but the primary culprits (and the primary victims) are programmers who don't know the code well but are tasked, in the future, with creating new subclasses of Bicycle.

The pattern of code in this hierarchy requires that subclasses not only know what they do but also how they are supposed to interact with their superclass. It makes sense that subclasses know the specializations they contribute (they are obviously the only classes who *can* know them), but forcing a subclass to know how to interact with its abstract superclass causes many problems.

It pushes knowledge of the algorithm down into the subclasses, forcing each to explicitly send super to participate. It causes duplication of code across subclasses, requiring that all send super in exactly the same places. And it raises the chance that future programmers will create errors when writing new subclasses, because programmers can be relied upon to include the correct specializations but can easily forget to send super.

When a subclass sends super it's effectively declaring that it knows the algorithm; it *depends* on this knowledge. If the algorithm changes, then the subclasses may break even if their own specializations are not otherwise affected.

Decoupling Subclasses Using Hook Messages

All of these problems can be avoided with one final refactoring. Instead of allowing subclasses to know the algorithm and requiring that they send super, superclasses can instead send *hook* messages, ones that exist solely to provide subclasses a place to contribute information by implementing matching methods. This strategy removes knowledge of the algorithm from the subclass and returns control to the superclass.

In the following example, this technique is used to give subclasses a way to contribute to initialization. Bicycle's initialize method now sends post_initialize and, as always, implements the matching method, one that in this case does nothing.

RoadBike supplies its own specialized initialization by overriding post_initialize, as you see here:

```
1  class Bicycle
2
3    def initialize(args={})
4      @size      = args[:size]
5      @chain     = args[:chain]      || default_chain
6      @tire_size = args[:tire_size]  || default_tire_size
7
8      post_initialize(args)      # Bicycle both sends
9    end
10
11   def post_initialize(args) # and implements this
12     nil
13   end
14   # ...
```

```
15 end
16
17 class RoadBike < Bicycle
18
19   def post_initialize(args)        # RoadBike can
20     @tape_color = args[:tape_color] # optionally
21   end                               # override it
22   # ...
23 end
```

This change doesn't just remove the send of `super` from `RoadBike`'s `initialize` method, it removes the `initialize` method altogether. `RoadBike` no longer controls initialization; it instead contributes specializations to a larger, abstract algorithm. That algorithm is defined in the abstract superclass `Bicycle`, which in turn is responsible for sending `post_initialize`.

`RoadBike` is still responsible for *what* initialization it needs but is no longer responsible for *when* its initialization occurs. This change allows `RoadBike` to know less about `Bicycle`, reducing the coupling between them and making each more flexible in the face of an uncertain future. `RoadBike` doesn't know when its `post_initialize` method will be called and it doesn't care what object actually sends the message. `Bicycle` (or any other object) could send this message at any time, there is no requirement that it be sent during object initialization.

Putting control of the timing in the superclass means the algorithm can change without forcing changes upon the subclasses.

This same technique can be used to remove the send of `super` from the `spares` method. Instead of forcing `RoadBike` to know that `Bicycle` implements spares and that `Bicycle`'s implementation returns a hash, you can loosen coupling by implementing a hook that gives control back to `Bicycle`.

The following example changes `Bicycle`'s `spares` method to send `local_spares`. `Bicycle` provides a default implementation, one that returns an empty hash. `RoadBike` takes advantage of this hook and overrides it to return its own version of `local_spares`, adding road bike specific spare parts.

```
1 class Bicycle
2   # ...
3   def spares
4     { tire_size: tire_size,
5       chain:     chain}.merge(local_spares)
6   end
```

```
7
8    # hook for subclasses to override
9    def local_spares
10     {}
11   end
12
13 end
14
15 class RoadBike < Bicycle
16   # ...
17   def local_spares
18     {tape_color: tape_color}
19   end
20
21 end
```

RoadBike's new implementation of local_spares replaces its former implementation of spares. This change preserves the specialization supplied by RoadBike but reduces its coupling to Bicycle. RoadBike no longer has to know that Bicycle implements a spares method; it merely expects that its own implementation of local_spares will be called, by some object, at some time.

After making similar changes to MountainBike, the final hierarchy looks like this:

```
1  class Bicycle
2    attr_reader :size, :chain, :tire_size
3
4    def initialize(args={})
5      @size      = args[:size]
6      @chain     = args[:chain]     || default_chain
7      @tire_size = args[:tire_size] || default_tire_size
8      post_initialize(args)
9    end
10
11   def spares
12     { tire_size: tire_size,
13       chain:     chain}.merge(local_spares)
14   end
15
16   def default_tire_size
17     raise NotImplementedError
18   end
19
```

```
20    # subclasses may override
21    def post_initialize(args)
22      nil
23    end
24
25    def local_spares
26      {}
27    end
28
29    def default_chain
30      '10-speed'
31    end
32
33 end
34
35 class RoadBike < Bicycle
36   attr_reader :tape_color
37
38    def post_initialize(args)
39      @tape_color = args[:tape_color]
40    end
41
42    def local_spares
43      {tape_color: tape_color}
44    end
45
46    def default_tire_size
47      '23'
48    end
49 end
50
51 class MountainBike < Bicycle
52   attr_reader :front_shock, :rear_shock
53
54    def post_initialize(args)
55      @front_shock = args[:front_shock]
56      @rear_shock =  args[:rear_shock]
57    end
58
59    def local_spares
60      {rear_shock:  rear_shock}
61    end
62
```

```
63    def default_tire_size
64      '2.1'
65    end
66  end
```

RoadBike and MountainBike are more readable now that they contain only special-izations. It's clear at a glance what they do, and it's clear that they are specializations of Bicycle.

New subclasses need only implement the template methods. This final example illustrates how simple it is to create a new subclass, even for someone unfamiliar with the application. Here is class RecumbentBike, a new specialization of Bicycle:

```
1  class RecumbentBike < Bicycle
2    attr_reader :flag
3
4    def post_initialize(args)
5      @flag = args[:flag]
6    end
7
8    def local_spares
9      {flag: flag}
10   end
11
12   def default_chain
13     "9-speed"
14   end
15
16   def default_tire_size
17     '28'
18   end
19 end
20
21 bent = RecumbentBike.new(flag: 'tall and orange')
22 bent.spares
23 # -> {:tire_size => "28",
24 #     :chain     => "9-speed",
25 #     :flag      => "tall and orange"}
```

The code in RecumbentBike is transparently obvious and is so regular and predictable that it might have come off of an assembly line. It illustrates the strength and value of inheritance; when the hierarchy is correct, anyone can successfully create a new subclass.

Summary

Inheritance solves the problem of related types that share a great deal of common behavior but differ across some dimension. It allows you to isolate shared code and implement common algorithms in an abstract class, while also providing a structure that permits subclasses to contribute specializations.

The best way to create an abstract superclass is by pushing code up from concrete subclasses. Identifying the correct abstraction is easiest if you have access to at least three existing concrete classes. This chapter's simple example relied on just two but in the real world you are often better served to wait for the additional information that three cases supply.

Abstract superclasses use the template method pattern to invite inheritors to supply specializations, and use hook methods to allow these inheritors to contribute these specializations without being forced to send super. Hook methods allow subclasses to contribute specializations without knowing the abstract algorithm. They remove the need for subclasses to send `super` and therefore reduce the coupling between layers of the hierarchy and increase its tolerance for change.

Well-designed inheritance hierarchies are easy to extend with new subclasses, even for programmers who know very little about the application. This ease of extension is inheritance's greatest strength. When your problem is one of needing numerous specializations of a stable, common abstraction, inheritance can be an extremely low-cost solution.

CHAPTER 7

Sharing Role Behavior with Modules

The previous chapter ended on a high note, with code that looked so promising you may be wondering where it's been all your life. However, before you decide to use classical inheritance to solve every imaginable design problem, consider this: What will happen when FastFeet develops a need for recumbent mountain bikes?

If the solution to this new design problem feels elusive, that's perfectly understandable. Creation of a recumbent mountain bike subclass requires combining the qualities of two existing subclasses, something that inheritance cannot readily accommodate. Even more distressing is the fact that this failure illustrates just *one* of several ways in which inheritance can go wrong.

To reap benefits from using inheritance you must understand not only how to write inheritable code but also when it makes sense to do so. Use of classical inheritance is always optional; every problem that it solves can be solved another way. Because no design technique is free, creating the most cost-effective application requires making informed tradeoffs between the relative costs and likely benefits of alternatives.

This chapter explores an alternative that uses the techniques of inheritance to share a *role*. It begins with an example that uses a Ruby module to define a common role and then proceeds to give practical advice about how to write all inheritable code.

Understanding Roles

Some problems require sharing behavior among otherwise unrelated objects. This common behavior is orthogonal to class; it's a *role* an object plays. Many of the roles needed by an application will be obvious at design time, but it's also common to discover unanticipated roles as you write the code.

When formerly unrelated objects begin to play a common role, they enter into a relationship with the objects for whom they play the role. These relationships are not as visible as those created by the subclass/superclass requirements of classical inheritance but they exist nonetheless. Using a role creates dependencies among the objects involved and these dependencies introduce risks that you must take into account when deciding among design options.

This section unearths a hidden role and creates code to share its behavior among all players, while at the same time minimizing the dependencies thereby incurred.

Finding Roles

The `Preparer` duck type from Chapter 5, Reducing Costs with Duck Typing, is a role. Objects that implement `Preparer`'s interface play this role. `Mechanic`, `TripCoordinator`, and `Driver` each implement `prepare_trip`; therefore, other objects can interact with them as if they are `Preparers` without concern for their underlying class.

The existence of a `Preparer` role suggests that there's also a parallel `Preparable` role (these things often come in pairs). The `Trip` class acts as a `Preparable` in the Chapter 5 example; it implements the `Prepareable` interface. This interface includes all of the messages that any `Preparer` might expect to send to a `Preparable`, that is, the methods `bicycles`, `customers`, and `vehicle`. The `Preparable` role is not terribly obvious because `Trip` is its only player but it's important to recognize that it exists. Chapter 9, Designing Cost-Effective Tests, suggests techniques for testing and documenting the `Preparable` role so as to distinguish it from the `Trip` class.

Although the `Preparer` role has multiple players, it is so simple that it is entirely defined by its interface. To play this role all an object need do is implement its own personal version of `prepare_trip`. Objects that act as `Preparers` have only this interface in common. They share the method signature but no other code.

`Preparer` and `Preparable` are perfectly legitimate duck types. It's far more common, however, to discover more sophisticated roles, ones where the role requires not only specific message signatures, but also specific behavior. When a role needs shared behavior you're faced with the problem of organizing the shared code. Ideally this code would be defined in a single place but be usable by any object that wished to act as the duck type and play the role.

Many object-oriented languages provide a way to define a named group of methods that are independent of class and can be mixed in to any object. In Ruby, these mix-ins are called *modules*. Methods can be defined in a module and then the module can be added to any object. Modules thus provide a perfect way to allow objects of different classes to play a common role using a single set of code.

When an object includes a module, the methods defined therein become available via automatic delegation. If this sounds like classical inheritance, it also looks like it, at least from the point of view of the including object. From that object's point of view, messages arrive, it doesn't understand them, they get automatically routed somewhere else, the correct method implementation is magically found, it is executed, and the response is returned.

Once you start putting code into modules and adding modules to objects, you expand the set of messages to which an object can respond and enter a new realm of design complexity. An object that directly implements few methods might still have a very large response set. The total set of messages to which an object can respond includes

- Those it implements
- Those implemented in all objects above it in the hierarchy
- Those implemented in any module that has been added to it
- Those implemented in all modules added to any object above it in the hierarchy

If this seems like a frighteningly large and potentially confusing response set, you have a clear grasp of the problem. Acquiring an understanding of the behavior of a deeply nested hierarchy is at best intimidating, at worst, impossible.

Organizing Responsibilities

Now that you have a sufficiently somber view of the possibilities, it's time to look at a manageable example. Just as with classical inheritance, before you can choose whether to create a duck type and put shared behavior into a module, you have to know how to do it correctly. Fortunately, the classical inheritance example in Chapter 6, Acquiring Behavior Through Inheritance, is about to pay off; this example builds on those techniques and is significantly shorter.

Consider the problem of scheduling a trip. Trips occur at specific points in time and involve bicycles, mechanics, and motor vehicles. Bikes, mechanics, and vehicles are real things in the physical world that can't be in two places at once. FastFeet needs a way to arrange all of these objects on a schedule so that it can determine, for any point in time, which objects are available and which are already committed.

Determining if an unscheduled bike, mechanic, or vehicle is available to participate in a trip is not as simple as looking to see if it's idle throughout the interval during which the trip is scheduled. These real-world things need a bit of downtime between trips, they cannot finish a trip on one day and start another the next. Bicycles and motor vehicles must undergo maintenance, and mechanics need a rest from being nice to customers and a chance to do their laundry.

The requirements are that bicycles have a minimum of one day between trips, vehicles a minimum of three days, and mechanics, four days.

The code to schedule these objects can be written in many ways, and, as has been true throughout the book, this example will evolve. It begins with some rather alarming code and works it way to a satisfactory solution, all in the interest of exposing likely antipatterns.

Assume that a `Schedule` class exists. Its interface already includes these three methods:

```
scheduled?(target, starting, ending)
add(target, starting, ending)
remove(target, starting, ending)
```

Each of the above methods takes three arguments: the target object and the start and end dates for the period of interest. The `Schedule` is responsible for knowing if its incoming `target` argument is already scheduled and for adding and removing `targets` from the schedule. These responsibilities rightly belong here in the `Schedule` itself.

These methods are fine, but unfortunately there's a gap in this code. It is true that knowing if an object is scheduled during some interval is all the information needed to prevent over-scheduling an already busy object. However, knowing that a object is *not* scheduled during an interval isn't enough information to know if it *can* be scheduled during that same interval. To properly determine if an object can be scheduled, some object, somewhere, must take lead time into account.

Figure 7.1 shows an implementation where the `Schedule` itself takes responsibility for knowing the correct lead time. The `schedulable?` method knows all the possible values and it checks the class of its incoming `target` argument to decide which lead time to use.

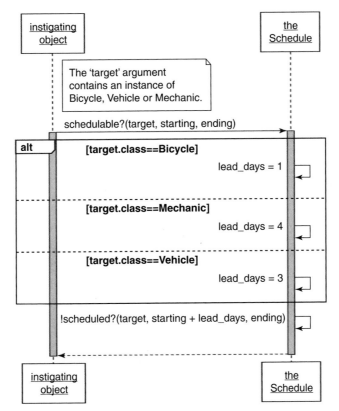

Figure 7.1   The schedule knows the lead time for other objects.

You've seen the pattern of checking class to know what *message* to send; here the Schedule checks class to know what *value* to use. In both cases Schedule knows too much. This knowledge doesn't belong in Schedule, it belongs in the classes whose names Schedule is checking.

This implementation cries out for a simple and obvious improvement, one suggested by the pattern of the code. Instead of knowing details about other classes, the Schedule should send them messages.

Removing Unnecessary Dependencies

The fact that the Schedule checks many class names to determine what value to place in one variable suggests that the variable name should be turned into a message, which in turn should be sent to each incoming object.

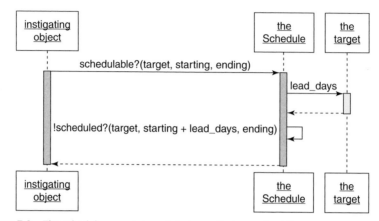

Figure 7.2   The schedule expects targets to know their own lead time.

Discovering the Schedulable Duck Type

Figure 7.2 shows a sequence diagram for new code that removes the check on class from the `schedulable?` method and alters the method to instead send the `lead_days` message to its incoming `target` argument. This change replaces an `if` statement that checks the class of an object with a message sent to that same object. It simplifies the code and pushes responsibility for knowing the correct number of lead days into the last object that could possibly know the correct answer, which is exactly where this responsibility belongs.

A close look at Figure 7.2 reveals something interesting. Notice that this diagram contains a box labeled "the target." The boxes on sequence diagrams are meant to represent objects and are commonly named after classes, as in "the Schedule" or "a Bicycle." In Figure 7.2, the `Schedule` intends to send `lead_days` to its `target`, but `target` could be an instance of any of a number of classes. Because `target`'s class is unknown, it's not obvious how to label the box for the receiver of this message.

The easiest way to draw the diagram is to sidestep this issue by labeling the box after the name of the variable and sending the `lead_days` message to that "target" without being precise about its class. The `Schedule` clearly does not care about `target`'s class, instead it merely expects it to respond to a specific message. This message-based expectation transcends class and exposes a role, one played by all `targets` and made explicitly visible by the sequence diagram.

The `Schedule` expects its `target` to behave like something that understands `lead_days`, that is, like something that is "schedulable." You have discovered a duck type.

Right now this new duck type is shaped much like the `Preparer` duck type from Chapter 5; it consists only of this interface. `Schedulables` must implement `lead_days` but currently have no other code in common.

Letting Objects Speak for Themselves

Discovering and using this duck type improves the code by removing the `Schedule`'s dependency on specific class names, which makes the application more flexible and easier to maintain. However, Figure 7.2 still contains unnecessary dependencies that should be removed.

It's easiest to illustrate these dependencies with an extreme example. Imagine a `StringUtils` class that implements utility methods for managing strings. You can ask `StringUtils` if a string is empty by sending `StringUtils.empty?(some_string)`.

If you have written much object-oriented code you will find this idea ridiculous. Using a separate class to manage strings is patently redundant; strings are objects, they have their own behavior, they manage themselves. Requiring that other objects know about a third party, `StringUtils`, to get behavior from a string complicates the code by adding an unnecessary dependency.

This specific example illustrates the general idea that objects should manage themselves; they should contain their own behavior. If your interest is in object B, you should not be forced to know about object A if your only use of it is to find things out about B.

The sequence diagram in Figure 7.2 violates this rule. The instigator is trying to ascertain if the `target` object is schedulable. Unfortunately, it doesn't ask this question of `target` itself, it instead asks a third party, `Schedule`. Asking `Schedule` if a target is schedulable is just like asking `StringUtils` if a string is empty. It forces the instigator to know about and thus depend upon the `Schedule`, even though its only real interest is in the target.

Just as strings respond to `empty?` and can speak for themselves, targets should respond to `schedulable?`. The `schedulable?` method should ·be added to the interface of the `Schedulable` role.

Writing the Concrete Code

As it currently stands, the `Schedulable` role contains only an interface. Adding the `schedulable?` method to this role requires writing some code and it's not immediately obvious where this code should reside. You are faced with two decisions; you must decide what the code should do and where the code should live.

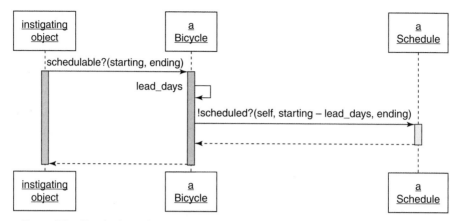

Figure 7.3   Bicycle classes know if they are schedulable.

The simplest way to get started is to separate the two decisions. Pick an arbitrary concrete class (for example, `Bicycle`) and implement the `schedulable?` method directly in that class. Once you have a version that works for `Bicycle` you can refactor your way to a code arrangement that allows all `Schedulables` to share the behavior.

Figure 7.3 shows a sequence diagram where this new code is in `Bicycle`. `Bicycle` now responds to messages about its own "schedulability."

Before this change, every instigating object had to know about and thus had a dependency on the `Schedule`. This change allows bicycles to speak for themselves, freeing instigating objects to interact with them without the aid of a third party.

The code to implement this sequence diagram is straightforward. Here's a very simple `Schedule`. This is clearly not a production-worthy implementation but it provides a good enough stand-in for the rest of the example.

```
1 class Schedule
2   def scheduled?(schedulable, start_date, end_date)
3     puts "This #{schedulable.class} " +
4         "is not scheduled\n" +
5         " between #{start_date} and #{end_date}"
6     false
7   end
8 end
```

This next example shows `Bicycle`'s implementation of `schedulable?`. `Bicycle` knows its own scheduling lead time (defined on line 23 and referenced on line 13 below), and delegates `scheduled?` to the `Schedule` itself.

```ruby
 1 class Bicycle
 2   attr_reader :schedule, :size, :chain, :tire_size
 3
 4   # Inject the Schedule and provide a default
 5   def initialize(args={})
 6     @schedule = args[:schedule] || Schedule.new
 7     # ...
 8   end
 9
10   # Return true if this bicycle is available
11   # during this (now Bicycle specific) interval.
12   def schedulable?(start_date, end_date)
13     !scheduled?(start_date - lead_days, end_date)
14   end
15
16   # Return the schedule's answer
17   def scheduled?(start_date, end_date)
18     schedule.scheduled?(self, start_date, end_date)
19   end
20
21   # Return the number of lead_days before a bicycle
22   # can be scheduled.
23   def lead_days
24     1
25   end
26
27   # ...
28 end
29
30 require 'date'
31 starting = Date.parse("2015/09/04")
32 ending   = Date.parse("2015/09/10")
33
34 b = Bicycle.new
35 b.schedulable?(starting, ending)
36 # This Bicycle is not scheduled
37 #   between 2015-09-03 and 2015-09-10
38 #   => true
```

Running the code (lines 30–35) confirms that `Bicycle` has correctly adjusted the starting date to include the bicycle specific lead days.

This code hides knowledge of who the `Schedule` is and what the `Schedule` does inside of `Bicycle`. Objects holding onto a `Bicycle` no longer need know about the existence or behavior of the `Schedule`.

Extracting the Abstraction

The code above solves the first part of current problem in that it decides what the `schedulable?` method should do, but `Bicycle` is not the only kind of thing that is "schedulable." `Mechanic` and `Vehicle` also play this role and therefore need this behavior. It's time to rearrange the code so that it can be shared among objects of different classes.

The following example shows a new `Schedulable` module, which contains an abstraction extracted from the `Bicycle` class above. The `schedulable?` (line 8) and `scheduled?` (line 12) methods are exact copies of the ones formerly implemented in `Bicycle`.

```ruby
 1 module Schedulable
 2   attr_writer :schedule
 3
 4   def schedule
 5     @schedule ||= ::Schedule.new
 6   end
 7
 8   def schedulable?(start_date, end_date)
 9     !scheduled?(start_date - lead_days, end_date)
10   end
11
12   def scheduled?(start_date, end_date)
13     schedule.scheduled?(self, start_date, end_date)
14   end
15
16   # includers may override
17   def lead_days
18     0
19   end
20
21 end
```

Two things have changed from the code as it previously existed in `Bicycle`. First, a `schedule` method (line 4) has been added. This method returns an instance of the overall `Schedule`.

Back in Figure 7.2 the instigating object depended on the `Schedule`, which meant there might be many places in the application that needed knowledge of the `Schedule`. In the next iteration, Figure 7.3, this dependency was transferred to `Bicycle`, reducing its reach into the application. Now, in the code above, the dependency on `Schedule` has been removed from `Bicycle` and moved into the `Schedulable` module, isolating it even further.

The second change is to the `lead_days` method (line 17). `Bicycle`'s former implementation returned a bicycle specific number, the module's implementation now returns a more generic default of zero days.

Even if there were no reasonable application default for lead days, the `Schedulable` module must still implement the `lead_days` method. The rules for modules are the same as for classical inheritance. If a module sends a message it must provide an implementation, even if that implementation merely raises an error indicating that users of the module must implement the method.

Including this new module in the original `Bicycle` class, as shown in the example below, adds the module's methods to `Bicycle`'s response set. The `lead_days` method is a hook that follows the template method pattern. `Bicycle` overrides this hook (line 4) to provide a specialization.

Running the code reveals that `Bicycle` retains the same behavior as when it directly implemented this role.

```
1  class Bicycle
2    include Schedulable
3
4    def lead_days
5      1
6    end
7
8    # ...
9  end
10
11 require 'date'
12 starting = Date.parse("2015/09/04")
13 ending   = Date.parse("2015/09/10")
14
```

```
15 b = Bicycle.new
16 b.schedulable?(starting, ending)
17 # This Bicycle is not scheduled
18 #    between 2015-09-03 and 2015-09-10
19 #  => true
20
```

Moving the methods to the `Schedulable` module, including the module and overriding `lead_days`, allows `Bicycle` to continue to behave correctly. Additionally, now that you have created this module other objects can make use of it to become `Schedulable` themselves. They can play this role without duplicating the code.

The pattern of messages has changed from that of sending `schedulable?` to a `Bicycle` to sending `schedulable?` to a `Schedulable`. You are now committed to the duck type and the sequence diagram shown in Figure 7.3 can be altered to look like the one in Figure 7.4.

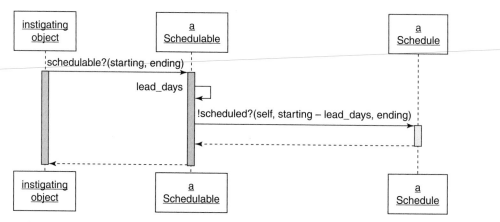

Figure 7.4   The schedulable duck type.

Once you include this module in all of the classes that can be scheduled, the pattern of code becomes strongly reminiscent of inheritance. The following example shows `Vehicle` and `Mechanic` including the `Schedulable` module and responding to the `schedulable?` message.

```
1 class Vehicle
2   include Schedulable
3
4   def lead_days
5     3
```

```
 6     end
 7
 8     # ...
 9 end
10
11 class Mechanic
12     include Schedulable
13
14     def lead_days
15         4
16     end
17
18     # ...
19 end
20
21 v = Vehicle.new
22 v.schedulable?(starting, ending)
23 # This Vehicle is not scheduled
24 #     between 2015-09-01 and 2015-09-10
25 #   => true
26
27 m = Mechanic.new
28 m.schedulable?(starting, ending)
29 # This Mechanic is not scheduled
30 #     between 2015-02-29 and 2015-09-10
31 #   => true
```

The code in Schedulable *is* the abstraction and it uses the template method pattern to invite objects to provide specializations to the algorithm it supplies. Schedulables override lead_days to supply those specializations. When schedulable? arrives at any Schedulable, the message is automatically delegated to the method defined in the module.

This may not fit the strict definition of classical inheritance, but in terms of how the code should be written and how the messages are resolved, it certainly acts like it. The coding techniques are the same because method lookup follows the same path.

This chapter has been careful to maintain a distinction between classical inheritance and sharing code via modules. This *is-a* versus *behaves-like-a* difference definitely matters, each choice has distinct consequences. However, the coding techniques for these two things are very similar and this similarity exists because both techniques rely on automatic message delegation.

Looking Up Methods

Understanding the similarities between classical inheritance and module inclusion is easier if you understand how object-oriented languages, in general, and Ruby, in particular, find the method implementation that matches a message send.

A Gross Oversimplification

When an object receives a message, the OO language first looks in that object's *class* for a matching method implementation. This makes perfect sense; method definitions would otherwise need to be duplicated within every instance of every class. Storing the methods known to an object inside of its class means that all instances of a class can share the same set of method definitions; definitions that need then exist in only one place.

Throughout this book there has been little concern with explicitly stating whether the object under discussion is an instance of a class or the class itself, expecting that the intent will be clear from the context and that you are comfortable with the notion that classes themselves are objects in their own right. Describing how method lookup works is going to require a bit more precision.

As stated above, the search for a method begins in the class of the receiving object. If this class does not implement the message, the search proceeds to its superclass. From here on only superclasses matter, the search proceeds up the superclass chain, looking in one superclass after another, until it reaches the top of the hierarchy.

Figure 7.5 shows how a generic object-oriented language would look up the `spares` method of the `Bicycle` hierarchy that you created in Chapter 6. For the purposes of this discussion, class `Object` sits at the top of the hierarchy. Please note

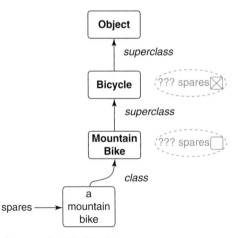

Figure 7.5 A generalization of method lookup.

that the specifics of method lookup in Ruby will turn out to be more involved, but this is a reasonable first model.

In Figure 7.5, the spares message is sent to an *instance* of MountainBike. The OO language first looks for a matching spares method in the MountainBike class. Upon failing to find method spares in that class, the search proceeds to MountainBike's superclass, Bicycle.

Because Bicycle implements spares, this example's search stops here. However, in the case where no superclass implementation exists, the search proceeds from one superclass to the next until it reaches the top of the hierarchy and searches in Object. If all attempts to find a suitable method fail, you might expect the search to stop, but many languages make a second attempt to resolve the message.

Ruby gives the original receiver a second chance by sending it a new message, method_missing, and passing :spares as an argument. Attempts to resolve this new message restart the search along the same path, except now the search is for method_missing rather than spares.

A More Accurate Explanation

The previous section explains only how methods are looked up for classical inheritance. This next section expands the explanation to encompass methods defined in a Ruby module. Figure 7.6 adds the Schedulable module to the method lookup path.

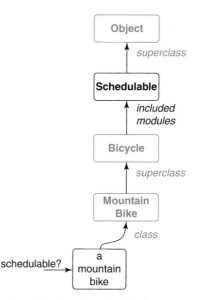

Figure 7.6   A more accurate explanation of method lookup.

The object hierarchy in Figure 7.6 looks much like the one from Figure 7.5. It differs only in that Figure 7.6 shows the `Schedulable` module highlighted between the `Bicycle` and `Object` classes.

When `Bicycle` includes `Schedulable`, all of the methods defined in the module become part of `Bicycle`'s response set. The module's methods go into the method lookup path directly *above* methods defined in `Bicycle`. Including this module doesn't change `Bicycle`'s superclass (that's still `Object`), but as far as method lookup is concerned, it may as well have. Any message received by an instance of `MountainBike` now stands a chance of being satisfied by a method defined in the `Schedulable` module.

This has enormous implications. If `Bicycle` implements a method that is also defined in `Schedulable`, `Bicycle`'s implementation overrides `Schedulable`'s. If `Schedulable` sends methods that it does not implement, instances of `MountainBike` may encounter confusing failures.

Figure 7.6 shows the `schedulable?` message being sent to an instance of `MountainBike`. To resolve this message, Ruby first looks for a matching method in the `MountainBike` class. The search then proceeds along the method lookup path, which now contains modules as well as superclasses. An implementation of `schedulable?` is eventually found in `Schedulable`, which lies in the lookup path between `Bicycle` and `Object`.

A Very Nearly Complete Explanation

Now that you've seen how modules fit into the method lookup path, it's time to complicate the picture further.

It's entirely possible for a hierarchy to contain a long chain of superclasses, each of which includes many modules. When a single class includes several different modules, the modules are placed in the method lookup path in *reverse* order of module inclusion. Thus, the methods of the last included module are encountered first in the lookup path.

This discussion has, until now, been about including modules into *classes* via Ruby's `include` keyword. As you have already seen, including a module into a class adds the module's methods to the response set for all instances of that class. For example, in Figure 7.6 the `Schedulable` module was included into the `Bicycle` class, and, as a result, instances of `MountainBike` gain access to the methods defined therein.

However, it is also possible to add a module's methods to a single object, using Ruby's `extend` keyword. Because `extend` adds the module's behavior directly to an object, extending a class with a module creates class methods *in that class* and extending an instance of a class with a module creates instance methods *in that instance*. These two things are exactly the same; classes are, after all, just plain old objects, and `extend` behaves the same for all.

Finally, any object can also have ad hoc methods added directly to its own personal "Singleton class." These ad hoc methods are unique to this specific object.

Each of these alternatives adds to an object's response set by placing method definitions in specific and unambiguous places along the method lookup path. Figure 7.7 illustrates the complete list of possibilities.

Before continuing, here's a word of warning. Figure 7.7 is accurate enough to guide the behavior of most designers, but it is not the complete story. For most application

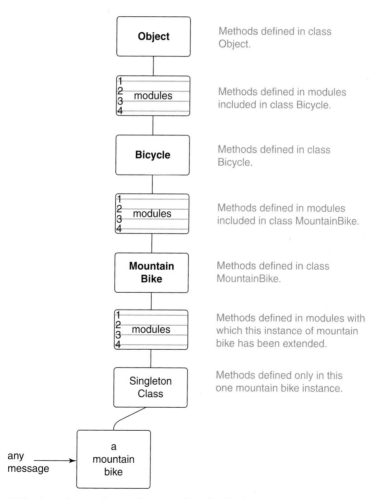

Figure 7.7 A nearly complete explanation of method lookup.

code it is perfectly adequate to behave as if class Object is the top of the hierarchy but, depending on your version of Ruby, this may not be technically true. If you are writing code for which you think this issue might matter, make sure you understand the object hierarchy of the Ruby in question.

Inheriting Role Behavior

Now that you've seen how to define a role's shared code in a module and how a module's code gets inserted into the method lookup path, you are equipped to write some truly frightening code. Imagine the possibilities. You can write modules that include other modules. You can write modules that override the methods defined in other modules. You can create deeply nested class inheritance hierarchies and then include these various modules at different levels of the hierarchy.

You can write code that is impossible to understand, debug, or extend.

This is powerful stuff, and dangerous in untutored hands. However, because this very same power is what allows you to create simple structures of related objects that elegantly fulfill the needs of your application, your task is not to avoid these techniques but to learn to use them for the right reasons, in the right places, in the correct way.

This first step along this path is to write properly inheritable code.

Writing Inheritable Code

The usefulness and maintainability of inheritance hierarchies and modules is in direct proportion to the quality of the code. More so than with other design strategies, sharing inherited behavior requires very specific coding techniques, which are covered in the following sections.

Recognize the Antipatterns

There are two antipatterns that indicate that your code might benefit from inheritance.

First, an object that uses a variable with a name like type or category to determine what message to send to self contains two highly related but slightly different types. This is a maintenance nightmare; the code must change every time a new type is added. Code like this can be rearranged to use classical inheritance by putting the common code in an abstract superclass and creating subclasses for the different types. This rearrangement allows you to create new subtypes by adding new subclasses. These subclasses extend the hierarchy without changing the existing code.

Second, when a sending object checks the class of a receiving object to determine what message to send, you have overlooked a duck type. This is another maintenance nightmare; the code must change every time you introduce a new class of receiver. In this situation all of the possible receiving objects play a common role. This role should be codified as a duck type and receivers should implement the duck type's interface. Once they do, the original object can send one single message to every receiver, confident that because each receiver plays the role it will understand the common message.

In addition to sharing an interface, duck types might also share behavior. When they do, place the shared code in a module and include that module in each class or object that plays the role.

Insist on the Abstraction

All of the code in an abstract superclass should apply to every class that inherits it. Superclasses should not contain code that applies to some, but not all, subclasses. This restriction also applies to modules: the code in a module must apply to all who use it.

Faulty abstractions cause inheriting objects to contain incorrect behavior; attempts to work around this erroneous behavior will cause your code to decay. When interacting with these awkward objects, programmers are forced to know their quirks and into dependencies that are better avoided.

Subclasses that override a method to raise an exception like "does not implement" are a symptom of this problem. While it is true that expediency pays for all and that it is sometimes most cost effective to arrange code in just this way, you should be reluctant to do so. When subclasses override a method to declare that they *do not do that thing* they come perilously close to declaring that they *are not that thing*. Nothing good can come of this.

If you cannot correctly identify the abstraction there may not be one, and if no common abstraction exists then inheritance is not the solution to your design problem.

Honor the Contract

Subclasses agree to a *contract*; they promise to be substitutable for their superclasses. Substitutability is possible only when objects behave as expected and subclasses are *expected* to conform to their superclass's interface. They must respond to every message in that interface, taking the same kinds of inputs and returning the same kinds of outputs. They are not permitted to do anything that forces others to check their type in order to know how to treat them or what to expect of them.

Where superclasses place restrictions on input arguments and return values, subclasses can indulge in a slight bit of freedom without violating their contract. Subclasses may accept input parameters that have broader restrictions and may return results that have narrower restrictions, all while remaining perfectly substitutable for their superclasses.

Subclasses that fail to honor their contract are difficult to use. They're "special" and cannot be freely substituted for their superclasses. These subclasses are declaring that they are not really a *kind-of* their superclass and cast doubt on the correctness of the entire hierarchy.

Liskov Substitution Principle (LSP)

When you honor the contract, you are following the Liskov Substitution Principle, which is named for its creator, Barbara Liskov, and supplies the "L" in the SOLID design principles. Her principle states:

> Let $q(x)$ be a property provable about objects x of type T. Then $q(y)$ should be true for objects y of type S where S is a subtype of T.

Mathematicians will instantly comprehend this statement; everyone else should understand it to say that in order for a type system to be sane, subtypes must be substitutable for their supertypes.

Following this principle creates applications where a subclass can be used anywhere its superclass would do, and where objects that include modules can be trusted to interchangeably play the module's role.

Use the Template Method Pattern

The fundamental coding technique for creating inheritable code is the template method pattern. This pattern is what allows you to separate the abstract from the concrete. The abstract code defines the algorithms and the concrete inheritors of that abstraction contribute specializations by overriding these template methods.

The template methods represent the parts of the algorithm that vary and creating them forces you to make explicit decisions about what varies and what does not.

Preemptively Decouple Classes

Avoid writing code that requires its inheritors to send `super`; instead use hook messages to allow subclasses to participate while absolving them of responsibility for knowing the abstract algorithm. Inheritance, by its very nature, adds powerful dependencies on the structure and arrangement of code. Writing code that requires subclasses to send `super` adds an additional dependency; avoid this if you can.

Hook methods solve the problem of sending `super`, but, unfortunately, only for adjacent levels of the hierarchy. For example, in Chapter 6, `Bicycle` sent hook method `local_spares` that `MountainBike` overrode to provide specializations. This hook method serves its purpose admirably, but the original problem reoccurs if you add another level to the hierarchy by creating subclass `MonsterMountainBike` under `MountainBike`. In order to combine its own spare parts with those of its parent, `MonsterMountainBike` would be forced to override `local_spares`, and within it, send `super`.

Create Shallow Hierarchies

The limitations of hook methods are just one of the many reasons to create shallow hierarchies.

Every hierarchy can be thought of a pyramid that has both depth and breadth. An object's depth is the number of superclasses between it and the top. Its breadth is the number of its direct subclasses. A hierarchy's shape is defined by its overall breadth and depth and it is this shape that determines ease of use, maintenance, and extension. Figure 7.8 illustrates a few of the possible variations of shape.

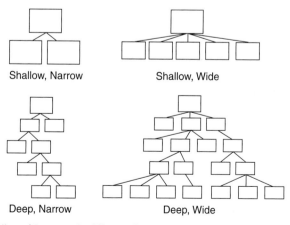

Shallow, Narrow   Shallow, Wide

Deep, Narrow   Deep, Wide

Figure 7.8   Hierarchies come in different shapes.

Shallow, narrow hierarchies are easy to understand. Shallow, wide hierarchies are slightly more complicated. Deep, narrow hierarchies are a bit more challenging and unfortunately have a natural tendency to get wider, strictly as a side effect of their depth. Deep, wide hierarchies are difficult to understand, costly to maintain, and should be avoided.

The problem with deep hierarchies is that they define a very long search path for message resolution and provide numerous opportunities for objects in that path to add behavior as the message passes by. Because objects depend on *everything* above them, a deep hierarchy has a large set of built-in dependencies, each of which might someday change.

Another problem with deep hierarchies is that programmers tend to be familiar with just the classes at their tops and bottoms; that is, they tend to understand only the behavior implemented at the boundaries of the search path. The classes in the middle get short shrift. Changes to these vaguely understood middle classes stand a greater chance of introducing errors.

Summary

When objects that play a common role need to share behavior, they do so via a Ruby module. The code defined in a module can be added to any object, be it an instance of a class, a class itself, or another module.

When a class includes a module, the methods in that module get put into the same lookup path as methods acquired via inheritance. Because module methods and inherited methods interleave in the lookup path, the coding techniques for modules mirror those of inheritance. Modules, therefore, should use the template method pattern to invite those that `include` them to supply specializations, and should implement hook methods to avoid forcing `includers` to send `super` (and thus know the algorithm).

When an object acquires behavior that was defined elsewhere, regardless of whether this *elsewhere* is a superclass or an included module, the acquiring object makes a commitment to honoring an implied contract. This contract is defined by the Liskov Substitution Principle, which in mathematical terms says that a subtype should be substitutable for its supertype, and in Ruby terms this means that an object should act like what it claims to be.

CHAPTER 8

Combining Objects with Composition

Composition is the act of combining distinct parts into a complex whole such that the whole becomes more than the sum of its parts. Music, for example, is composed.

You may not think of your software as music but the analogy is apt. The musical score of Beethoven's Fifth Symphony is a long list of distinct and independent notes. You need hear them only once to understand that while it *contains* the notes, it is *not* the notes. It is something more.

You can create software this same way, by using object-oriented composition to combine simple, independent objects into larger, more complex wholes. In composition, the larger object is connected to its parts via a *has-a* relationship. A bicycle has parts. Bicycle is the containing object, the parts are contained within a bicycle. Inherent in the definition of composition is the idea that, not only does a bicycle have parts, but it communicates with them via an interface. Part is a *role* and bicycles are happy to collaborate with any object that plays the role.

This chapter teaches the techniques of OO composition. It starts with an example, moves on to a discussion of the relative strengths and weakness of composition and inheritance, and then concludes with recommendations about how to choose between alternative design techniques.

Composing a Bicycle of Parts

This section begins where the `Bicycle` example in Chapter 6, Acquiring Behavior Through Inheritance, ended. If that code is no longer in the forefront of your mind, it's worth flipping back to the end of Chapter 6 and refreshing your memory. This section takes that example and moves it through several refactorings, gradually replacing inheritance with composition.

Updating the Bicycle Class

The `Bicycle` class is currently an abstract superclass in an inheritance hierarchy and you'd like to convert it to use composition. The first step is to ignore the existing code and think about how a bicycle should be composed.

The `Bicycle` class is responsible for responding to the `spares` message. This `spares` message should return a list of spare parts. Bicycles have parts, the bicycle–parts relationship quite naturally feels like composition. If you created an object to hold all of a bicycle's parts, you could delegate the spares message to that new object.

It's reasonable to name this new class `Parts`. The `Parts` object can be responsible for holding a list of the bike's parts and for knowing which of those parts needs spares. Notice that this object represents a collection of parts, not a single part.

The sequence diagram in Figure 8.1 illustrates this idea. Here, a `Bicycle` sends the `spares` message to its `Parts` object.

Every `Bicycle` needs a `Parts` object; part of what it means to be a `Bicycle` is to *have-a* `Parts`. The class diagram in Figure 8.2 illustrates this relationship.

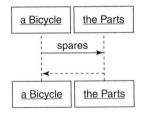

Figure 8.1   A *Bicycle* asks *Parts* for *spares*.

Figure 8.2   A *Bicycle* has-a *Parts*.

This diagram shows the `Bicycle` and `Parts` classes connected by a line. The line attaches to `Bicycle` with a black diamond; this black diamond indicates *composition*, it means that a `Bicycle` is composed of `Parts`. The `Parts` side of the line has the number "1." This means there's just one `Parts` object per `Bicycle`.

It's easy to convert the existing `Bicycle` class to this new design. Remove most of its code, add a `parts` variable to hold the `Parts` object, and delegate `spares` to `parts`. Here's the new `Bicycle` class.

```ruby
class Bicycle
  attr_reader :size, :parts

  def initialize(args={})
    @size       = args[:size]
    @parts      = args[:parts]
  end

  def spares
    parts.spares
  end
end
```

`Bicycle` is now responsible for three things: knowing its `size`, holding onto its `Parts`, and answering its `spares`.

Creating a Parts Hierarchy

That was easy, but only because there wasn't much bicycle related behavior in the `Bicycle` class to begin with; most of the code in `Bicycle` dealt with parts. You still need the parts behavior that you just removed from `Bicycle`, and the simplest way to get this code working again is to simply fling that code into a new hierarchy of `Parts`, as shown below.

```ruby
class Parts
  attr_reader :chain, :tire_size

  def initialize(args={})
    @chain      = args[:chain]     || default_chain
    @tire_size  = args[:tire_size] || default_tire_size
    post_initialize(args)
  end
```

```ruby
 9
10    def spares
11      { tire_size: tire_size,
12        chain:     chain}.merge(local_spares)
13    end
14
15    def default_tire_size
16      raise NotImplementedError
17    end
18
19    # subclasses may override
20    def post_initialize(args)
21      nil
22    end
23
24    def local_spares
25      {}
26    end
27
28    def default_chain
29      '10-speed'
30    end
31  end
32
33  class RoadBikeParts < Parts
34    attr_reader :tape_color
35
36    def post_initialize(args)
37      @tape_color = args[:tape_color]
38    end
39
40    def local_spares
41      {tape_color: tape_color}
42    end
43
44    def default_tire_size
45      '23'
46    end
47  end
48
49  class MountainBikeParts < Parts
50    attr_reader :front_shock, :rear_shock
51
```

```
52   def post_initialize(args)
53     @front_shock = args[:front_shock]
54     @rear_shock =  args[:rear_shock]
55   end
56
57   def local_spares
58     {rear_shock:  rear_shock}
59   end
60
61   def default_tire_size
62     '2.1'
63   end
64 end
```

This code is a near exact copy of the `Bicycle` hierarchy from Chapter 6; the differences are that the classes have been renamed and the `size` variable has been removed.

The class diagram in Figure 8.3 illustrates this transition. There is now an abstract `Parts` class. `Bicycle` is composed of `Parts`. `Parts` has two subclasses, `RoadBikeParts` and `MountainBikeParts`.

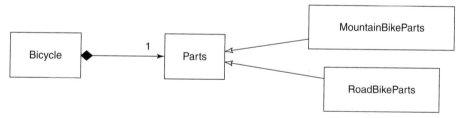

Figure 8.3   A hierarchy of `Parts`.

After this refactoring, everything still works. As you can see below, regardless of whether it has `RoadBikeParts` or `MountainBikeParts`, a bicycle can still correctly answer its `size` and `spares`.

```
1 road_bike =
2   Bicycle.new(
3     size: 'L',
4     parts: RoadBikeParts.new(tape_color: 'red'))
5
6 road_bike.size    # -> 'L'
7
```

```
 8  road_bike.spares
 9  # -> {:tire_size=>"23",
10  #       :chain=>"10-speed",
11  #       :tape_color=>"red"}
12
13  mountain_bike =
14    Bicycle.new(
15      size:  'L',
16      parts: MountainBikeParts.new(rear_shock: 'Fox'))
17
18  mountain_bike.size    # -> 'L'
19
20  mountain_bike.spares
21  # -> {:tire_size=>"2.1",
22  #       :chain=>"10-speed",
23  #       :rear_shock=>"Fox"}
```

This wasn't a big change and it isn't much of an improvement. However, this refactoring did reveal one useful thing; it made it blindingly obvious just how little
Bicycle specific code there was to begin with. Most of the code above deals with
individual parts; the Parts hierarchy now cries out for another refactoring.

Composing the Parts Object

By definition a parts list contains a list of individual parts. It's time to add a class to
represent a single part. The class name for an individual part clearly ought to be *Part*
but introducing a Part class when you already have a Parts class makes conversation
a challenge. It is confusing to use the word "parts" to refer to a collection of Part
objects, when that same word already refers to a single Parts object. However, the
previous phrase illustrates a technique that side steps the communication problem;
when discussing Part and Parts, you can follow the class name with the word
"object" and pluralize "object" as necessary.

You can also avoid the communication problem from the beginning by choosing
different class names, but other names might not be as expressive and may well introduce communication problems of their own. This Parts/Part situation is common
enough that it's worth dealing with head-on. Choosing these class names requires a
precision of communication that's a worthy goal in itself.

Thus, there's a Parts object, and it may contain many Part objects—simple as
that.

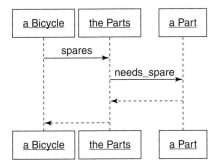

Figure 8.4 *Bicycle* sends *spares* to *Parts*, *Parts* sends *needs_spare* to each *Part*.

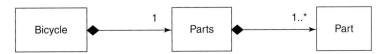

Figure 8.5 *Bicycle* holds one *Parts* object, which in turn holds many *Part* objects.

Creating a Part

Figure 8.4 shows a new sequence diagram that illustrates the conversation between `Bicycle` and its `Parts` object, and between a `Parts` object and its `Part` objects. `Bicycle` sends `spares` to `Parts` and then the `Parts` object sends `needs_spare` to each `Part`.

Changing the design in this way requires creating a new `Part` object. The `Parts` object is now composed of `Part` objects, as illustrated by the class diagram in Figure 8.5. The "1..*" on the line near `Part` indicates that a `Parts` will have one or more `Part` objects.

Introducing this new `Part` class simplifies the existing `Parts` class, which now becomes a simple wrapper around an array of `Part` objects. `Parts` can filter its list of `Part` objects and return the ones that need spares. The code below shows three classes: the existing `Bicycle` class, the updated `Parts` class, and the newly introduced `Part` class.

```
1  class Bicycle
2    attr_reader :size, :parts
3
4    def initialize(args={})
5      @size      = args[:size]
6      @parts     = args[:parts]
```

```
 7     end
 8
 9   def spares
10      parts.spares
11   end
12 end
13
14 class Parts
15   attr_reader :parts
16
17   def initialize(parts)
18     @parts = parts
19   end
20
21   def spares
22     parts.select {|part| part.needs_spare}
23   end
24 end
25
26 class Part
27   attr_reader :name, :description, :needs_spare
28
29   def initialize(args)
30     @name        = args[:name]
31     @description = args[:description]
32     @needs_spare = args.fetch(:needs_spare, true)
33   end
34 end
```

Now that these three classes exist you can create individual `Part` objects. The following code creates a number of different parts and saves each in an instance variable.

```
 1 chain =
 2   Part.new(name: 'chain', description: '10-speed')
 3
 4 road_tire =
 5   Part.new(name: 'tire_size',  description: '23')
 6
 7 tape =
 8   Part.new(name: 'tape_color', description: 'red')
 9
10 mountain_tire =
```

```
11    Part.new(name: 'tire_size',  description: '2.1')
12
13 rear_shock =
14    Part.new(name: 'rear_shock', description: 'Fox')
15
16 front_shock =
17    Part.new(
18      name: 'front_shock',
19      description: 'Manitou',
20      needs_spare: false)
```

Individual `Part` objects can be grouped together into a `Parts`. The code below combines the road bike `Part` objects into a road bike suitable `Parts`.

```
1 road_bike_parts =
2    Parts.new([chain, road_tire, tape])
```

Of course, you can skip this intermediate step and simply construct the `Parts` object on the fly when creating a `Bicycle`, as shown in lines 4–6 and 22–25 below.

```
1 road_bike =
2    Bicycle.new(
3      size:  'L',
4      parts: Parts.new([chain,
5                        road_tire,
6                        tape]))
7
8 road_bike.size     # -> 'L'
9
10 road_bike.spares
11 # -> [#<Part:0x00000101036770
12 #           @name="chain",
13 #           @description="10-speed",
14 #           @needs_spare=true>,
15 #       #<Part:0x0000010102dc60
16 #           @name="tire_size",
17 #       etc ...
18
19 mountain_bike =
20    Bicycle.new(
21      size:  'L',
```

```
22      parts: Parts.new([chain,
23                         mountain_tire,
24                         front_shock,
25                         rear_shock]))
26
27 mountain_bike.size      # -> 'L'
28
29 mountain_bike.spares
30 # -> [#<Part:0x00000101036770
31 #          @name="chain",
32 #          @description="10-speed",
33 #          @needs_spare=true>,
34 #       #<Part:0x0000010101b678
35 #          @name="tire_size",
36 #          etc ...
```

As you can see from lines 8–17, and 27–34 above, this new code arrangement works just fine, and it behaves *almost* exactly like the old Bicycle hierarchy. There is one difference: Bicycle's old spares method returned a hash, but this new spares method returns an array of Part objects.

While it may be tempting to think of these objects as instances of Part, composition tells you to think of them as objects that play the Part role. They don't have to be a *kind-of* the Part class, they just have to act like one; that is, they must respond to name, description, and needs_spare.

Making the Parts Object More Like an Array

This code works but there's definitely room for improvement. Step back for a minute and think about the parts and spares methods of Bicycle. These messages feel like they ought to return the same sort of thing, yet the objects that come back don't behave in the same way. Look at what happens when you ask each for its size.

In line 1 below, spares is happy to report that its size is 3. However, asking this same question of parts doesn't turn out so well, as you can see from lines 2–4.

```
1 mountain_bike.spares.size # -> 3
2 mountain_bike.parts.size
3 # -> NoMethodError:
4 #      undefined method 'size' for #<Parts:...>
```

Line 1 works because `spares` returns an array (of `Part` objects) and `Array` understands `size`. Line 2 fails because `parts` returns instance of `Parts`, which does not.

Failures like this will chase you around for as long as you own this code. These two things both *seem* like arrays. You will inevitably treat them as if they are, despite the fact that exactly one half of the time, the result will be like stepping on the proverbial rake in the yard. The `Parts` object does *not* behave like an array and all attempts to treat it as one will fail.

You can fix the proximate problem by adding a `size` method to `Parts`. This is a simple matter of implementing a method to delegate `size` to the actual array, as shown here:

```
1  def size
2    parts.size
3  end
```

However, this change starts the `Parts` class down a slippery slope. Do this, and it won't be long before you'll want `Parts` to respond to `each`, and then `sort`, and then everything else in `Array`. This never ends; the more array-like you make `Parts`, the more like an array you'll expect it to be.

Perhaps `Parts` *is* an `Array`, albeit one with a bit of extra behavior. You could make it one; the next example shows a new version of the `Parts` class, now as a subclass of `Array`.

```
1  class Parts < Array
2    def spares
3      select {|part| part.needs_spare}
4    end
5  end
```

The above code is a very straightforward expression of the idea that `Parts` is a specialization of `Array`; in a perfect object-oriented language this solution would be exactly correct. Unfortunately, the Ruby language has not quite achieved perfection and this design contains a hidden flaw.

This next example illustrates the problem. When `Parts` subclasses `Array`, it inherits all of `Array`'s behavior. This behavior includes methods like `+`, which adds two arrays together and returns a third. Lines 3 and 4 below show `+` combining two existing instances of `Parts` and saving the result into the `combo_parts` variable.

This appears to work; `combo_parts` now contains the correct number of parts (line 7). However, something is clearly not right. As line 12 shows, `combo_parts` cannot answer its `spares`.

The root cause of the problem is revealed by lines 15–17. Although the objects that got +'d together were instances of `Parts`, the object that + returned was an instance of `Array`, and `Array` does not understand `spares`.

```
 1  #   Parts inherits '+' from Array, so you can
 2  #      add two Parts together.
 3  combo_parts =
 4     (mountain_bike.parts + road_bike.parts)
 5
 6  # '+' definitely combines the Parts
 7  combo_parts.size               # -> 7
 8
 9  # but the object that '+' returns
10  #   does not understand 'spares'
11  combo_parts.spares
12  # -> NoMethodError: undefined method 'spares'
13  #         for #<Array:...>
14
15  mountain_bike.parts.class    # -> Parts
16  road_bike.parts.class        # -> Parts
17  combo_parts.class            # -> Array !!!
```

It turns out that there are many methods in `Array` that return new arrays, and unfortunately these methods return new instances of the `Array` class, not new instances of your subclass. The `Parts` class is still misleading and you have just swapped one problem for another. Where once you were disappointed to find that `Parts` did not implement `size`, now you might be surprised to find that adding two `Parts` together returns a result that does not understand `spares`.

You've seen three different implementations of `Parts`. The first answers only the `spares` and `parts` messages; it does not act like an array, it merely contains one. The second `Parts` implementation adds `size`, a minor improvement that just returns the size of its internal array. The most recent `Parts` implementation subclasses `Array` and therefore gives the appearance of fully behaving like an array, but as the example above shows, an instance of `Parts` still displays unexpected behavior.

It has become clear that there is no perfect solution; it's therefore time to make a difficult decision. Even though it cannot respond to `size`, the original `Parts` implementation may be good enough; if so, you can accept its lack of array-like behavior and revert to that version. If you need `size` and `size` alone, it may be best to add just this one method and so settle for the second implementation. If you can tolerate the possibility of confusing errors or you know with absolute certainty that you'll never encounter them, it might make sense to subclass `Array` and walk quietly away.

Somewhere in the middle ground between complexity and usability lies the following solution. The `Parts` class below delegates `size` and `each` to its `@parts` array and includes `Enumerable` to get common traversal and searching methods. This version of `Parts` does not have all of the behavior of `Array`, but at least everything that it claims to do actually works.

```
 1  require 'forwardable'
 2  class Parts
 3    extend Forwardable
 4    def_delegators :@parts, :size, :each
 5    include Enumerable
 6
 7    def initialize(parts)
 8      @parts = parts
 9    end
10
11    def spares
12      select {|part| part.needs_spare}
13    end
14  end
```

Sending + to an instance of *this* `Parts` results in a `NoMethodError` exception. However, because `Parts` now responds to `size`, `each`, and all of `Enumerable`, and obligingly raises errors when you mistakenly treat it like an actual `Array`, this code may be good enough. The following example shows that `spares` and `parts` can now both respond to `size`.

```
 1  mountain_bike =
 2    Bicycle.new(
 3      size: 'L',
 4      parts: Parts.new([chain,
 5                        mountain_tire,
 6                        front_shock,
```

```
 7                           rear_shock]))
 8
 9  mountain_bike.spares.size   # -> 3
10  mountain_bike.parts.size    # -> 4
```

You again have a workable version of the `Bicycle`, `Parts`, and `Part` classes. It's time to reevaluate the design.

Manufacturing Parts

Look back at lines 4–7 above. The `Part` objects held in the `chain`, `mountain_tire`, and so on, variables were created so long ago that you may already have forgotten them. Think about the body of knowledge that these four lines represent. Somewhere in your application, some object had to know how to create these `Part` objects. And here, on lines 4–7 above, *this* place has to know that these four specific objects go with mountain bikes.

This is a lot of knowledge and it can easily leak all over your application. This leakage is both unfortunate and unnecessary. Although there are lots of different individual parts, there are only a few valid combinations of parts. Everything would be easier if you could describe the different bikes and then use your descriptions to magically manufacture the correct `Parts` object for any bike.

It's easy to describe the combination of parts that make up a specific bike. The code below does this with a simple 2-dimensional array, where each row contains three possible columns. The first column contains the part name (`'chain'`, `'tire_size'`, etc.), the second, the part description (`'10-speed'`, `'23'`, etc.) and the third (which is optional), a Boolean that indicates whether this part needs a spare. Only `'front_shock'` on line 9 below puts a value in this third column, the other parts would like to default to `true`, as they require spares.

```
 1  road_config =
 2    [['chain',        '10-speed'],
 3     ['tire_size',    '23'],
 4     ['tape_color',   'red']]
 5
 6  mountain_config =
 7    [['chain',        '10-speed'],
 8     ['tire_size',    '2.1'],
 9     ['front_shock',  'Manitou', false],
10     ['rear_shock',   'Fox']]
```

Unlike a hash, this simple 2-dimensional array provides no structural information. However, *you* understand how this structure is organized and you can encode your knowledge into a new object that manufactures `Parts`.

Creating the PartsFactory

As discussed in Chapter 3, Managing Dependencies, an object that manufactures other objects is a factory. Your past experience in other languages may predispose you to flinch when you hear this word, but think of this as an opportunity to reclaim it. The word *factory* does not mean difficult, or contrived, or overly complicated; it's merely the word OO designers use to concisely communicate the idea of an object that creates other objects. Ruby factories are simple and there's no reason to avoid this intention revealing word.

The code below shows a new `PartsFactory` module. Its job is to take an array like one of those listed above and manufacture a `Parts` object. Along the way it may well create `Part` objects, but this action is private. Its public responsibility is to create a `Parts`.

This first version of `PartsFactory` takes three arguments, a `config`, and the names of the classes to be used for `Part`, and `Parts`. Line 6 below creates the new instance of `Parts`, initializing it with an array of `Part` objects built from the information in the `config`.

```
1  module PartsFactory
2    def self.build(config,
3                      part_class  = Part,
4                      parts_class = Parts)
5
6      parts_class.new(
7        config.collect {|part_config|
8          part_class.new(
9            name:         part_config[0],
10           description:  part_config[1],
11           needs_spare:  part_config.fetch(2, true))})
12   end
13 end
```

This factory knows the structure of the `config` array. In lines 9–11 above it expects `name` to be in the first column, `description` to be in the second, and `needs_spare` to be in the third.

Putting knowledge of config's structure in the factory has two consequences. First, the config can be expressed very tersely. Because PartsFactory understands config's internal structure, config can be specified as an array rather than a hash. Second, once you commit to keeping config in an array, you should *always* create new Parts objects using the factory. To create new Parts via any other mechanism requires duplicating the knowledge that is encoded in lines 9–11 above.

Now that PartsFactory exists, you can use the configuration arrays defined above to easily create new Parts, as shown here:

```
 1 road_parts = PartsFactory.build(road_config)
 2 # -> [#<Part:0x00000101825b70
 3 #        @name="chain",
 4 #        @description="10-speed",
 5 #        @needs_spare=true>,
 6 #      #<Part:0x00000101825b20
 7 #        @name="tire_size",
 8 #          etc ...
 9
10 mountain_parts = PartsFactory.build(mountain_config)
11 # -> [#<Part:0x0000010181ea28
12 #        @name="chain",
13 #        @description="10-speed",
14 #        @needs_spare=true>,
15 #      #<Part:0x0000010181e9d8
16 #        @name="tire_size",
17 #          etc ...
```

PartsFactory, combined with the new configuration arrays, isolates all the knowledge needed to create a valid Parts. This information was previously dispersed throughout the application but now it is contained in this one class and these two arrays.

Leveraging the PartsFactory

Now that the PartsFactory is up and running, have another look at the Part class (repeated below). Part is simple. Not only that, the only even *slightly* complicated line of code (the fetch on line 7 below) is duplicated in PartsFactory. If PartsFactory created every Part, Part wouldn't need this code. And if you remove this code from Part, there's almost nothing left; you can replace the whole Part class with a simple OpenStruct.

```
1  class Part
2    attr_reader :name, :description, :needs_spare
3
4    def initialize(args)
5      @name        = args[:name]
6      @description = args[:description]
7      @needs_spare = args.fetch(:needs_spare, true)
8    end
9  end
```

Ruby's OpenStruct class is a lot like the Struct class that you've already seen, it provides a convenient way to bundle a number of attributes into an object. The difference between the two is that Struct takes position order initialization arguments while OpenStruct takes a hash for its initialization and then derives attributes from the hash.

There are good reasons to remove the Part class; this simplifies the code and you may never again need anything as complicated as what you currently have. You can remove all trace of Part by deleting the class and then changing PartsFactory to use OpenStruct to create an object that plays the Part *role*. The following code shows a new version of PartFactory where part creation has been refactored into a method of its own (line 9).

```
1  require 'ostruct'
2  module PartsFactory
3    def self.build(config, parts_class = Parts)
4      parts_class.new(
5        config.collect {|part_config|
6          create_part(part_config)})
7    end
8
9    def self.create_part(part_config)
10     OpenStruct.new(
11       name:        part_config[0],
12       description: part_config[1],
13       needs_spare: part_config.fetch(2, true))
14   end
15 end
```

Line 13 above is now the only place in the application that defaults needs_spare to true, so PartsFactory must be solely responsible for manufacturing Parts.

This new version of `PartsFactory` works. As shown below, it returns a `Parts` that contains an array of `OpenStruct` objects, each of which plays the `Part` role.

```
1  mountain_parts = PartsFactory.build(mountain_config)
2  # -> <Parts:0x000001009ad8b8 @parts=
3  #        [#<OpenStruct name="chain",
4  #                      description="10-speed",
5  #                      needs_spare=true>,
6  #        #<OpenStruct name="tire_size",
7  #                      description="2.1",
8  #                      etc ...
```

The Composed Bicycle

The following code shows that `Bicycle` now uses composition. It shows `Bicycle`, `Parts`, and `PartsFactory` and the configuration arrays for road and mountain bikes.

`Bicycle` *has-a* `Parts`, which in turn *has-a* collection of `Part` objects. `Parts` and `Part` may exist as classes, but the objects in which they are contained think of them as roles. `Parts` is a class that plays the `Parts` role; it implements `spares`. The role of `Part` is played by an `OpenStruct`, which implements `name`, `description` and `needs_spare`.

The following 54 lines of code completely replace the 66-line inheritance hierarchy from Chapter 6.

```
1  class Bicycle
2    attr_reader :size, :parts
3
4    def initialize(args={})
5      @size       = args[:size]
6      @parts      = args[:parts]
7    end
8
9    def spares
10      parts.spares
11    end
12  end
13
14  require 'forwardable'
15  class Parts
16    extend Forwardable
```

```
17    def_delegators :@parts, :size, :each
18    include Enumerable
19
20    def initialize(parts)
21      @parts = parts
22    end
23
24    def spares
25      select {|part| part.needs_spare}
26    end
27  end
28
29  require 'ostruct'
30  module PartsFactory
31    def self.build(config, parts_class = Parts)
32      parts_class.new(
33        config.collect {|part_config|
34          create_part(part_config)})
35    end
36
37    def self.create_part(part_config)
38      OpenStruct.new(
39        name:         part_config[0],
40        description:  part_config[1],
41        needs_spare:  part_config.fetch(2, true))
42    end
43  end
44
45  road_config =
46    [['chain',        '10-speed'],
47     ['tire_size',    '23'],
48     ['tape_color',   'red']]
49
50  mountain_config =
51    [['chain',        '10-speed'],
52     ['tire_size',    '2.1'],
53     ['front_shock',  'Manitou', false],
54     ['rear_shock',   'Fox']]
```

This new code works much like the prior `Bicycle` hierarchy. The only difference is
that the `spares` message now returns an array of `Part`-like objects instead of a hash,
as you can see on lines 7 and 15 below.

```
1  road_bike =
2    Bicycle.new(
3      size: 'L',
4      parts: PartsFactory.build(road_config))
5
6  road_bike.spares
7  # -> [#<OpenStruct name="chain", etc ...
8
9  mountain_bike =
10   Bicycle.new(
11     size: 'L',
12     parts: PartsFactory.build(mountain_config))
13
14 mountain_bike.spares
15 # -> [#<OpenStruct name="chain", etc ...
```

Now that these new classes exist, it's very easy to create a new kind of bike.

Adding support for recumbent bikes took 19 new lines of code in Chapter 6. This task can now be accomplished with 3 lines of configuration (lines 2–4 below).

```
1  recumbent_config =
2    [['chain',       '9-speed'],
3     ['tire_size',   '28'],
4     ['flag',        'tall and orange']]
5
6  recumbent_bike =
7    Bicycle.new(
8      size: 'L',
9      parts: PartsFactory.build(recumbent_config))
10
11 recumbent_bike.spares
12 # -> [#<OpenStruct
13 #        name="chain",
14 #        description="9-speed",
15 #        needs_spare=true>,
16 #      #<OpenStruct
17 #        name="tire_size",
18 #        description="28",
19 #        needs_spare=true>,
20 #      #<OpenStruct
21 #        name="flag",
22 #        description="tall and orange",
23 #        needs_spare=true>]
```

As shown in lines 11–23 above, you can now create a new bike by simply describing its parts.

Aggregation: A Special Kind of Composition

You already know the term *delegation*; delegation is when one object receives a message and merely forwards it to another. Delegation creates dependencies; the receiving object must recognize the message *and* know where to send it.

Composition often involves delegation but the term means something more. A *composed* object is made up of parts with which it expects to interact via well-defined interfaces.

Composition describes a *has-a* relationship. Meals have appetizers, universities have departments, bicycles have parts. Meals, universities, and bicycles are composed objects. Appetizers, departments, and parts are roles. The composed object depends on the interface of the role.

Because meals interact with appetizers using an interface, new objects that wish to act as appetizers need only implement this interface. Unanticipated appetizers fit seamlessly and interchangeably into existing meals.

The term *composition* can be a bit confusing because it gets used for two slightly different concepts. The definition above is for the broadest use of the term. In most cases when you see *composition* it will indicate nothing more than this general *has-a* relationship between two objects.

However, as formally defined it means something a bit more specific; it indicates a *has-a* relationship where the contained object has no life independent of its container. When used in this stricter sense you know not only that meals have appetizers, but also that once the meal is eaten the appetizer is also gone.

This leaves a gap in the definition that is filled by the term *aggregation*. Aggregation is exactly like composition except that the contained object has an independent life. Universities have departments, which in turn have professors. If your application manages many universities and knows about thousands of professors, it's quite reasonable to expect that although a department completely disappears when its university goes defunct, its professors continue to exist.

The university–department relationship is one of composition (in its strictest sense) and the department–professor relationship is aggregation.

Destroying a department does not destroy its professors; they have an existence and life of their own.

This distinction between composition and aggregation may have little practical effect on your code. Now that you are familiar with both terms you can use *composition* to refer to both kinds of relationships and be more explicit only if the need arises.

Deciding Between Inheritance and Composition

Remember that classical inheritance is a *code arrangement technique*. Behavior is dispersed among objects and these objects are organized into class relationships such that automatic delegation of messages invokes the correct behavior. Think of it this way: For the cost of arranging objects in a hierarchy, you get message delegation for free.

Composition is an alternative that reverses these costs and benefits. In composition, the relationship between objects is not codified in the class hierarchy; instead objects stand alone and as a result must explicitly know about and delegate messages to one another. Composition allows objects to have structural independence, but at the cost of explicit message delegation.

Now that you've seen examples of inheritance and composition you can begin to think about when to use them. The general rule is that, faced with a problem that composition can solve, you should be biased towards doing so. If you cannot explicitly defend inheritance as a better solution, use composition. Composition contains far fewer built-in dependencies than inheritance; it is very often the best choice.

Inheritance *is* a better solution when its use provides high rewards for low risk. This section examines the costs and benefits of inheritance versus composition and provides guidelines for choosing the best relationship.

Accepting the Consequences of Inheritance

Making wise choices about using inheritance requires a clear understanding of its costs and benefits.

Benefits of Inheritance

Chapter 2, Designing Classes with a Single Responsibility, outlined four goals for code: it should be transparent, reasonable, usable, and exemplary. Inheritance, when correctly applied, excels at the second, third, and fourth goals.

Methods defined near the top of inheritance hierarchies have widespread influence because the height of the hierarchy acts as a lever that multiplies their effects. Changes made to these methods ripple down the inheritance tree. Correctly modeled hierarchies are thus extremely *reasonable*; big changes in behavior can be achieved via small changes in code.

Use of inheritance results in code that can be described as *open–closed*; hierarchies are open for extension while remaining closed for modification. Adding a new subclass to an existing hierarchy requires no changes to existing code. Hierarchies are thus *usable*; you can easily create new subclasses to accommodate new variants.

Correctly written hierarchies are easy to extend. The hierarchy embodies the abstraction and every new subclass plugs in a few concrete differences. The existing pattern is easy to follow and replicating it will be the natural choice of any programmer charged with creating new subclasses. Hierarchies are therefore *exemplary*; by their nature they provide guidance for writing the code to extend them.

You need look no farther than the source of object-oriented languages themselves to see the value of organizing code using inheritance. In Ruby, the `Numeric` class provides an excellent example. `Integer` and `Float` are modeled as subclasses of `Numeric`; this *is-a* relationship is exactly right. Integers and floats are fundamentally *numbers*. Allowing these two classes to share a common abstraction is the most parsimonious way to organize code.

Costs of Inheritance

Concerns about the use of inheritance fall into two different areas. The first fear is that you might be fooled into choosing inheritance to solve the wrong kind of problem. If you make this mistake a day will come when you need to add behavior but find there's no easy way do so. Because the model is incorrect, the new behavior won't fit; in this case you'll be forced to duplicate or restructure code.

Second, even when inheritance makes sense for the problem, you might be writing code that will be used by others for purposes you did not anticipate. These other programmers want the behavior you have created but may not be able to tolerate the dependencies that inheritance demands.

The previous section on the benefits of inheritance was careful to qualify its assertions as applying only to a "correctly modeled hierarchy." Imagine *reasonable*, *usable* and *exemplary* as two-sided coins. The benefit side represents the wonderful gains that inheritance provides. If you apply inheritance to a problem for which it is not suited, you effectively flip these coins over and encounter a parallel detriment.

The flip side of the *reasonable* coin is the very high cost of making changes near the top of an incorrectly modeled hierarchy. In this case, the leveraging effect works to your disadvantage; small changes break everything.

The opposing side of the *usable* coin is the impossibility of adding behavior when new subclasses represent a mixture of types. The `Bicycle` hierarchy in Chapter 6 failed when the need for recumbent mountain bikes appeared. This hierarchy already contains subclasses for `MountainBike` and `RecumbentBike`; combining the qualities of these two classes into a single object is not possible in the hierarchy as it currently exists. You cannot reuse existing behavior without changing it.

The other side of the *exemplary* coin is the chaos that ensues when novice programmers attempt to extend incorrectly modeled hierarchies. These inadequate hierarchies should not be extended, they need to be refactored, but novices do not have the skills to do so. Novices are forced to duplicate existing code or to add dependencies on class names, both of which serve to exacerbate existing design problems.

Inheritance, therefore, is a place where the question "What will happen when I'm wrong?" assumes special importance. Inheritance by definition comes with a deeply embedded set of dependencies. Subclasses depend on the methods defined in their superclasses *and* on the automatic delegation of messages to those superclasses. This is classical inheritance's greatest strength and biggest weakness; subclasses are bound, irrevocably and by design, to the classes above them in the hierarchy. These built-in dependencies amplify the effects of modifications made to superclasses. Enormous, broad-reaching changes of behavior can be achieved with very small changes in code.

This is true, for better or for worse, whether you come to regret it or not.

Finally, your consideration of the use of inheritance should be tempered by your expectations about the population who will use your code. If you are writing code for an in-house application in a domain with which you are intimately familiar, you may be able to predict the future well enough to be confident that your design problem is one for which inheritance is a cost-effective solution. As you write code for a wider audience, your ability to anticipate needs necessarily decreases and the suitability of requiring inheritance as part of the interface goes down.

Avoid writing frameworks that require users of your code to subclass your objects in order to gain your behavior. Their application's objects may already be arranged in a hierarchy; inheriting from your framework may not be possible.

Accepting the Consequences of Composition

Objects built using composition differ from those built using inheritance in two basic ways. Composed objects do not depend on the structure of the class hierarchy, and they delegate their own messages. These differences confer a different set of costs and benefits.

Benefits of Composition

When using composition, the natural tendency is to create many small objects that contain straightforward responsibilities that are accessible through clearly defined interfaces. These well-composed objects excel when measured against several of Chapter 2's goals for code.

These small objects have a single responsibility and specify their own behavior. They are *transparent*; it's easy to understand the code and it's clear what will happen if it changes. Also, the composed object's independence from the hierarchy means that it inherits very little code and so is generally immune from suffering side effects as a result of changes to classes above it in the hierarchy.

Because composed objects deal with their parts via an interface, adding a new kind of part is a simple matter of plugging in a new object that honors the interface. From the point of view of the composed object, adding a new variant of an existing part is *reasonable* and requires no changes to its code.

By their very nature, objects that participate in composition are small, structurally independent, and have well-defined interfaces. This allows their seamless transition into pluggable, interchangeable components. Well-composed objects are therefore easily *usable* in new and unexpected contexts.

At its best, composition results in applications built of simple, pluggable objects that are easy to extend and have a high tolerance for change.

Costs of Composition

Composition's strengths, as with most things in life, contribute to its weaknesses.

A composed object relies on its many parts. Even if each part is small and easily understood, the combined operation of the whole may be less than obvious. While every individual part may indeed be *transparent*, the whole may not be.

The benefits of structural independence are gained at the cost of automatic message delegation. The composed object must explicitly know which messages to delegate and to whom. Identical delegation code may be needed by many different objects; composition provides no way to share this code.

As these costs and benefits illustrate, composition is excellent at prescribing rules for assembling an object made of parts but doesn't provide as much help for the problem of arranging code for a collection of parts that are very nearly identical.

Choosing Relationships

Classical inheritance (Chapter 6), behavior sharing via modules (Chapter 7, Sharing Role Behavior with Modules) and composition are each the perfect solution for the problem they solve. The trick to lowering your application costs is to apply each technique to the right problem.

Some of the grand masters of object-oriented design have given advice about using inheritance and composition.

- "Inheritance is specialization."—Bertrand Meyer, *Touch of Class: Learning to Program Well with Objects and Contracts*

- "Inheritance is best suited to adding functionally to existing classes when you will use most of the old code and add relatively small amounts of new code." —— Erich Gamma, Richard Helm, Ralph Johnson, and John Vlissides, *Design Patterns: Elements of Reusable Object-Oriented Software*

- "Use composition when the behavior is more than the sum of its parts."—paraphrase of Grady Booch, *Object-Oriented Analysis and Design*

Use Inheritance for *is-a* Relationships

When you select inheritance over composition you are placing a bet that the benefits thereby accrued will outweigh the costs. Some bets are more likely to pay off than others. Small sets of real-world objects that fall naturally into static, transparently obvious specialization hierarchies are candidates to be modeled using classical inheritance.

Imagine a game where players race bicycles. Players assemble their bikes by "buying" parts. One of the parts they can buy is a shock. The game provides six nearly identical shocks; each differs slightly in cost and behavior.

All of these shocks are, well, *shocks*. Their "shock-ness" is at the core of their identity. Shocks exist in no more atomic category. Variants of shocks are far more alike than they are different. The most accurate and descriptive statement that you can make about any one of the variants is that it *is-a* shock.

Inheritance is perfect for this problem. Shocks can be modeled as a shallow narrow hierarchy. The hierarchy's small size makes it understandable, intention revealing, and easily extendable. Because these objects meet the criteria for successful use of inheritance, the risk of being wrong is low, but in the unlikely event that you *are* wrong, the cost of changing your mind is also low. You can achieve the benefits of inheritance while exposing yourself to few of its risks.

In terms of this Chapter's example, each different shock plays the role of `Part`. It inherits common shock behavior *and* the `Part` role from its abstract `Shock` super-class. The `PartsFactory` currently assumes that every part can be represented by the `Part OpenStruct`, but you could easily extend the part configuration array to supply the class name for a specific shock. Because you already think of `Part` as an interface, it's easy to plug in a new kind of part, even if this part uses inheritance to get some of its behavior.

If requirements change such that there is an explosion in the kinds of shocks, reassess this design decision. Perhaps it still holds, perhaps not. If modeling a bevy of new shocks requires dramatically expanding the hierarchy, or if the new shocks don't conveniently fit into the existing code, reconsider alternatives *at that time*.

Use Duck Types for *behaves-like-a* Relationships

Some problems require many different objects to play a common role. In addition to their core responsibilities, objects might play roles like *schedulable, preparable, printable,* or *persistable.*

There are two key ways to recognize the existence of a role. First, although an object plays it, the role is not the object's main responsibility. A bicycle *behaves-like-a* schedulable but it *is-a* bicycle. Second, the need is widespread; many otherwise unrelated objects share a desire to play the same role.

The most illuminating way to think about roles is from the outside, from the point of view of a holder of a role player rather than that of a player of a role. The holder of a *schedulable* expects it to implement `Schedulable`'s interface and to honor `Schedulable`'s contract. All *schedulables* are alike in that they must meet these expectations.

Your design task is to recognize that a role exists, define the interface of its duck type and provide an implementation of that interface for every possible player. Some roles consist only of their interface, others share common behavior. Define the common behavior in a Ruby module to allow objects to play the role without duplicating the code.

Use Composition for *has-a* Relationships

Many objects contain numerous parts but are more than the sums of those parts. `Bicycles` *have-a* `Parts`, but the bike itself is something more. It has behavior that is separate from and in addition to the behavior of its parts. Given the current requirements of the bicycle example, the most cost-effective way to model the `Bicycle` object is via composition.

This *is-a* versus *has-a* distinction is at the core of deciding between inheritance and composition. The more parts an object has, the more likely it is that it should be modeled with composition. The deeper you drill down into individual parts, the more likely it is that you'll discover a specific part that has a few specialized variants and is thus a reasonable candidate for inheritance. For every problem, assess the costs and benefits of alternative design techniques and use your judgment and experience to make the best choice.

Summary

Composition allows you to combine small parts to create more complex objects such that the whole becomes more than the sum of its parts. Composed objects tend to consist of simple, discrete entities that can easily be rearranged into new combinations. These simple objects are easy to understand, reuse, and test, but because they combine into a more complicated whole, the operation of the bigger application may not be as easy to understand as that of the individual parts.

Composition, classical inheritance, and behavior sharing via modules are competing techniques for arranging code. Each has different costs and benefits; these differences predispose them to be better at solving slightly different problems.

These techniques are tools, nothing more, and you'll become a better designer if you practice each of them. Learning to use them properly is a matter of experience and judgment, and one of the best ways to gain experience is to learn from your own mistakes. The key to improving your design skills is to attempt these techniques, accept your errors cheerfully, remain detached from past design decisions, and refactor mercilessly.

As you gain experience, you'll get better at choosing the correct technique the first time, your costs will go down, and your applications will improve.

CHAPTER 9

Designing Cost-Effective Tests

Writing changeable code is an art whose practice relies on three different skills.

First, you must understand object-oriented design. Poorly designed code is naturally difficult to change. From a practical point of view, changeability is the only design metric that matters; code that's easy to change *is* well-designed. Because you have read this far it's only fair to assume that your efforts will pay off and that you have acquired a foundation from which to begin the practice of designing changeable code.

Second, you must be skilled at refactoring code. Not in the casual sense of "go into the application and fling some things around," but in the real, grown-up, bullet-proof sense defined by Martin Fowler in *Refactoring: Improving the Design of Existing Code*:

> Refactoring is the process of changing a software system in such a way that it does not alter the external behavior of the code yet improves the internal structure.

Notice the phrase *does not alter the external behavior of the code*. Refactoring, as formally defined, does not add new behavior, it improves existing structure. It's a precise process that alters code via tiny, crab-like steps and carefully, incrementally, and unerringly transforms one design into another.

Good design preserves maximum flexibility at minimum cost by putting off decisions at every opportunity, deferring commitments until more specific requirements arrive. When that day comes, *refactoring* is how you morph the current code structure into one that will accommodate the new requirements. New features will be added only after you have successfully refactored the code.

If your refactoring skills are weak, improve them. The need for ongoing refactoring is an outgrowth of good design; your design efforts will pay full dividends only when you can refactor with ease.

Finally, the art of writing changeable code requires the ability to write high-value tests. Tests give you confidence to refactor constantly. Efficient tests prove that altered code continues to behave correctly without raising overall costs. Good tests weather code refactorings with aplomb; they are written such that changes to the code do not force rewrites of the tests.

Writing tests that can perform this trick is a matter of design and is the topic of this chapter.

An understanding of object-oriented design, good refactoring skills, and the ability to write efficient tests form a three-legged stool upon which changeable code rests. Well-designed code is easy to change, refactoring is how you change from one design to the next, and tests free you to refactor with impunity.

Intentional Testing

The most common arguments for having tests are that they reduce bugs and provide documentation, and that writing tests *first* improves application design.

These benefits, however valid, are proxies for a deeper goal. The true purpose of testing, just like the true purpose of design, is to reduce costs. If writing, maintaining, and running tests consumes more time than would otherwise be needed to fix bugs, write documentation, and design applications tests are clearly not worth writing and no rational person would argue otherwise.

It is common for programmers who are new to testing to find themselves in the unhappy state where the tests they write *do* cost more than the value those tests provide, and who therefore want to argue about the worth of tests. These are programmers who believed themselves highly productive in their former test-not lives but who have crashed into the test-first wall and stumbled to a halt. Their attempts at test-first programming result in less output, and their desire to regain productivity drives them to revert to old habits and forgo writing tests.

The solution to the problem of costly tests, however, is not to stop testing but instead to get better at it. Getting good value from tests requires clarity of intention and knowing what, when, and how to test.

Knowing Your Intentions

Testing has many potential benefits, some obvious, others more obscure. A thorough understanding of these benefits will increase your motivation to achieve them.

Finding Bugs

Finding faults, or bugs, early in the development process yields big dividends. Not only is it easier to find and fix a bug nearer in time to its creation, but getting the code right earlier rather than later can have unexpected positive effects on the resulting design. Knowing that you can (or can't) do something early on may cause you to choose alternatives in the present that alter the design options available in the future. Also, as code accumulates, embedded bugs acquire dependencies. Fixing these bugs late in the process may necessitate changing a lot of dependent code. Fixing bugs early always lowers costs.

Supplying Documentation

Tests provide the only reliable documentation of design. The story they tell remains true long after paper documents become obsolete and human memory fails. Write your tests as if you expect your future self to have amnesia. Remember that you will forget; write tests that remind you of the story once you have.

Deferring Design Decisions

Tests allow you to safely defer design decisions. As your design skills improve you will begin to write applications that are sprinkled with places where you know the design needs *something* but you don't yet have enough information to know exactly what. These are the places where you are awaiting additional information, valiantly resisting the forces that compel you to commit to a specific design.

These "pending" decision points are often coded as slightly embarrassing, extremely concrete hacks hidden behind totally presentable interfaces. This situation occurs when you are aware of just one concrete case in the present but you fully expect new cases to arrive in the near future. You know that at some point you will be better served by code that handles these many concrete cases as a single abstraction, but right now you don't have enough information to anticipate what that abstraction will be.

When your tests depend on interfaces you can refactor the underlying code with reckless abandon. The tests verify the continued good behavior of the interface and changes to the underlying code do not force rewrites of the tests. Intentionally depending on interfaces allows you to use tests to put off design decisions safely and without penalty.

Supporting Abstractions

When more information finally arrives and you make the next design decision, you'll change the code in ways that increase its level of abstraction. Herein lies another of the benefits of tests on design.

Good design naturally progresses toward small independent objects that rely on abstractions. The behavior of a well-designed application gradually becomes the result of interactions among these abstractions. Abstractions are wonderfully flexible design components but the improvements they provide come at one slight cost: While each individual abstraction might be easy to understand, there is no single place in the code that makes obvious the behavior of the whole.

As the code base expands and the number of abstractions grows, tests become increasingly necessary. There is a level of design abstraction where it is almost impossible to safely make any change unless the code has tests. Tests are your record of the interface of every abstraction and as such they are the wall at your back. They let you put off design decisions and create abstractions to any useful depth.

Exposing Design Flaws

The next benefit of tests is that they expose design flaws in the underlying code. If a test requires painful setup, the code expects too much context. If testing one object drags a bunch of others into the mix, the code has too many dependencies. If the test is hard to write, other objects will find the code difficult to reuse.

Tests are the canary in the coal mine; when the design is bad, testing is hard.

The inverse, however, is not guaranteed to be true. Costly tests do not necessarily mean that the application is poorly designed. It is quite technically possible to write bad tests for well-designed code. Therefore, for tests to lower your costs, both the underlying application *and* the tests must be well-designed.

Your goal is to gain all of the benefits of testing for the least cost possible. The best way to achieve this goal is to write loosely coupled tests about only the things that matter.

Knowing What to Test

Most programmers write too many tests. This is not always obvious because in many cases the cost of these unnecessary tests is so high that the programmers involved have given up testing altogether. It's not that they don't have tests. They have a big, but out-of-date test suite; it just never runs. One simple way to get better value from tests is to write fewer of them. The safest way to accomplish this is to test everything just once and in the proper place.

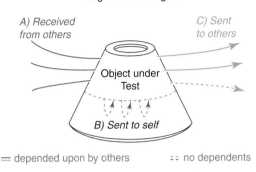

Figure 9.1   Objects under test are like space capsules, messages breach their boundaries.

Removing duplication from testing lowers the cost of changing tests in reaction to application changes, and putting tests in the right place guarantees they'll be forced to change only when absolutely necessary. Distilling your tests to their essence requires having a very clear idea about what you intend to test, one that can be derived from design principles you already know.

Think of an object-oriented application as a series of messages passing between a set of black boxes. Dealing with every object as a black box puts constraints on what others are permitted to know and limits the public knowledge about any object to the messages that pierce its boundaries.

Well-designed objects have boundaries that are very strong. Each is like the space capsule shown in Figure 9.1. Nothing on the outside can see in, nothing on the inside can see out and only a few explicitly agreed upon messages can pass through the predefined airlocks.

This willful ignorance of the internals of every other object is at the core of design. Dealing with objects as if they are only and exactly the messages to which they respond lets you design a changeable application, and it is your understanding of the importance of this perspective that allows you to create tests that provide maximum benefit at minimum cost.

The design principles you are enforcing in your application apply to your tests as well. Each test is merely another application object that needs to use an existing class. The more the test gets coupled to that class, the more entangled the two become and the more vulnerable the test is to unnecessarily being forced to change.

Not only should you limit couplings, but the few you allow should be to stable things. The most stable thing about any object is its public interface; it logically follows that the tests you write should be for messages that are defined in public interfaces. The

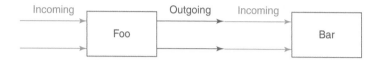

Figure 9.2   One object's outgoing message is another's incoming.

most costly and least useful tests are those that blast holes in an object's containment walls by coupling to unstable internal details. These over-eager tests prove nothing about the overall correctness of an application but nonetheless raise costs because they break with every refactoring of underlying class.

Tests should concentrate on the incoming or outgoing messages that cross an object's boundaries. The incoming messages make up the public interface of the receiving object. The outgoing messages, by definition, are incoming into other objects and so are part of some other object's interface, as illustrated in Figure 9.2.

In Figure 9.2, messages that are incoming into Foo make up Foo's public interface. Foo is responsible for testing its own interface and it does so by making assertions about the results that these messages return. Tests that make assertions about the values that messages return are tests of *state.* Such tests commonly assert that the results returned by a message equal an expected value.

Figure 9.2 also shows Foo sending messages to Bar. A message sent by Foo to Bar is outgoing from Foo but incoming to Bar. This message is part of Bar's public interface and all tests of state should thus be confined to Bar. Foo need not, and should not, test these outgoing messages for state. The general rule is that objects should make assertions about state *only* for messages in their own public interfaces. Following this rule confines tests of message return values to a single place and removes unnecessary duplication, DRYing out your tests and lowering maintenance costs.

The fact that you need not test outgoing messages for state does not mean outgoing messages need no tests at all. There are two flavors of outgoing messages, and one of them requires a different kind of test.

Some outgoing messages have no side effects and thus matter only to their senders. The sender surely cares about the result it gets back (why else send the message?), but no other part of the application cares if the message gets sent. Outgoing messages like this are known as *queries* and they need not be tested by the sending object. Query messages are part of the public interface of their receiver, which already implements every necessary test of state.

However, many outgoing messages *do* have side effects (a file gets written, a database record is saved, an action is taken by an observer) upon which your application depends. These messages are *commands* and it is the responsibility of the sending object to prove that they are properly sent. Proving that a message gets sent is a test of behavior, not state, and involves assertions about the number of times, and with what arguments, the message is sent.

Here, then, are the guidelines for what to test: Incoming messages should be tested for the state they return. Outgoing command messages should be tested to ensure they get sent. Outgoing query messages should not be tested.

As long as your application's objects deal with one another strictly via public interfaces, your tests need know nothing more. When you test this minimal set of messages, no change in the private behavior of any object can affect any test. When you test outgoing command messages only to prove they get sent, your loosely coupled tests can tolerate application changes without being forced to change in turn. As long as the public interfaces remain stable, you can write tests once and they will keep you safe forever.

Knowing When to Test

You should write tests first, whenever it makes sense to do so.

Unfortunately, judging when it makes sense to do so can be a challenge for novice designers, rendering this advice less than helpful. Novices often write code that is far too coupled; they combine unrelated responsibilities and bind many dependencies into every object. Their applications are tightly woven tapestries of entangled code where no object lives in isolation. It is very hard to retroactively test these applications because *tests are reuse* and this code can't be reused.

Writing tests first forces a modicum of reusability to be built into an object from its inception; it would otherwise be impossible to write tests at all. Therefore, novice designers are best served by writing test-first code. Their lack of design skills may make this bafflingly difficult but if they persevere they will at least have testable code, something that may not otherwise be true.

Be warned, however, that writing tests first is no substitute for and does not guarantee a well-designed application. The reusability that results from test-first is an improvement over nothing at all but the resulting application can still fall far short of good design. Well-intentioned novices often write expensive, duplicative tests around messy, tightly coupled code. It is an unfortunate truth that the most complex code is usually written by the least qualified person. This does not reflect an innate complexity of the underlying task, rather a lack of experience on the part of the programmer. Novice programmers don't yet have the skills to write simple code.

The overcomplicated applications these novices produce should be viewed as triumphs of perseverance; it's a miracle these applications work at all. The code is *hard*. The applications are difficult to change and every refactoring breaks all the tests. This high cost of change can easily start a downward productivity spiral that is discouraging for all concerned. Changes cascade throughout the application, and the maintenance cost of tests makes them seem costly relative to their worth.

If you are a novice and in this situation, it's important to sustain faith in the value of tests. Done at the correct time and in the right amounts, testing, and writing code test-first, will lower your overall costs. Gaining these benefits requires applying object-oriented design principles everywhere, both to the code of your application *and* to the code in your tests. Your new-found knowledge of design already makes it easier to write testable code, most of the remainder of this chapter illustrates how to apply these design principles during the construction of tests. Because well-designed applications are easy to change, and well-designed tests may very well avoid change altogether, these overall design improvements pay off dramatically.

Experienced designers garner subtler improvements from testing-first. It's not that they can't benefit from it or that they'll never discover something unexpected by following its dictates, rather that the gains accrued from forced reuse are ones they already have. These programmers already write loosely coupled, reusable code; tests add value in other ways.

It is not unheard of for experienced designers to "spike" a problem, that is, to do experiments where they just write code. These experiments are exploratory, for problems about whose solution they are uncertain. Once clarity is gained and a design suggests itself, these programmers then revert to test-first for production code.

Your overall goal is to create well-designed applications that have acceptable test coverage. The best way to reach this goal varies according to the strengths and experience of the programmer.

This license to use your own judgment is not permission to skip testing. Poorly designed code without tests is just legacy code that can't be tested. Don't overestimate your strengths and use an inflated self-view as an excuse to avoid tests. While it sometimes makes sense to write a bit of code the old fashioned way, you should err on the side of test-first.

Knowing How to Test

Anyone can create a new Ruby testing framework and sometimes it seems that everyone has. The next shiny new framework may contain a feature that you just can't live without; if you understand the costs and benefits, feel free to choose any framework that suits you.

However, there are many good reasons to stay within the testing mainstream. The frameworks with the most use have the best support. They are speedily updated to ensure compatibility with new releases of Ruby (and of Rails) and so present no obstacle to keeping current. Their large user base biases them towards maintaining backward compatibility; it's unlikely they'll change in such a way as to force a rewrite of all your tests. And because they are widely adopted, it's easy to find programmers who have experience using them.

As of this writing, the mainstream frameworks are MiniTest, from Ryan Davis and seattle.rb and bundled with Ruby as of version 1.9, and RSpec, from David Chelimsky and the RSpec team. These frameworks have different philosophies and while you may naturally lean towards one or the other, both are excellent choices.

Not only must you choose a framework, you must grapple with alternative styles of testing: Test Driven Development (TDD) and Behavior Driven Development (BDD). Here the decision is not so clear-cut. TDD and BDD may appear to be in opposition but they are best viewed as on a continuum like Figure 9.3, where your values and experience dictate the choice of where to stand.

Both styles create code by writing tests first. BDD takes an outside-in approach, creating objects at the boundary of an application and working its way inward, mocking as necessary to supply as-yet-unwritten objects. TDD takes an inside-out approach, usually starting with tests of domain objects and then reusing these newly created domain objects in the tests of adjacent layers of code.

Past experience or inclination may render one style more suitable for you than the other, but both are completely acceptable. Each has costs and benefits, some of which will be explored in the next sections on writing tests.

When testing, it's useful to think of your application's objects as divided into two major categories. The first category contains the object that you're testing,

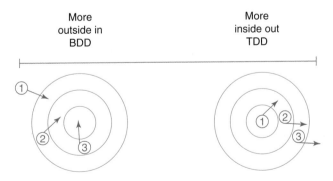

Figure 9.3   BDD and TDD should be viewed as on a continuum.

referred to from now on as the *object under test*. The second category contains everything else.

Your tests must obviously know things about the first category, that is, about the object under test, but they should remain as ignorant as possible about the second. Pretend that the rest of the application is opaque, that the only information available during the test is that which can be gained from looking at the object under test.

Once you dial your testing focus down to the specific object under test, you'll need to choose a testing point-of-view. Your tests *could* stand completely inside of the object under test, with effective access to all of its internals. This is a bad idea, however, because it allows knowledge that should be private to the object to leak into the tests, increasing coupling between them and raising the likelihood that changes to code will require changes in tests. It's better for tests to assume a viewpoint that sights along the edges of the object under test, where they can know only about messages that come and go.

MiniTest Framework

The tests in this chapter are written using MiniTest. This is not an endorsement of one framework over another, rather a recognition of the fact that examples written in MiniTest will run anywhere Ruby 1.9 or above is installed. You can duplicate and experiment with these examples without installing additional software.

By the time you read this chapter MiniTest may have changed. Perfect strangers may well have improved this software and given you those improvements free of charge; such is the life of the open source developer. Regardless of how MiniTest may have evolved, the principles illustrated below hold true. Don't get distracted by changes in syntax; concentrate on understanding the underlying goals of the tests. Once you understand these goals, you can achieve them via any testing framework.

Testing Incoming Messages

Incoming messages make up an object's public interface, the face it presents to the world. These messages need tests because other application objects depend on their signatures and on the results they return.

These first tests use code from the examples in Chapter 3, Managing Dependencies. Following is a reminder of those `Wheel` and `Gear` classes, as they were when entangled together. `Gear` creates an instance of the `Wheel` class deep inside its `gear_inches` method, on line 24 below.

> **Note**
>
> The remainder of this chapter contains tests for code that appeared previously in this book. These code samples served earlier to explain the principles of object-oriented design; here they will illustrate how to test different components of design. The following tests don't cover every line of code you've seen, but they do test every concept you've learned in this book.

```ruby
 1 class Wheel
 2   attr_reader :rim, :tire
 3   def initialize(rim, tire)
 4     @rim        = rim
 5     @tire       = tire
 6   end
 7
 8   def diameter
 9     rim + (tire * 2)
10   end
11 # ...
12 end
13
14 class Gear
15   attr_reader :chainring, :cog, :rim, :tire
16   def initialize(args)
17     @chainring = args[:chainring]
18     @cog       = args[:cog]
19     @rim       = args[:rim]
20     @tire      = args[:tire]
21   end
22
23   def gear_inches
24     ratio * Wheel.new(rim, tire).diameter
25   end
```

```
26
27   def ratio
28      chainring / cog.to_f
29   end
30 # ...
31 end
```

Table 9.1 shows the messages (other than those that return simple attributes) that cross these object's boundaries. `Wheel` responds to one incoming message, `diameter` (which in turn is sent by, or outgoing from, `Gear`) and `Gear` responds to two incoming messages, `gear_inches` and `ratio`.

The opening paragraph of this section stated that every incoming message is part of an object's public interface and so must be tested. Now it's time to add a slight caveat to this rule.

Deleting Unused Interfaces

Incoming messages ought to have dependents. As you can see from Table 9.1, this is true for `diameter`, `gear_inches`, and `ratio` where they are incoming messages. Some object *other than the original implementer* depends on each of these messages.

If you draw this table for the object under test and find a purported incoming message that does not have dependents, you should view that message with great suspicion. What purpose is served by implementing a message that no one sends? It's not really *incoming* at all, it's a speculative implementation that reeks of guessing about the future and clearly anticipates requirements that do not exist.

Do not test an incoming message that has no dependents; delete it. You application is improved by ruthlessly eliminating code that is not actively being used. Such code is negative cash flow, it adds testing and maintenance burdens but provides no value. Deleting unused code saves money right now, if you do not do so you must test it.

Table 9.1   Incoming and Outgoing Messages by Object.

Object	Incoming Messages	Outgoing Messages	Has Dependents?
Wheel	diameter		Yes
Gear		diameter	No
	gear_inches		Yes
	ratio		Yes

Overcome any reluctance that you feel; practicing this pruning will teach you its value. Until such time as you are completely convinced of the rightness of this strategy you may console yourself with the knowledge that in extremity you can recover deleted code from revision control. Regardless of whether you do it with joy or in pain, delete the code. Unused code costs more to keep than to recover.

Proving the Public Interface

Incoming messages are tested by making assertions about the value, or state, that their invocation returns. The first requirement for testing an incoming message is to prove that it returns the correct value in every possible situation.

The following code shows a test of Wheel's diameter method. Line 4 creates an instance of Wheel and line 6 asserts that this Wheel has a diameter of 29.

```
 1  class WheelTest < MiniTest::Unit::TestCase
 2
 3    def test_calculates_diameter
 4      wheel = Wheel.new(26, 1.5)
 5
 6      assert_in_delta(29,
 7                      wheel.diameter,
 8                      0.01)
 9    end
10  end
```

This test is extremely simple and it invokes very little code. Wheel has no hidden dependencies so no other application objects get created as a side effect of running this test. Wheel's design allows you to test it independently of every other class in your application.

Testing Gear is a bit more interesting. Gear requires a few more arguments than Wheel, but even so the overall structure of these two tests is very similar. In the gear_inches test below, line 4 creates a new instance of Gear and line 10 makes assertions about the results of the method.

```
 1  class GearTest < MiniTest::Unit::TestCase
 2
 3    def test_calculates_gear_inches
 4      gear =  Gear.new(
 5                chainring: 52,
```

```
 6                    cog:        11,
 7                    rim:        26,
 8                    tire:       1.5 )
 9
10        assert_in_delta(137.1,
11                        gear.gear_inches,
12                        0.01)
13    end
14 end
```

This new gear_inches test looks a lot like Wheel's diameter test but don't be fooled by appearances. This test has entanglements that the diameter test did not have. Gear's implementation of gear_inches unconditionally creates and uses another object, Wheel. Gear and Wheel are coupled in the code *and* in the tests, though it's not obvious here.

The fact that Gear's gear_inches method creates and uses another object affects how long this test runs and how likely it is to suffer unintended consequences as a result of changes to unrelated parts of the application. The coupling that creates this problem, however, is hidden inside of Gear and so totally invisible in this test. The test's purpose is to prove that gear_inches returns the right result and it certainly fulfills that requirement, but the way the underlying code is structured adds hidden risk.

If Wheels are expensive to create, the Gear test pays that cost even though it has no interest in Wheel. If Gear is correct but Wheel is broken, the Gear test might fail in a misleading way, at a place far distant from the code you're trying to test.

Tests run fastest when they execute the least code and the volume of external code that a test invokes is directly related to your design. An application constructed of tightly coupled, dependent-laden objects is like a tapestry where pulling on one thread drags the entire rug along. When tightly coupled objects are tested, a test of one object runs code in many others. If the code were such that Wheel were also coupled to other objects, this problem is magnified; running the Gear test would then create a large network of objects, any of which might break in a maddeningly confusing way.

These problems are manifested in, but are not unique to, the tests. Because tests are the first reuse of code, this problem is but a harbinger of things to come for your application as a whole.

Isolating the Object Under Test

Gear is a simple object but attempts to test its gear_inches method have already unearthed hidden complexity. The goal of this test is to ensure that gear inches are calculated correctly but it turns out that running gear_inches relies on code in objects other than Gear.

This exposes a broader design problem; when you can't test Gear in isolation, it bodes ill for the future. This difficulty in isolating Gear for testing reveals that it is bound to a specific context, one that imposes limitations that will interfere with reuse.

Chapter 3 broke this binding by removing the creation of Wheel from Gear. Here's a copy of the code that made that transition; Gear now expects to be injected with an object that understands diameter.

```ruby
 1  class Gear
 2    attr_reader :chainring, :cog, :wheel
 3    def initialize(args)
 4      @chainring = args[:chainring]
 5      @cog       = args[:cog]
 6      @wheel     = args[:wheel]
 7    end
 8
 9    def gear_inches
10      # The object in the'wheel' variable
11      #   plays the 'Diameterizable' role.
12      ratio * wheel.diameter
13    end
14
15    def ratio
16      chainring / cog.to_f
17    end
18  # ...
19  end
```

This transition of code is paralleled by a transition of thought. Gear no longer cares about the class of the injected object, it merely expects that it implement diameter. The diameter method is part of the public interface of a *role*, one that might reasonably be named Diameterizable.

Now that Gear is decoupled from Wheel, you must inject an instance of Diameterizable during every Gear creation. However, because Wheel is the only application class that plays this role, your runtime options are severely limited. In real life, as the code currently exists, every Gear that you create will of necessity be injected with an instance of Wheel.

As circular as this sounds, injecting a Wheel into Gear is not the same as injecting a Diameterizable. The application code looks exactly the same, granted, but its logical meaning differs. The difference is not in the characters that you type but in your thoughts about what they mean. Freeing your imagination from an attachment to the class of the incoming object opens design *and testing* possibilities that are otherwise unavailable. Thinking of the injected object as an instance of its role gives you more choices about what kind of Diameterizable to inject into Gear during your tests.

One possible Diameterizable is, obviously, Wheel, because it clearly implements the correct interface. The next example makes this very prosaic choice; it updates the existing test to accommodate the changes to the code by injecting an instance of Wheel (line 6) during the test.

```
1  class GearTest < MiniTest::Unit::TestCase
2    def test_calculates_gear_inches
3      gear =  Gear.new(
4                 chainring: 52,
5                 cog:       11,
6                 wheel:     Wheel.new(26, 1.5))
7
8      assert_in_delta(137.1,
9                        gear.gear_inches,
10                       0.01)
11   end
12 end
```

Using a Wheel for the injected Diameterizable results in test code that exactly mirrors the application. It is now obvious, both in the application and in the tests, that Gear is using Wheel. The invisible coupling between these classes has been publicly exposed.

This test is fast enough but this adequate speed is quite by accident. It's not that the gear_inches test has been carefully isolated and thus decoupled from other code; not at all, it's just that all the code coupled to this test runs quickly as well.

Notice also that it's not obvious here (or anywhere else for that matter) that Wheel is playing the Diameterizable role. The role is virtual, it's all in your head. Nothing about the code guides future maintainers to think of Wheel as a Diameterizable.

However, despite the invisibility of the role and this coupling to Wheel, structuring the test in this way has one very real advantage, as the next section shows.

Injecting Dependencies Using Classes

When the code in your test uses the same collaborating objects as the code in your application, your tests always break when they should. The value of this cannot be underestimated.

Here's a simple example. Imagine that Diameterizable's public interface changes. Another programmer goes into the Wheel class and changes the diameter method's name to width, as shown in line 8 below.

```
 1 class Wheel
 2   attr_reader :rim, :tire
 3   def initialize(rim, tire)
 4     @rim        = rim
 5     @tire       = tire
 6   end
 7
 8   def width   # <— used to be 'diameter'
 9     rim + (tire * 2)
10   end
11 # ...
12 end
```

Imagine further that this programmer failed to update the name of the sent message in Gear. Gear still sends diameter in its gear_inches method, as you can see in this reminder of Gear's current code:

```
1 class Gear
2   # ...
3   def gear_inches
4     ratio * wheel.diameter # <— obsolete
5   end
6 end
```

Because the `Gear` test injects an instance of `Wheel` and `Wheel` implements `width` but Gear sends `diameter`, the test now fails:

```
1  Gear
2    ERROR test_calculates_gear_inches
3          undefined method 'diameter'
```

This failure is unsurprising, it is exactly what should happen when two concrete objects collaborate and the receiver of a message changes but its sender does not. `Wheel` has changed and as a result `Gear` needs to change. This test fails as it should.

The test is simple and the failure obvious because the code is so concrete, but like all concretions it works only for this specific case. Here, for this code, the test above is good enough, but there are other situations in which you are better served to locate and test the abstraction.

A more extreme example illuminates the problem. If there are hundreds of `Diameterizables`, how do you decide which is most intention revealing to inject during the test? What if `Diameterizables` are extremely costly, how do you avoid running lots of unnecessary, time-consuming code? Common sense suggests that if `Wheel` is the only `Diameterizable` and it is fast enough, the test should just inject a `Wheel`, but what if your choice is less obvious?

Injecting Dependencies as Roles

The `Wheel` class and the `Diameterizable` role are so closely aligned that it's hard to see them as separate concepts, but understanding what happened in the previous test requires making a distinction. `Gear` and `Wheel` both have relationships with a third thing, the `Diameterizable` role. As you can see in Figure 9.4, `Diameterizable` is depended on by `Gear` and implemented by `Wheel`.

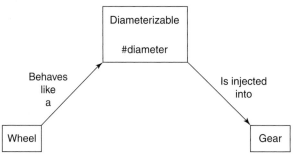

Figure 9.4   *Gear* depends upon *Diameterizable*; *Wheel* implements it.

This role is an abstraction of the idea that disparate objects can have diameters. As with all abstractions, it is reasonable to expect this abstract role to be more stable than the concretion from which it came. However in the specific case above the opposite is true.

There are two places in the code where an object depends on knowledge of `Diameterizable`. First, `Gear` thinks that it knows `Diameterizable`'s interface; that is, it believes it can send `diameter` to the injected object. Second, the code that created the object to be injected believes that `Wheel` implements this interface; that is, it expects `Wheel` to implement `diameter`. Now that `Diameterizable` has changed, there's a problem. `Wheel` has been updated to implement the new interface but unfortunately `Gear` still expects the old one.

The whole point of dependency injection is that it allows you to substitute different concrete classes without changing existing code. You can assemble new behavior by creating new objects that play existing roles and injecting these objects where those roles are expected. Object-oriented design tells you to inject dependencies because it believes that specific concrete classes will vary more than these roles, or conversely, roles will be more stable than the classes from which they were abstracted.

Unfortunately, the opposite just happened. In this example it was not the class of the injected object that changed, it was the interface of the role. It is still correct to inject a `Wheel` but now incorrect to send that `Wheel` the `diameter` message.

When a role has a single player, that one concrete player and the abstract role are so closely aligned that the boundaries between them are easily blurred and it is a practical fact that sometimes this blurring doesn't matter. In this case `Wheel` is the only player of `Diameterizable` and you don't currently expect to have others. If `Wheel`s are cheap, injecting an actual `Wheel` has little negative effect on your tests.

When the application code can only be written one way, mirroring that arrangement is often the most effective way to write tests. Doing so permits tests to correctly fail regardless of whether the concretion (the name of the `Wheel` class) or the abstraction (the interface to the `diameter` method) changes.

However, this is not always true. Sometimes there are forces at work that drive you to wish to forgo the use of `Wheel` in your tests. If your application contains many different `Diameterizable`s you might want to create an idealized one so your tests clearly convey the idea of this role. If all `Diameterizable`s are expensive, you may want to fake a cheap one to make your tests run faster. If you are doing BDD, your application might not yet contain any object that plays this role; you may be forced to manufacture *something* just to write the test.

Creating Test Doubles

This next example explores the idea of creating a fake object, or *test double*, to play the Diameterizable role. For this test, assume Diameterizable's interface has reverted to the original diameter method and that diameter is again correctly implemented by Wheel and sent by Gear. Line 2 below creates a fake, DiameterDouble. Line 13 injects this fake into Gear.

```
 1  # Create a player of the 'Diameterizable' role
 2  class DiameterDouble
 3    def diameter
 4      10
 5    end
 6  end
 7
 8  class GearTest < MiniTest::Unit::TestCase
 9    def test_calculates_gear_inches
10      gear =  Gear.new(
11              chainring: 52,
12              cog:       11,
13              wheel:     DiameterDouble.new)
14
15      assert_in_delta(47.27,
16                      gear.gear_inches,
17                      0.01)
18    end
19  end
```

A test double is a stylized instance of a role player that is used exclusively for testing. Doubles like this are very easy to make; nothing hinders you from creating one for every possible situation. Each variation is like an artist's sketch. It emphasizes a single interesting feature and allows the underlying object's other details to recede to the background.

This double *stubs* diameter, that is, it implements a version of diameter that returns a canned answer. DiameterDouble is quite limited, but that's the whole point. The fact that it always returns 10 for diameter is perfect. This stubbed return value provides a dependable foundation on which to construct the test.

Many test frameworks have built-in ways to create doubles and to stub return values. These specialized mechanisms can be handy, but for simple test doubles it's fine to use plain old Ruby objects, as does the example above.

`DiameterDouble` is *not* a mock. It's easy to slip into the habit of using the word "mock" to describe this double, but mocks are something else entirely and will be covered later in this chapter in the section Testing Outgoing Messages.

Injecting this double decouples the `Gear` test from the `Wheel` class. It no longer matters if `Wheel` is slow because `DiameterDouble` is always fast. This test works just fine, as running it shows:

```
1 GearTest
2     PASS test_calculates_gear_inches
```

This test uses a test double and is therefore simple, fast, isolated, and intention revealing; what could possibly go wrong?

Living the Dream

Imagine now that the code undergoes the same alterations as before: `Diameterizable`'s interface changes from `diameter` to `width` and `Wheel` gets updated but `Gear` does not. This change once again breaks the application. Remember that the previous `Gear` test (which injected a `Wheel` instead of using a double) noticed this problem right away and began to fail with an `undefined method` `'diameter'` error.

Now that you're injecting `DiameterDouble`, however, here's what happens when you re-run the test:

```
1 GearTest
2     PASS test_calculates_gear_inches
```

The test *continues to pass* even though the application is definitely broken. This application cannot possibly work; `Gear` sends `diameter` but `Wheel` implements `width`.

You have created an alternate universe, one in which tests cheerfully report that all is well despite the fact that the application is manifestly incorrect. The possibility of creating this universe is what causes some to warn that stubbing (and mocking) makes for brittle tests. However, as is always true, the fault here is with the programmer, not the tool. Writing better code requires understanding the root cause of this problem, which in turn necessitates a closer look at its components.

The application contains a `Diameterizable` role. This role originally had one player, `Wheel`. When `GearTest` created `DiameterDouble`, it introduced *a second player of the role*. When the interface of a role changes, all players of the role must adopt the new interface. It's easy, however, to overlook role players that were constructed specifically for tests and that is exactly what happened here. Wheel got updated with the new interface but DiameterDouble did not.

Using Tests to Document Roles

It's no wonder this problem occurs; the role is nearly invisible. There's no place in the application where you can point your finger and say "This defines Diameterizable." When remembering that the role even exists is a challenge, forgetting that test doubles play it is inevitable.

One way to raise the role's visibility is to assert that Wheel plays it. Line 6 below does just this; it documents the role and proves that Wheel correctly implements its interface.

```
 1 class WheelTest < MiniTest::Unit::TestCase
 2   def setup
 3     @wheel = Wheel.new(26, 1.5)
 4   end
 5
 6   def test_implements_the_diameterizable_interface
 7     assert_respond_to(@wheel, :diameter)
 8   end
 9
10   def test_calculates_diameter
11     wheel = Wheel.new(26, 1.5)
12
13     assert_in_delta(29,
14                     wheel.diameter,
15                     0.01)
16   end
17 end
```

The implements_the_diameterizable_interface test introduces the idea of tests for roles but is not a completely satisfactory solution. It is, in fact, woefully incomplete. First, it cannot be shared with other Diameterizables. Other players of this role would have to duplicate this test. Next, it does nothing to help with the "living the dream" problem from the Gear test. Wheel's assertion that it plays this role does not prevent Gear's DiameterDouble from becoming obsolete and allowing the gear_inches test to erroneously pass.

Fortunately, the problem of documenting and testing roles has a simple solution, one that will be thoroughly covered in the subsequent section, Proving the

Correctness of Ducks. For now it's enough to recognize that roles need tests of their own.

The goal of this section was to prove public interfaces by testing incoming messages. `Wheel` was cheap to test. The original `Gear` test was more expensive because it depended on a hidden coupling to `Wheel`. Replacing that coupling with an injected dependency on `Diameterizable` isolated the object under test but created a dilemma about whether to inject a real or a fake object.

This choice between injecting real or fake objects has far-reaching consequences. Injecting the same objects at test time as are used at runtime ensures that tests break correctly but may lead to long running tests. Alternatively, injecting doubles can speed tests but leave them vulnerable to constructing a fantasy world where tests work but the application fails.

Notice that the act of testing did not, by itself, force an improvement in design. Nothing about testing *made* you remove the coupling and inject the dependency. While it's true that the outside-in approach of BDD provides more guidance than does TDD, neither practice prevents a naïve designer from writing `Wheel` and then embedding the creation of a `Wheel` deep inside of `Gear`. This coupling doesn't make tests impossible, it just raises costs. Reducing the coupling is up to you and relies on your understanding of the principles of design.

Testing Private Methods

Sometimes the object under test sends messages to itself. Messages sent to `self` invoke methods that are defined in the receiver's private interface. These private messages are like proverbial trees falling in empty forests; they do not exist, at least as far as the rest of your application is concerned. Because sends of private methods cannot be seen from outside of the black box of the object under test, in the pristine world of idealized design they need not be tested.

However, the real world is not so neat and this simple rule does not completely suffice. Dealing with private methods requires judgment and flexibility.

Ignoring Private Methods During Tests

There are many excellent reasons to omit tests of private methods.

First, such tests are redundant. Private methods are hidden inside the object under test and their results cannot be seen by others. These private methods are invoked by public methods *that already have tests*. A bug in a private method can certainly break the overall application but this failure will always be exposed by an existing test. Testing private methods is never necessary.

Second, private methods are unstable. Tests of private methods are therefore coupled to application code that is likely to change. When the application changes the tests will be forced to change in turn. It's easy to create a situation where precious time is spent performing ongoing maintenance on unnecessary tests.

Finally, testing private methods can mislead others into using them. Tests provide documentation about the object under test. They tell a story about how it expects to interact with the world at large. Including private methods in this story distracts the readers from its main purpose and encourages them to break encapsulation and to depend on these methods. Your tests should hide private methods, not expose them.

Removing Private Methods from the Class Under Test

One way to sidestep this entire problem is to avoid private methods altogether. If you have no private methods, you need not be concerned for their tests.

An object with many private methods exudes the design smell of having too many responsibilities. If your object has so many private methods that you dare not leave them untested, consider extracting the methods into new object. The extracted methods form the core of the responsibilities of the new object and so make up its public interface, which is (theoretically) stable and thus safe to depend upon.

This strategy is a good one, but unfortunately is only truly helpful if the new interface is indeed stable. Sometimes the new interface is not, and it is at this point that theory and practice part ways. This new public interface will be exactly as stable (or as unstable) as was the original private interface. Methods don't magically become more reliable just because they got moved. It is costly to couple to unstable methods—regardless of whether they are portrayed as public or private.

Choosing to Test a Private Method

Times of great uncertainly call for drastic measures. It is therefore occasionally defensible to fling a bit of smelly code into place and hide the mess until better information arrives. Hiding messes is easily done; just wrap the offending code in a private method.

If you create a mess and never fix it your costs will eventually go up, but in the short term, for the right problem, having enough confidence to write embarrassing code can save money. When your intention is to defer a design decision, do the simplest thing that solves today's problem. Isolate the code behind the best interface you can conceive and hunker down and wait for more information.

Applying this strategy can result in private methods that are wildly unstable. Once you've made this leap it's reasonable to consider compounding your sins by testing these unstable methods. The application code is ugly and will undergo frequent change; the risk of breaking something is ever-present. These tests are costly and will likely be forced to change in lock-step with the underlying code, but every other option for keeping things running may be more expensive.

These tests of private methods aren't necessary in order to know that a change broke something, the public interface tests still serve that purpose admirably. Tests of private methods produce error messages that directly pinpoint the failing parts of private code. These more specific errors are tight couplings that increase maintenance costs, but they make it easier to understand the effects of changes and so they take some of the pain out of refactoring complex private code.

Reducing the barriers to refactoring is important, because refactor you will. That's the whole point. The mess is temporary, you intend to refactor out of it. As more design information arrives, these private methods will improve. Once the fog clears and a design reveals itself, the methods will become more stable. As stability improves, the cost of maintaining *and* the need for tests will go down. Eventually it will be possible to extract the private methods into a separate class and safely expose them to the world.

The rules-of-thumb for testing private methods are thus: Never write them, and if you do, never ever test them, unless of course it makes sense to do so. Therefore, be biased against writing these tests but do not fear to do so if this would improve your lot.

Testing Outgoing Messages

Outgoing messages, as you know from the "What to Test" section, are either *queries* or *commands*. Query messages matter only to the object that sends them, while command messages have effects that are visible to other objects in your application.

Ignoring Query Messages

Messages that have no side effects are known as `query` messages. Here's a simple example, where Gear's `gear_inches` method sends `diameter`.

```
1  class Gear
2    # ...
3    def gear_inches
4      ratio * wheel.diameter
5    end
6  end
```

Nothing in the application other than the gear_inches method cares that diameter gets sent. The diameter method has no side effects, running it leaves no visible trace, and no other objects depend on its execution.

In the same way that tests should ignore messages sent to self, they also should ignore outgoing query messages. The consequences of sending diameter are hidden inside of Gear. Because the overall application does not need this message to be sent, your tests need not care.

Gear's gear_inches method depends on the result that diameter returns, but tests to prove the correctness of diameter belong in Wheel, not here in Gear. It is redundant for Gear to duplicate those tests, maintenance costs will increase if it does. Gear's only responsibility is to prove that gear_inches works correctly and it can do this by simply testing that gear_inches always returns appropriate results.

Proving Command Messages

Sometimes, however, it *does* matter that a message get sent; other parts of your application depend on something that happens as a result. In this case the object under test is responsible for sending the message and your tests must prove it does so.

Illustrating this problem requires a new example. Imagine a game where players race virtual bicycles. These bicycles, obviously, have gears. The Gear class is now responsible for letting the application know when a player changes gears so the application can update the bicycle's behavior.

In the following code, Gear meets this new requirement by adding an observer. When a player shifts gears the set_cog or set_chainring methods execute. These methods save the new value and then invoke Gear's changed method (line 20). This method then sends changed to observer, passing along the current chainring and cog.

```
 1  class Gear
 2    attr_reader :chainring, :cog, :wheel, :observer
 3    def initialize(args)
 4      # ...
 5      @observer  = args[:observer]
 6    end
 7
 8    # ...
 9
10    def set_cog(new_cog)
11      @cog = new_cog
12      changed
```

```
13      end
14
15      def set_chainring(new_chainring)
16        @chainring = new_chainring
17        changed
18      end
19
20      def changed
21        observer.changed(chainring, cog)
22      end
23  # ...
24  end
```

Gear has a new responsibility; it must notify observer when cogs or chainrings change. This new responsibility is just as important as its previous obligation to calculate gear inches. When a player changes gears the application will be correct only if Gear sends changed to observer. Your tests should prove this message gets sent.

Not only should they prove it, but they also should do so without making assertions about the result that observer's changed method returns. Just as Wheel's tests claimed sole responsibility for making assertions about the results of its own diameter method, observer's tests are responsible for making assertions about the results of its changed method. The responsibility for testing a message's return value lies with its receiver. Doing so anywhere else duplicates tests and raises costs.

To avoid duplication you need a way to prove that Gear sends changed to observer that does not force you to rely on checking what comes back when it does. Fortunately, this is easy; you need a *mock*. Mocks are tests of behavior, as opposed to tests of state. Instead of making assertions about what a message returns, mocks define an expectation that a message will get sent.

The test below proves that Gear fulfills its responsibilities and it does so without binding itself to details about how observer behaves. The test creates a mock (line 4) that it injects in place of the observer (line 8). Each test method tells the mock to expect to receive the changed message (lines 12 and 17) and then verifies that it did so (lines 14 and 20).

```
1  class GearTest < MiniTest::Unit::TestCase
2
3    def setup
4      @observer = MiniTest::Mock.new
```

```
 5      @gear      = Gear.new(
 6                      chainring: 52,
 7                      cog:       11,
 8                      observer:  @observer)
 9    end
10
11    def test_notifies_observers_when_cogs_change
12      @observer.expect(:changed, true, [52, 27])
13      @gear.set_cog(27)
14      @observer.verify
15    end
16
17    def test_notifies_observers_when_chainrings_change
18      @observer.expect(:changed, true, [42, 11])
19      @gear.set_chainring(42)
20      @observer.verify
21    end
22  end
```

This is the classic usage pattern for a mock. In the notifies_observers_when_
cogs_change test above, line 12 tells the mock what message to expect, line 13 triggers the behavior that should cause this expectation to be met, and then line 14 asks
the mock to verify that it indeed was. The test passes only if sending set_chainring
to gear does something that causes observer to receive changed with the given
arguments.

Notice that all the mock did with the message was remember that it received it. If
the object under test depends on the result it gets back when observer receives
changed, the mock can be configured to return an appropriate value. This return
value, however, is beside the point. Mocks are meant to prove messages get sent, they
return results only when necessary to get tests to run.

The fact that Gear works just fine even after you mock observer's changed
method such that it does absolutely nothing proves that Gear doesn't care what that
method actually does. Gear's only responsibility is to send the message; this test
should restrict itself to proving Gear does so.

In a well-designed application, testing outgoing messages is simple. If you have
proactively injected dependencies, you can easily substitute mocks. Setting expectations on these mocks allows you to prove that the object under test fulfills its responsibilities without duplicating assertions that belong elsewhere.

Testing Duck Types

The Testing Incoming Messages section in this chapter wandered into the territory of testing roles, but while it introduced the issue, it did not provide a satisfactory resolution. It's time to return to that topic and examine how to test duck types. This section shows how to create tests that role players can share and then returns to the original problem and uses shareable tests to prevent test doubles from becoming obsolete.

Testing Roles

The code for this first example comes from the `Preparer` duck type of Chapter 5, Reducing Costs with Duck Typing. These first few code samples repeat part of the lesson from Chapter 5; feel free to skim down to the first test if you have a clear memory of the problem.

Here's a reminder of the original `Mechanic`, `TripCoordinator`, and `Driver` classes:

```
 1 class Mechanic
 2   def prepare_bicycle(bicycle)
 3     #...
 4   end
 5 end
 6
 7 class TripCoordinator
 8   def buy_food(customers)
 9     #...
10   end
11 end
12
13 class Driver
14   def gas_up(vehicle)
15     #...
16   end
17   def fill_water_tank(vehicle)
18     #...
19   end
20 end
```

Each of these classes has a reasonable public interface, yet when `Trip` used these interfaces to prepare a trip it was forced to check the class of each object to determine which message to send, as shown here:

```
1  class Trip
2    attr_reader :bicycles, :customers, :vehicle
3
4    def prepare(preparers)
5      preparers.each {|preparer|
6        case preparer
7        when Mechanic
8          preparer.prepare_bicycles(bicycles)
9        when TripCoordinator
10         preparer.buy_food(customers)
11       when Driver
12         preparer.gas_up(vehicle)
13         preparer.fill_water_tank(vehicle)
14       end
15     }
16   end
17 end
```

The `case` statement above couples `prepare` to three existing concrete classes. Imagine trying to test the `prepare` method or the consequences of adding a new kind of `preparer` into this mix. This method is painful to test and expensive to maintain.

If you come upon code that uses this antipattern but does not have tests, consider refactoring to a better design before writing them. It's always dangerous to make changes in the absence of tests, but this teetering pile of code is so fragile that refactoring it first might well be the most cost-effective strategy. The refactoring that fixes this problem is simple and makes all subsequent change easier.

The first part of the refactoring is to decide on `Preparer`'s interface and to implement that interface in every player of the role. If the public interface of `Preparer` is `prepare_trip`, the following changes allow `Mechanic`, `TripCoordinator`, and `Driver` to play the role:

```
1  class Mechanic
2    def prepare_trip(trip)
3      trip.bicycles.each {|bicycle|
4        prepare_bicycle(bicycle) }
```

```
 5    end
 6
 7    # ...
 8  end
 9
10  class TripCoordinator
11    def prepare_trip(trip)
12      buy_food(trip.customers)
13    end
14
15    # ...
16  end
17
18  class Driver
19    def prepare_trip(trip)
20      vehicle = trip.vehicle
21      gas_up(vehicle)
22      fill_water_tank(vehicle)
23    end
24    # ...
25  end
```

Now that `Preparers` exist, `Trip`'s prepare method can be vastly simplified. The following refactoring alters `Trip`'s prepare method to collaborate with `Preparers` instead of sending unique messages to each specific class:

```
1  class Trip
2    attr_reader :bicycles, :customers, :vehicle
3
4    def prepare(preparers)
5      preparers.each { |preparer|
6        preparer.prepare_trip(self) }
7    end
8  end
```

Having done these refactorings you are positioned to write tests. The above code contains a collaboration between `Preparers` and a `Trip`, which can now be thought of as a `Preparable`. Your tests should document the existence of the `Preparer` role, prove that each of its players behaves correctly, and show that `Trip` interacts with them appropriately.

Because several different classes act as `Preparers`, the role's test should be written once and shared by every player. `MiniTest` is a low ceremony testing framework and it supports sharing tests in the simplest possible way, via Ruby modules.

Here's a module that tests and documents the `Preparer` interface:

```
1  module PreparerInterfaceTest
2    def test_implements_the_preparer_interface
3      assert_respond_to(@object, :prepare_trip)
4    end
5  end
```

This module proves that `@object` responds to `prepare_trip`. The test below uses this module to prove that `Mechanic` is a `Preparer`. It includes the module (line 2) and provides a `Mechanic` during setup via the `@object` variable (line 5).

```
1  class MechanicTest < MiniTest::Unit::TestCase
2    include PreparerInterfaceTest
3
4    def setup
5      @mechanic = @object = Mechanic.new
6    end
7
8    # other tests which rely on @mechanic
9  end
```

The `TripCoordinator` and `Driver` tests follow this same pattern. They also include the module (lines 2 and 10 below) and initialize `@object` in their setup methods (lines 5 and 13).

```
1  class TripCoordinatorTest < MiniTest::Unit::TestCase
2    include PreparerInterfaceTest
3
4    def setup
5      @trip_coordinator = @object = TripCoordinator.new
6    end
7  end
8
9  class DriverTest < MiniTest::Unit::TestCase
10   include PreparerInterfaceTest
11
```

```
12   def setup
13     @driver = @object =  Driver.new
14   end
15 end
```

Running these three tests produces a satisfying result:

```
1 DriverTest
2     PASS test_implements_the_preparer_interface
3
4 MechanicTest
5     PASS test_implements_the_preparer_interface
6
7 TripCoordinatorTest
8     PASS test_implements_the_preparer_interface
```

Defining the PreparerInterfaceTest as a module allows you to write the test once and then reuse it in every object that plays the role. The module serves as a test and as documentation. It raises the visibility of the role and makes it easy to prove that any newly created Preparer successfully fulfills its obligations.

The test_implements_the_preparer_interface method tests an incoming message and as such belongs with the receiving object's tests, which is why the module gets included in the tests of Mechanic, TripCoordinator, and Driver. Incoming messages, however, go hand-in-hand with outgoing messages and you must test both sides of this equation. You have proven that all receivers correctly implement prepare_trip, now you must also prove that Trip correctly sends it.

As you know, proving that an outgoing message gets sent is done by setting expectations on a mock. The following test creates a mock (line 4), tells it to expect prepare_trip (line 6), triggers Trip's prepare method (line 8), and then verifies that the mock received the proper message (line 9).

```
1 class TripTest < MiniTest::Unit::TestCase
2
3   def test_requests_trip_preparation
4     @preparer = MiniTest::Mock.new
5     @trip     = Trip.new
6     @preparer.expect(:prepare_trip, nil, [@trip])
7
8     @trip.prepare([@preparer])
```

```
 9        @preparer.verify
10    end
11 end
```

The `test_requests_trip_preparation` test lives directly in `TripTest`. `Trip` is the only `Preparable` in the application so there's no other object with which to share this test. If other `Preparables` arise the test should be extracted into a module and shared among `Preparables` at that time.

Running this test proves that `Trip` collaborates with `Preparers` using the correct interface:

```
1 TripTest
2     PASS test_requests_trip_preparation
```

This completes the tests of the `Preparer` role. It's now possible to return to the problem of brittleness when using doubles to play roles in tests.

Using Role Tests to Validate Doubles

Now that you know how to write reusable tests that prove an object correctly plays a role you can use this technique to reduce the brittleness caused by stubbing.

The earlier section, Testing Incoming Messages, introduced the "living the dream" problem. The final test in that section contained a misleading false positive, in which a test that should have failed instead passed because of a test double that stubbed an obsolete method. Here's a reminder of that faultily passing test:

```
 1 class DiameterDouble
 2
 3   def diameter  # The interface changed to 'width',
 4     10          # but this double and Gear both
 5   end           # still use 'diameter'.
 6 end
 7
 8 class GearTest < MiniTest::Unit::TestCase
 9   def test_calculates_gear_inches
10     gear =  Gear.new(
11             chainring: 52,
```

```
12                    cog:        11,
13                    wheel:      DiameterDouble.new)
14
15        assert_in_delta(47.27,
16                        gear.gear_inches,
17                        0.01)
18    end
19 end
```

The problem with this test is that DiameterDouble purports to play the Diameterizable role but it does so incorrectly. Now that Diameterizable's interface has changed DiameterDouble is out-of-date. This obsolete double enables the test to bumble along in the mistaken belief that Gear works correctly, when in actual fact GearTest only works when combined with its similarly confused test double. The application is broken but you cannot tell it by running this test.

You last saw WheelTest in the Using Tests to Document Roles section, where it was attempting to counter this problem by raising the visibility of Diameterizable's interface. Here's an example where line 6 proves that Wheel acts like a Diameterizable that implements width:

```
 1 class WheelTest < MiniTest::Unit::TestCase
 2   def setup
 3     @wheel = Wheel.new(26, 1.5)
 4   end
 5
 6   def test_implements_the_diameterizable_interface
 7     assert_respond_to(@wheel, :width)
 8   end
 9
10   def test_calculates_diameter
11     # ...
12   end
13 end
```

With this test, you now hold all the pieces needed to solve the brittleness problem. You know how to share tests among players of a role, you recognize that you have two players of the Diameterizable role, and you have a test that any object can use to prove that it correctly plays the role.

The first step in solving the problem is to extract `test_implements_the_di-ameterizable_interface` from `Wheel` into a module of its own:

```
1  module DiameterizableInterfaceTest
2    def test_implements_the_diameterizable_interface
3      assert_respond_to(@object, :width)
4    end
5  end
```

Once this module exists, reintroducing the extracted behavior back into `WheelTest` is a simple matter of including the module (line 2) and initializing `@object` with a `Wheel` (line 5):

```
 1  class WheelTest < MiniTest::Unit::TestCase
 2    include DiameterizableInterfaceTest
 3
 4    def setup
 5      @wheel = @object = Wheel.new(26, 1.5)
 6    end
 7
 8    def test_calculates_diameter
 9      # ...
10    end
11  end
```

At this point `WheelTest` works just as it did before the extraction, as you can see by running the test:

```
1  WheelTest
2    PASS test_implements_the_diameterizable_interface
3    PASS test_calculates_diameter
```

It's gratifying that the `WheelTest` still passes but this refactoring serves a broader purpose than that of merely rearranging the code. Now that you have an independent module that proves that a `Diameterizable` behaves correctly, you can use the module to prevent test doubles from silently becoming obsolete.

The `GearTest` below has been updated to use this new module. Lines 9 through 15 define a new test class, `DiameterDoubleTest`. `DiameterDoubleTest` is not about

Gear per se, its purpose is to prevent test brittleness by ensuring the ongoing soundness of the double.

```
 1 class DiameterDouble
 2   def diameter
 3     10
 4   end
 5 end
 6
 7 # Prove the test double honors the interface this
 8 #   test expects.
 9 class DiameterDoubleTest < MiniTest::Unit::TestCase
10   include DiameterizableInterfaceTest
11
12   def setup
13     @object = DiameterDouble.new
14   end
15 end
16
17 class GearTest < MiniTest::Unit::TestCase
18   def test_calculates_gear_inches
19     gear =  Gear.new(
20               chainring: 52,
21               cog:       11,
22               wheel:     DiameterDouble.new)
23
24     assert_in_delta(47.27,
25                     gear.gear_inches,
26                     0.01)
27   end
28 end
```

The fact that DiameterDouble and Gear are both incorrect has been allowing previous versions of this test to pass. Now that the double is being tested to ensure it honestly plays its role, running the test finally produces an error:

```
1 DiameterDoubleTest
2   FAIL test_implements_the_diameterizable_interface
3         Expected #<DiameterDouble:...> (DiameterDouble)
4           to respond to #width.
5 GearTest
6   PASS test_calculates_gear_inches
```

The `GearTest` still passes erroneously but that's not a problem because `DiameterDoubleTest` now informs you that `DiameterDouble` is wrong. This failure causes you to correct `DiameterDouble` to implement `width`, as shown on line 2 below:

```
1  class DiameterDouble
2    def width
3      10
4    end
5  end
```

After this change, re-running the test produces a failure in `GearTest`:

```
 1  DiameterDoubleTest
 2      PASS test_implements_the_diameterizable_interface
 3
 4  GearTest
 5    ERROR test_calculates_gear_inches
 6         undefined method 'diameter'
 7           for #<DiameterDouble:0x0000010090a7f8>
 8             gear_test.rb:35:in 'gear_inches'
 9             gear_test.rb:86:in 'test_calculates_gear_inches'
10
```

Now that `DiameterDoubleTest` passes, `GearTest` fails. This failure points directly to the offending line of code in `Gear`. The tests finally tell you to change `Gear`'s `gear_inches` method to send `width` instead of `diameter`, as in this example:

```
1  class Gear
2
3    def gear_inches
4                # finally, 'width' instead of 'diameter'
5      ratio * wheel.width
6    end
7
8  # ...
9  end
```

Once you make this final change, the application is correct and all tests correctly pass:

```
1  DiameterDoubleTest
2      PASS test_implements_the_diameterizable_interface
```

```
 3
 4 GearTest
 5    PASS test_calculates_gear_inches
```

Not only does this test pass, but it will continue to pass (or fail) appropriately, no matter what happens to the `Diameterizable` interface. When you treat test doubles as you would any other role player and test them to prove their correctness, you avoid test brittleness and can stub without fear of consequence.

The desire to test duck types creates a need for shareable tests for roles, and once you acquire this role-based perspective you can use it to your advantage in many situations. From the point of view of the object under test, every other object is a role and dealing with objects as if they are representatives of the roles they play loosens coupling and increases flexibility, both in your application and in your tests.

Testing Inherited Code

You've finally arrived at the last challenge, testing inherited code. This section is much like the previous ones in that it recapitulates a previously seen example and then proceeds to test it. The example used here is the final `Bicycle` hierarchy from Chapter 6, Acquiring Behavior Through Inheritance. Even though that hierarchy eventually proved unsuitable for inheritance, the underlying code is fine and serves admirably as a basis for these tests.

Specifying the Inherited Interface

Here's the `Bicycle` class as you last saw it in Chapter 6:

```
 1 class Bicycle
 2   attr_reader :size, :chain, :tire_size
 3
 4   def initialize(args={})
 5     @size      = args[:size]
 6     @chain     = args[:chain]      || default_chain
 7     @tire_size = args[:tire_size]  || default_tire_size
 8     post_initialize(args)
 9   end
10
11   def spares
12     { tire_size: tire_size,
13       chain:     chain}.merge(local_spares)
```

```
14     end
15
16     def default_tire_size
17       raise NotImplementedError
18     end
19
20     # subclasses may override
21     def post_initialize(args)
22       nil
23     end
24
25     def local_spares
26       {}
27     end
28
29     def default_chain
30       '10-speed'
31     end
32   end
```

Here is the code for RoadBike, one of Bicycle's subclasses:

```
1  class RoadBike < Bicycle
2    attr_reader :tape_color
3
4    def post_initialize(args)
5      @tape_color = args[:tape_color]
6    end
7
8    def local_spares
9      {tape_color: tape_color}
10   end
11
12   def default_tire_size
13     '23'
14   end
15 end
```

The first goal of testing is to prove that all objects in this hierarchy honor their contract. The Liskov Substitution Principle declares that subtypes should be substitutable for their supertypes. Violations of Liskov result in unreliable objects that don't behave as expected. The easiest way to prove that every object in the hierarchy obeys Liskov is to write a shared test for the common contract and include this test in every object.

The contract is embodied in a shared interface. The following test articulates the interface and therefore defines what it means to be a Bicycle:

```ruby
 1 module BicycleInterfaceTest
 2   def test_responds_to_default_tire_size
 3     assert_respond_to(@object, :default_tire_size)
 4   end
 5
 6   def test_responds_to_default_chain
 7     assert_respond_to(@object, :default_chain)
 8   end
 9
10   def test_responds_to_chain
11     assert_respond_to(@object, :chain)
12   end
13
14   def test_responds_to_size
15     assert_respond_to(@object, :size)
16   end
17
18   def test_responds_to_tire_size
19     assert_respond_to(@object, :tire_size)
20   end
21
22   def test_responds_to_spares
23     assert_respond_to(@object, :spares)
24   end
25 end
```

Any object that passes the BicycleInterfaceTest can be trusted to act like a Bicycle. All of the classes in the Bicycle hierarchy must respond to this interface and should be able to pass this test. The following example includes this interface test in the abstract superclass BicycleTest (line 2), and in the concrete subclass RoadBikeTest (line 10):

```ruby
 1 class BicycleTest < MiniTest::Unit::TestCase
 2   include BicycleInterfaceTest
 3
 4   def setup
```

```
 5        @bike = @object = Bicycle.new({tire_size: 0})
 6    end
 7 end
 8
 9 class RoadBikeTest < MiniTest::Unit::TestCase
10    include BicycleInterfaceTest
11
12    def setup
13        @bike = @object = RoadBike.new
14    end
15 end
```

Running the test tells a story:

```
 1 BicycleTest
 2    PASS test_responds_to_default_chain
 3    PASS test_responds_to_size
 4    PASS test_responds_to_tire_size
 5    PASS test_responds_to_chain
 6    PASS test_responds_to_spares
 7    PASS test_responds_to_default_tire_size
 8
 9 RoadBikeTest
10    PASS test_responds_to_chain
11    PASS test_responds_to_tire_size
12    PASS test_responds_to_default_chain
13    PASS test_responds_to_spares
14    PASS test_responds_to_default_tire_size
15    PASS test_responds_to_size
```

> **Note**
>
> Don't be alarmed that the parts of `BicycleTest` and `RoadBikeTest` run in different orders; random test ordering is a feature of `MiniTest`.

The `BicycleInterfaceTest` will work for every kind of `Bicycle` and can be easily included in any new subclass. It documents the interface and prevents accidental regressions.

Specifying Subclass Responsibilities

Not only do all `Bicycles` share a common interface, the abstract `Bicycle` superclass imposes requirements upon its subclasses.

Confirming Subclass Behavior

Because there are many subclasses, they should share a common test to prove that each meets the requirements. Here's a test that documents the requirements for subclasses:

```
 1 module BicycleSubclassTest
 2   def test_responds_to_post_initialize
 3     assert_respond_to(@object, :post_initialize)
 4   end
 5
 6   def test_responds_to_local_spares
 7     assert_respond_to(@object, :local_spares)
 8   end
 9
10   def test_responds_to_default_tire_size
11     assert_respond_to(@object, :default_tire_size)
12   end
13 end
```

This test codifies the requirements for subclasses of `Bicycle`. It doesn't force subclasses to implement these methods, in fact, any subclass is free to inherit `post_initialize` and `local_spares`. This test just proves that a subclass does nothing so crazy that it causes these messages to fail. The only method that must be implemented by subclasses is `default_tire_size`. The superclass implementation of `default_tire_size` raises an error; this test will fail unless the subclass implements its own specialized version.

    `RoadBike` acts like a `Bicycle` so its test already includes the `BicycleInterfaceTest`. The test below has been changed to include the new `BicycleSubclassTest`; `RoadBike` should also act like a subclass of `Bicycle`.

```
 1 class RoadBikeTest < MiniTest::Unit::TestCase
 2   include BicycleInterfaceTest
 3   include BicycleSubclassTest
 4
 5   def setup
 6     @bike = @object = RoadBike.new
 7   end
 8 end
```

Running this modified test tells an enhanced story:

```
1  RoadBikeTest
2     PASS test_responds_to_default_tire_size
3     PASS test_responds_to_spares
4     PASS test_responds_to_chain
5     PASS test_responds_to_post_initialize
6     PASS test_responds_to_local_spares
7     PASS test_responds_to_size
8     PASS test_responds_to_tire_size
9     PASS test_responds_to_default_chain
```

Every subclass of `Bicycle` can share these same two modules, because every subclass should act both like a `Bicycle` and like a subclass of `Bicycle`. Even though it's been a while since you've seen the `MountainBike` subclass, you can surely appreciate the ability to ensure that `MountainBikes` are good citizens by simply adding these two modules to its test, as shown here:

```
1  class MountainBikeTest < MiniTest::Unit::TestCase
2    include BicycleInterfaceTest
3    include BicycleSubclassTest
4
5    def setup
6      @bike = @object = MountainBike.new
7    end
8  end
```

The `BicycleInterfaceTest` and the `BicycleSubclassTest`, combined, take all of the pain out of testing the common behavior of subclasses. These tests give you confidence that subclasses aren't drifting away from the standard, and they allow novices to create new subclasses in complete safety. Newly arrived programmers don't have to scour the superclasses to unearth requirements, they can just include these tests when they write new subclasses.

Confirming Superclass Enforcement

The `Bicycle` class should raise an error if a subclass does not implement `default_tire_size`. Even though this requirement applies to subclasses, the actual enforcement behavior is in `Bicycle`. This test is therefore placed directly in `BicycleTest`, as shown on line 8 below:

```
1  class BicycleTest < MiniTest::Unit::TestCase
2    include BicycleInterfaceTest
3
4    def setup
5      @bike = @object = Bicycle.new({tire_size: 0})
6    end
7
8    def test_forces_subclasses_to_implement_default_tire_size
9      assert_raises(NotImplementedError) {@bike.default_tire_size}
10   end
11 end
```

Notice that line 5 of `BicycleTest` supplies a tire size, albeit an odd one, at `Bicycle` creation time. If you look back at `Bicycle`'s `initialize` method you'll see why. The `initialize` method expects to either receive an input value for `tire_size` or to be able retrieve one by subsequently sending the `default_tire_size` message. If you remove the `tire_size` argument from line 5, this test dies in its `setup` method while creating a `Bicycle`. Without this argument, `Bicycle` can't successfully get through object initialization.

The `tire_size` argument is necessary because `Bicycle` is an abstract class that does not expect to receive the new message. `Bicycle` doesn't have a nice, friendly creation protocol. It doesn't need one because the actual application never creates instances of `Bicycle`. However, the fact that the application doesn't create new `Bicycles` doesn't mean this never happens. It surely does. Line 5 of the `BicycleTest` above clearly creates a new instance of this abstract class.

This problem is ubiquitous when testing abstract classes. The `BicycleTest` needs an object on which to run tests and the most obvious candidate is an instance of `Bicycle`. However, creating a new instance of an abstract class can range from difficult and impossible. This test is fortunate in that `Bicycle`'s creation protocol allows the test to create a concrete `Bicycle` instance by passing `tire_size`, but creating a testable object is not always this easy and you may find it necessary to employ a more sophisticated strategy. Fortunately, there's an easy way to overcome this general problem that will be covered below in the section Testing Abstract Superclass Behavior.

For now, supplying the `tire_size` argument works just fine. Running `BicycleTest` now produces output that looks more like that of an abstract superclass:

```
1  BicycleTest
2    PASS test_responds_to_default_tire_size
3    PASS test_responds_to_size
```

```
4    PASS test_responds_to_default_chain
5    PASS test_responds_to_tire_size
6    PASS test_responds_to_chain
7    PASS test_responds_to_spares
8    PASS test_forces_subclasses_to_implement_default_tire_size
```

Testing Unique Behavior

The inheritance tests have so far concentrated on testing common qualities. Most of the resulting tests were shareable and ended up being placed in modules (`BicycleInterfaceTest` and `BicycleSubclassTest`), although one test (`forces_subclasses_to_implement_default_tire_size`) did get placed directly into `BicycleTest`.

Now that you have dispensed with the common behavior, two gaps remain. There are as yet no tests for specializations, neither for the ones provided by the concrete subclasses nor for those defined in the abstract superclass. The following section concentrates on the first; it tests specializations supplied by individual subclasses. The section after moves the focus upward in the hierarchy and tests behavior that is unique to `Bicycle`.

Testing Concrete Subclass Behavior

Now is the time to renew your commitment to writing the absolute minimum number of tests. Look back at the `RoadBike` class. The shared modules already prove most of its behavior. The only thing left to test are the specializations that `RoadBike` supplies.

It's important to test these specializations without embedding knowledge of the superclass into the test. For example, `RoadBike` implements `local_spares` and also responds to `spares`. The `RoadBikeTest` should ensure that `local_spares` works while maintaining deliberate ignorance about the existence of the `spares` method. The shared `BicycleInterfaceTest` already proves that `RoadBike` responds correctly to `spares`, it is redundant and ultimately limiting to reference that method directly in this test.

The `local_spares` method, however, is clearly `RoadBike`'s responsibility. Line 9 below tests this specialization directly in `RoadBikeTest`:

```
1  class RoadBikeTest < MiniTest::Unit::TestCase
2    include BicycleInterfaceTest
3    include BicycleSubclassTest
4
5    def setup
6      @bike = @object = RoadBike.new(tape_color: 'red')
7    end
```

```
 8
 9  def test_puts_tape_color_in_local_spares
10    assert_equal 'red', @bike.local_spares[:tape_color]
11  end
12 end
```

Running `RoadBikeTest` now shows that it meets its common responsibilities and also supplies its own specializations:

```
 1 RoadBikeTest
 2   PASS test_responds_to_default_chain
 3   PASS test_responds_to_default_tire_size
 4   PASS test_puts_tape_color_in_local_spares
 5   PASS test_responds_to_spares
 6   PASS test_responds_to_size
 7   PASS test_responds_to_local_spares
 8   PASS test_responds_to_post_initialize
 9   PASS test_responds_to_tire_size
10   PASS test_responds_to_chain
```

Testing Abstract Superclass Behavior

Now that you have tested the subclass specializations it's time to step back and finish testing the superclass. Moving your focus up the hierarchy to `Bicycle` reintroduces a previously encountered problem; `Bicycle` is an abstract superclass. Creating an instance of `Bicycle` is not only hard but the instance might not have all the behavior you need to make the test run.

Fortunately, your design skills provide a solution. Because `Bicycle` used template methods to acquire concrete specializations you can stub the behavior that would normally be supplied by subclasses. Even better, because you understand the Liskov Substitution Principle, you can easily manufacture a testable instance of `Bicycle` by creating a new subclass for use solely by this test.

The test below follows just such a strategy. Line 1 defines a new class, `StubbedBike`, as a subclass of `Bicycle`. The test creates an instance of this class (line 15) and uses it to prove that `Bicycle` correctly includes the subclass's `local_spares` contribution in `spares` (line 23).

It remains convenient to sometimes create an instance of the abstract `Bicycle` class, even though this requires passing the `tire_size` argument, as on line 14. This instance of `Bicycle` continues to be used in the test on line 18 to prove that the abstract class forces subclasses to implement `default_tire_size`.

These two kinds of `Bicycles` coexist peacefully in the test, as you see here:

```
1  class StubbedBike < Bicycle
2    def default_tire_size
3      0
4    end
5    def local_spares
6      {saddle: 'painful'}
7    end
8  end
9
10 class BicycleTest < MiniTest::Unit::TestCase
11   include BicycleInterfaceTest
12
13   def setup
14     @bike = @object = Bicycle.new({tire_size: 0})
15     @stubbed_bike   = StubbedBike.new
16   end
17
18   def test_forces_subclasses_to_implement_default_tire_size
19     assert_raises(NotImplementedError) {
20       @bike.default_tire_size}
21   end
22
23   def test_includes_local_spares_in_spares
24     assert_equal @stubbed_bike.spares,
25                   { tire_size: 0,
26                     chain:    '10-speed',
27                     saddle:   'painful'}
28   end
29 end
```

The idea of creating a subclass to supply stubs can be helpful in many situations. As long as your new subclass does not violate Liskov, you can use this technique in any test you like.

Running `BicycleTest` now proves that it includes subclass contributions on the spares list:

```
1  BicycleTest
2    PASS test_responds_to_spares
3    PASS test_responds_to_tire_size
```

```
4     PASS test_responds_to_default_chain
5     PASS test_responds_to_default_tire_size
6     PASS test_forces_subclasses_to_implement_default_tire_size
7     PASS test_responds_to_chain
8     PASS test_includes_local_spares_in_spares
9     PASS test_responds_to_size
```

One last point: If you fear that StubbedBike will become obsolete and permit BicycleTest to pass when it should fail, the solution is close at hand. There is already a common BicycleSubclassTest. Just as you used the Diameterizable InterfaceTest to guarantee DiameterDouble's continued good behavior, you can use BicycleSubclassTest to ensure the ongoing correctness of StubbedBike. Add the following code to BicycleTest:

```
1  # Prove the test double honors the interface this
2  #    test expects.
3  class StubbedBikeTest < MiniTest::Unit::TestCase
4    include BicycleSubclassTest
5
6    def setup
7      @object = StubbedBike.new
8    end
9  end
```

After you make this change, running BicycleTest produces this additional output:

```
1  StubbedBikeTest
2     PASS test_responds_to_default_tire_size
3     PASS test_responds_to_local_spares
4     PASS test_responds_to_post_initialize
```

Carefully written inheritance hierarchies are easy to test. Write one shareable test for the overall interface and another for the subclass responsibilities. Diligently isolate responsibilities. Be especially careful when testing subclass specializations to prevent knowledge of the superclass from leaking down into the subclass's test.

Testing abstract superclasses can be challenging; use the Liskov Substitution Principle to your advantage. If you leverage Liskov and create new subclasses that are used exclusively for testing, consider requiring these subclasses to pass your subclass responsibility test to ensure they don't accidentally become obsolete.

Summary

Tests are indispensable. Well-designed applications are highly abstract and under constant pressure to evolve; without tests these applications can neither be understood nor safely changed. The best tests are loosely coupled to the underlying code and test everything once and in the proper place. They add value without increasing costs.

A well-designed application with a carefully crafted test suite is a joy to behold and a pleasure to extend. It can adapt to every new circumstance and meet any unexpected need.

Afterword

Responsibilities, dependencies, interfaces, ducks, inheritance, behavior sharing, composition, and testing—you've learned it all. You've immersed yourself in a world of objects, and if this book has achieved its goal, you think differently about objects now than when you first began.

Chapter 1, Object-Oriented Design, stated that object-oriented design is about managing dependencies; that statement is still true but it's just one truth about design. A deeper truth is that there is a way in which all objects are identical, regardless of whether they represent entire applications, major subsystems, individual classes, or simple methods. A single object never stands alone; applications consist of objects that are related to one another. Like a key and its lock, a hand and its glove, or a call and its response objects are defined, not by what they do, but by the messages that pass between them. Object-oriented design is fractal; the central problem is to define an extensible way for objects to communicate, and at every level of magnification this problem looks the same.

This book is full of rules about how to write code—rules for managing dependencies and creating interfaces. Now that you know these rules you can bend them to your own purposes. The tensions inherent in design mean that these rules are meant to be broken; learning to break them well is a designer's greatest strength.

The tenets of design are tools and with practice they will come naturally into your hand, allowing you to create changeable applications that serve their purpose and bring you joy. Your applications will not be perfect but do not be discouraged. Perfection is elusive, perhaps even unreachable; this should not impede your desire to achieve it. Persist. Practice. Experiment. Imagine. Do your best work, and all else will follow.

Index

| | = operator, 43, 48–49
Abstract
  behavior, promoting, 120–23
  classes, 117–20, 235, 237
  definition of, 54
  superclass, creating, 117–20
Abstractions
  extracting, 150–53
  finding, 116–29
  insisting on, in writing
      inheritable code, 159
  recognizing, 54–55
  separating from concretions,
      123–25
  supporting, in intentional testing,
      194
  template method pattern, 125–29
Across-class types, 86
Ad infinitum, 3
Aggregation, 183–84
Agile, 8–10
Antipattern
  definition of, 109, 111
  recognizing, 158–59
Argument-order dependencies,
      removing, 46–51
  defaults, explicitly defining, 48–49
  hashes for initialization
      arguments, using, 46–48
  multiparameter initialization,
      isolating, 49–51
Automatic message delegation,
      105–6

Behaves-like-a relationships, 189
Behavior
  acquired through inheritance,
      105–39
  confirming, 233–36
  data structures, hiding, 26–29
  depending on, instead of data,
      24–29
  instance variables, hiding,
      24–26
  set of, 19
  subclass, 233–39
  superclass, 234–39
  testing, 236–39
Behavior Driven Development
      (BDD), 199, 213
Big Up Front Design (BUFD), 8–9
Booch, Grady, 188
Break-even point, 11
Bugs, finding, 193

Case statements that switch on
      class, 96–98
  kind_of? and is_a?, 97
  responds_to?, 97
Category used in class, 111
Class. *See also* Single responsibility,
      classes with
  abstract, 117–20, 235, 237
  avoiding dependent-laden, 55
  bicycle, updating, 164–65
  case statements that switch on,
      96–98

code, organizing to allow for
      changes, 16–17
concrete, 106–9, 209
deciding what belongs in, 16–17
decoupling, in writing inheritable
      code, 161
dependent-laden, avoiding, 55
grouping methods into, 16
references to (*See* Loosely coupled
      code, writing)
responsibilities isolated in, 31–33
Ruby based *vs.* framework,
      53–54
type and *category* used in, 111
virtual, 61
Class-based OO languages, 12–13
Class class, 14
Classical inheritance, 105–6
Class of an object
  ambiguity about, 94–95
  checking, 97, 111, 146
Class under test, removing private
      methods from, 214
Code. *See also* Inheritable code,
      writing; Inherited code,
      testing
  concrete, writing, 147–50
  dependency injection to shape,
      41–42
  depending on behavior instead of
      data, 24–29
  embracing change, writing,
      24–33

Your purchase of **Practical Object-Oriented Design in Ruby** includes access to a free online edition for 45 days through the **Safari Books Online** subscription service. Nearly every Addison-Wesley Professional book is available online through **Safari Books Online**, along with thousands of books and videos from publishers such as Cisco Press, Exam Cram, IBM Press, O'Reilly Media, Prentice Hall, Que, Sams, and VMware Press.

Safari Books Online is a digital library providing searchable, on-demand access to thousands of technology, digital media, and professional development books and videos from leading publishers. With one monthly or yearly subscription price, you get unlimited access to learning tools and information on topics including mobile app and software development, tips and tricks on using your favorite gadgets, networking, project management, graphic design, and much more.

Activate your FREE Online Edition at
informit.com/safarifree

STEP 1:   Enter the coupon code: EFQGHFH.

STEP 2:   New Safari users, complete the brief registration form.
Safari subscribers, just log in.

If you have difficulty registering on Safari or accessing the online edition,
please e-mail customer-service@safaribooksonline.com